POLARITY MAGIC

THE SECRET HISTORY OF WESTERN RELIGION

ABOUT THE AUTHORS

Wendy Berg and Mike Harris are leading ritual magicians of the Western Mystery Tradition. They have accumulated some forty years of magical experience between them.

WRITE TO THE AUTHORS

If you wish to contact the authors or would like more information about this book, please write to the authors in care of Llewellyn Worldwide and we will forward your request. Both the authors and publisher appreciate hearing from you and learning of your enjoyment of this book and how it has helped you. Llewellyn Worldwide cannot guarantee that every letter written to the authors can be answered, but all will be forwarded. Please write to:

Wendy Berg and Mike Harris
⅄ Llewellyn Worldwide
P.O. Box 64383, Dept. 0-7387-0300-1
St. Paul, MN 55164-0383, U.S.A.

Please enclose a self-addressed stamped envelope for reply,
or $1.00 to cover costs. If outside U.S.A., enclose
international postal reply coupon.

Many of Llewellyn's authors have websites with additional information and resources. For more information, please visit our website at http://www.llewellyn.com.

POLARITY MAGIC

THE SECRET HISTORY OF WESTERN RELIGION

WENDY BERG AND MIKE HARRIS

2003
Llewellyn Publications
St. Paul, Minnesota 55164-0383, U.S.A.

First Edition
First Printing, 2003

Cover art © 2003 by Corel and Digital Stock
Cover design and interior illustrations by Lisa Novak

Library of Congress Cataloging-in-Publication Data
Berg, Wendy, 1951–
    Polarity magic: the secret history of western religion/Wendy Berg
    and Mike Harris.
      p.   cm.
    Includes bibliographical references.
    ISBN 0-7387-0300-1
      1. Magic—History. 2. Mysteries, Religious—History. 3. Mythology—
    History. 4. Occultism—History. I. Harris, Mike, 1947- II. Title.
    BF1589.B47 2003
    133.4'3—dc21   2003044687

Llewellyn Publications
A Division of Llewellyn Worldwide, Ltd.
P.O. Box 64383, Dept. 0-7387-0300-1
St. Paul, MN 55164-0383, U.S.A.
www.llewellyn.com

Printed in the United States of America

for Persephone and Silvanus in the deep green

CONTENTS

INTRODUCTION

This is a book about magic; not the magic that conjures rabbits out of hats or cures warts, but the magic that was practiced in the temples of Egypt, the stone circles of Bronze Age Britain, and, appearances notwithstanding, the Temple of Jerusalem.

Magic has undergone a remarkable revival in the last twenty-five years, and the ripples on the surface of that revival may be seen in a plethora of inner disciplines. These range from New Age therapeutics to quantum cosmology, and to a fascination with the spiritual methodology of early Western cultures. At the center of all these is a recognition of a long neglected "Western Mystery Tradition." At the heart of that tradition we find what magicians now coyly term "Polarity Magic," though few are aware of its theory and fewer still of its practice. Even so, polarity magic in its many forms constitutes the core of all mythology and the mystery teachings that mythology expounds. The late Dion Fortune stated that the aim of magic is "to effect changes in consciousness in conformity with will."[1] These changes are achieved through the subtle exchange and transformation of energies. Polarity magic recognizes that the most effective starting point for such exchanges is in the fundamental energies that exist and are exchanged between men and women. Polarity magic therefore tends to exalt, rather than negate, human sexuality in spiritual endeavor.

In doing so it gives equal credence to the feminine as well as the masculine aspects, not only of human priesthood but of the divinity that such priesthood mediates. With a new awareness of the divine feminine, the goddesses of ancient myth are now awoken on the lips of ordinary people and the Isis of many names walks the world again. She searches for her lost mate, the man-god Osiris, that the two may be one and the sacred child of the world's future may be conceived and brought to birth. In her search she travels through many lands, ages, and cultures, and in doing so she uses many names. She may call herself Mary and Miriam, Anat and Eve, Brigid and Ceridwen, Hathor and Gwenevere. She may walk the Atlantean hinterland between being and unbeing, or the groves of Olivet or the orchards of Avalon or the streets of London. For this is a book about the magic of the greater Isis, and that magic is not confined to either an Egypt of ancient ruins or the perceptual enclosures of modern neopaganism. She seeks that other half of herself, the potency for unity that ignorant priestcraft castrated and crucified to halt history in its own comfort zone. Now she has left the timeless deserts and the wistful groves to call to men and women of good will to be priests and priestesses to her marriage, and godparents to their own future.

The mandate of all priesthood is "the cure of souls": a mandate that embraces not only the souls of individuals but the folk souls of nations and, not least, the soul of creation itself. As magic enables men and women to be active in the otherwise intangible mysteries of creation, it is an essential activity of priesthood. It is, however, a very ancient activity, embracing pre-Christian beliefs and practices, and in the instances where a Christian viewpoint is maintained it is not surprisingly one that is radically at odds with that of orthodox Christianity. It has, therefore, attracted the label of heresy down the centuries.

The Oxford English Dictionary defines heresy as "an opinion that is contrary to the accepted beliefs of the Christian church."

Anybody who embraces the beliefs that this book expounds will therefore, by such a definition, be a heretic! There were of course heretics long before the rise of Christianity. Human nature being what it is, there have always been those who have held beliefs that are contrary to those of the status quo—those who knew that the travels of great Isis could not be halted at some hostel of self-satisfied religion. Such may seem to be of little consequence in these enlightened times, but it was not always so. Before English law embraced the tolerance that Christianity should have embraced, heresy, actual or presumed, cost many men and women their lives. We might therefore wonder what was so special about some of these "opinions contrary to the accepted beliefs of the Christian Church" that folks were prepared to die for them.

Judeo-Christian mythology found heresy from the very beginning in the story of Adam and Eve. Adam's and Eve's essential sin was to fly in the face of divinely-ordained accepted belief and practice. The post-exilic Hebrew priests who concocted the myth did so to support their theological stance by making sure that Eve was the primary human culprit. Her readiness to sympathize with the serpent hinted that female sexuality cannot be trusted, certainly not in any dialogue with the divine. Even today women may not sit with men in the synagogue and a menstruating woman is, by Old Testament precedent, considered to be spiritually unclean. Adam's story is an object lesson for the Judeo-Christian man to never trust his Eve, for to do so is to risk both the invalidation of humanity's contract with God and exile from that Paradisal state where heaven and earth rub shoulders.

The Edenic myth (of which there are several versions) was probably set in its present form just after the Hebrew Babylonian exile and marks a turning point in early Judaic belief that has stayed with us for the last 2,500 years. It took an ancient "Otherworld" theme of an Isis and an Osiris, a bride and bridegroom embraced in original innocence, and transformed it into an unhealthy obsession with original sin. Nakedness became a parable for sexual impropriety and "forbidden fruit" became a metaphor not only for the exercise of such impropriety but also for the acquisition of heretical and sinister knowledge.

To understand why the founding fathers of Judeo-Christian belief should have gone out of their way to blame the origination of all human sin on the archetypal woman, we must search in the footnotes of history and the mythological assumptions of prehistory. In "the cure of souls" we must conduct this search to arrive at a diagnosis before we may suggest remedies, and the remedies that we do suggest are inevitably holistic. The holistic approach attempts, of course, to address the causes rather than the effects of a disease. An example may be given from the recent acknowledgement by some denominations of institutional Christianity that there should be female as well as male "priests." This acknowledgment, laudable though it is, arises largely as a grudging realization of the power of political feminism. It is a reactive social bandage upon a deep and ancient wound, and without a true understanding of the spiritual dynamics of the role of the priestess it is an ineffectual remedy for the snubbing of Isis and the blaming of Eve. There can be no effectual priesthood on this planet if it is by men *or* by women; nature doesn't work that way. But there can and must be an effectual priesthood by men *and* women together, for both must be spiritually and magically mated to conceive the future. Likewise there can be no priesthood of inner *or* outer creation, of this part *or* of that part of belief, for all creation is a holism and human nature is part and parcel of all nature. There can be no question of magic *or* religion, only of magic *and* religion. We are of the stuff of angels and animals, of both cosmic awareness and self-centered pettiness, yet all these parts comprise one whole and no cure of souls may be satisfactory unless it is a holistic cure. For the complete Isis in all her aspects must be permitted to find and reintegrate her fragmented Osiris so that together they may initiate the marriage of heaven and earth.

It was to express and explain these convictions that we began to sketch out this book in 1998. At the time we were both members of a mystery school that worked at the cutting edge of the Western Qabalist tradition. Within that year we found ourselves translating our ideas for this book into actual magical practice, some of which is cited in the chapters that follow. Hence the reader will find Jesus Christ and Mary of Magdala happily rubbing shoulders not only with each other, but with Taliesin and Ceridwen, Isis and Osiris, Merlin and Gwenddydd, and others. For with the intentional talismanic removal of one divide, others come crashing down, and the traditional divisive labels of both magic and religion cease to hold us in their thrall.

But the time for labels, boxes, secrets, magical elitism, theological dogma, and all those stifling comforts of our spiritual adolescence must now be over. The supposed safety that such things afforded us are delusory, for spirituality is a risky business. As the initiate who wrote in the name of Paul of Tarsus recognized, a time comes when we must grow up and put away childish things.

The various traditions of magic and religion have always taken their cue from a mixture of myth, virtual history, and intuition, and we have tended to do the same. No magician may expect to follow the practical aspects of his or her work without recourse to the tradition from which it sprang, yet no tradition can hope to survive without the practical spiritual endeavors of its adherents. Magic and religion are all about belief and intention and can only be really effective at that point where the "how" and the "why" converge and motivate. We have therefore attempted to indicate the progression of the "why" (and the "why not!") through myth and the checkered history of its application, and provide the "how" in a mixture of pathworkings, rituals, and suggestions. It is our hope that this will yield the motivation for the seeker to dip his or her toe in the water.

For the more experienced swimmer in the Western Mystery School there are plenty of surprises. After some forty years of combined magical experience, we were certainly surprised by what began to emerge in these pages. Polarity magic has, for example, many precedents in mythology, but what if it is intended to *change* mythology? The more that we worked with the myths in this way, the more we realized that polarity magic begins with Eve's quantum "what if?" This makes the myths malleable, for polarity magic is archetypal mating, and the products of such a union appear to induce the conception and birth of new archetypal situations that advance the myths and overlay ancient assumptions with new insights. The mysteries have always acknowledged "the redemption of archetypes" but that has merely tended in practice to assure the consolidation of myth, whereas polarity magic rightly done appears to encourage its amendment. Such amendment may be seen in our approach to the Judeo-Christian tradition, which, religious dogma notwithstanding, is a rich source of myth. Indeed, it was the distillation of the mythologies of many ancient cultures that were brought to historical externalization in the events that attach to the conception, the birth, the life, and the death of Christ. These and other matters, such as the real versus the traditional role of the faery consort, began to come to light as we pursued *Polarity Magic,* and in no small way rocked our previously stable "boat of a million years."

For the more general reader we offer an inside view into a little-understood realm of human spiritual endeavor and some explanations for the curious twists of theology and religious history that have seeded a faith to which so many people are now indifferent. The Age of Dogma is passed, and with its passing comes an impatience for honesty and clarity. The twenty-first century cries out for something beyond the materialism of our little lives, yet no longer has patience for the trite phrases of the nineteenth-century pulpit. Here then are some alternatives that celebrate rather than confound God-given free will, and refuse, in an insidious culture of blame, to lay the blame for all human misery on Eve's precocious theft of fruit from the Tree of Life.

As we embarked upon this project we became acutely aware of those who had trodden this path before us. We were especially aware of a remarkable woman named Dion Fortune, from whom our own lodge may claim direct esoteric lineage, and of her teacher, Maiya Trenchell Hayes. We were also aware of Dion Fortune's pupil and occasional literary agent Christine Campbell Thomson, and of Colonel C. R. F. Seymour. To the man and woman in the street these names mean nothing. However, to those who have toiled through the degrees of any Western Mystery school worth the name, they carry considerable authority. Fredrick Bligh Bond, who impressed us with his affable, discarnate influence, is somewhat better known than those previously mentioned. He had worked briefly with Dion Fortune in her early days at Glastonbury when Maiya Trenchell Hayes, a senior member of the Hermetic Order of the Golden Dawn, was helping Dion Fortune set up her own mystery school. Colonel Seymour and Christine Campbell Thomson were later members of that school, and went on to develop a very effective magical partnership, cut short by the Second World War and Seymour's sudden death.

Fredrick Bligh Bond died in 1945, having lived in America for many years before retiring to Wales to spend the last years of his life in and around the Dolgellau area. Dion Fortune died in 1946 and was buried in Glastonbury. It is to the amicable and compassionate spirits of these pioneers that we owe a great deal. They had, we found, laid out most of the groundwork for us in their esoteric activities between the two world wars. They had also left a plethora of loose ends that the mystery schools of later and recent years have largely forgotten or ignored. For mystery schools are as much subject to spiritual complacency and inertia as their institutional religious counterparts. Yet it was from the following through of these loose ends that this book and the events surrounding its composition grew.

We set out to address the working relationship between priest and priestess, which is at the heart of all effective mystery working.

This has variously been described as "Western Tantra," "Polarity Magic," and, by the more sensationally inclined, "Sex Magick." But we ended up with something a good deal more substantial, not the least of which is a very real sense of where we come from. The largely invisible development of the mysteries over the last five thousand years has impacted and shaped the way that the Western psyche perceives itself and the world that it lives in. Whether we are pagans or Christians, rationalists or romantics, atheists or believers, we cannot deny the patterns that have been etched into our collective psyche. If we want to change those patterns and change the world, we are obliged to open "the door that has no key." Here is a key for men and women who together have the courage to use it.

CHAPTER ONE

AUTUMN IN ATLANTIS

LIES BREATHED THROUGH SILVER

The mysteries are born from myth. Myth is careless of chronology and is a form in which so-called "fact" founders—a form that C. S. Lewis described as "lies breathed through silver."[1]

Myth does not in fact take the trouble to lie about specific events in historical context; it simply can't be bothered with them. Its truth deals with the interaction of the soul of a people with the soul of creation. In doing so its function was never to keep, or pretend to keep, historical records. The mistaken belief that it did so has provided us with generations of biblical fundamentalists, a score of New Age fabulists, and enough theological nitpicking to fuel countless schisms and wars.

History and myth find themselves in the same perplexing relationship as Newtonian physics and quantum mechanics. The concrete events of so-called factual history take indisputable form in archaeological and historical record: what you see is what you get. Myth, by contrast, selects archetypal situations and relationships that underscore human experience and muses on their probabilities. Factual history is about *what was* and myth is about *what if?* Such quantum flexibility gives myth and the human spiritual evolution it anticipates an open ended, never-ending-story quality that invites human participation. Like the Edenic serpent, it suggests that humans will be allowed a hand in the game of creative consequences.

The historical roles of Julius Caesar and his mistress, Cleopatra, may be seen in part as a tragic participation in the archetypal weavings of myth. Caesar rose to be the half man, half god, divine king that the mythical Osiris had been. Cleopatra believed, through a sense of destiny rather than arrogance, that she was the very embodiment of Isis to her people. On the wall of the temple of Isis at Dendera it is Cleopatra who stands in its huge bas reliefs as Isis—not with the mythical child Horus, but with her own human child Caesarion, her child by Caesar. Yet she stands like the lone mother Isis, since her Caesar was butchered by conspirators as Osiris had been. Cleopatra believed and lived out the Isis mythology and drew Julius Caesar into her destiny with great historical resonance, almost as if the myth predicted their human fate.

Fate is bound to time, whereas myth may touch history but refuses to be cut and dried in singular historical events. Like the magical brew, the *Awen* in the cauldron of the Celtic goddess Ceridwen, its inspiring, regenerating, and transforming liquor bubbles constantly, ready for humanity to sip. Myth is therefore not about predicting what *will* happen, but what *can* happen in the time, space, and events of our lives if we have the courage and insight to sup from its cauldron. But even in the Celtic cauldron myths of Ceridwen and Bran, the cauldron is eventually misused and shattered, and infinite myth and infinite potential seep away into the arid earth of space/time and human expediency. The primitive, inspirational cauldron becomes replaced by the Holy Grail, but even that revised, creative wellspring of spiritual evolution is lost and its legends die. With the shattering of myth the nectar of inspiration and aspiration is lost. The world becomes set in the intellectual concrete of space/time, rendering the past unalterable, the present unpalatable, and the future unimaginable. The overpaternalistic censors of the Book of Genesis failed to recognize that dangerous fruit is better than no fruit at all.

It was at the hands of these scribes that Hebrew myth met its nemesis, its fall from eternal inspiration into human expediency, when their definitive version of the Old Testament appeared in about 440 B.C. The Old Testament is virtual history, a collection of myth salted with obligatory historical snippets set in convenient, rather than chronological, order. Its essential distinction from other collections of myth and virtual history is not its monotheism, but the fact that it is *canonical*. The word "canon" is taken from the Greek; it means "rule," and the rule of the Hebrew Bible is that it is the first and last word of God and may not be added to or revised in any way. Even so, some thousand years later the fathers of the Christian church added their own New Testament, but concluded it with the same canonical proviso that it may in no way be changed. This means that while the Bible may be theologically debated as having many and varied levels of meaning, the actual text itself, myth or not, is seen to have been related by God about God in such a way that it cannot be altered or amended, for the Bible is couched in that ultimate tool of human expediency: law.

In the Hebrew tradition, the priestly human scribes who wrote down the inspirational myths are considered to have been incidental. They were the legal secretaries whose only responsibility was to unquestioningly draft a contract with Yahweh. It is a scriptural axiom that God spoke and the prophets and scribes merely took dictation, even though human nature knows better! Myth became dogma, and a potential path of spiritual enlightenment became frozen in a legalistic Hebrew world view. From this time on even God had to observe the law, creating for six days, then, like a good Jew, resting on the Sabbath. "Truth" became the truth of the Deuteronomical law, and a splendid tapestry of Hebrew and Canaanite myth was reworked to conform to that law. While the rest of the world, the pagan world, continued to grope for divinity and human dialogue with that divinity through myth, Judaism fought shy of such "lies breathed through silver." The law of Deuteronomy had become divine law. When Job attempted to get a divine explanation for life, the universe, and everything that, as a human at the sharp end of it all, he may supposedly be entitled to, the reply was belittling and dismissive: "Where wast thou when I laid the foundations of the earth? Declare if thou hast understanding."[2]

Thus the unquestioning canonical boundaries became set for all revealed religion—Judaism, Christianity, and Islam—for the centuries that followed. Sections of myth that were intellectually and dogmatically digestible became theology (literally "Godspeak"), and the rest became "Tradition." The preciosities of Jewish intellect later allowed Tradition its diversions, particularly in Qabalah, but revealed religion was the religion of the peoples of the book, and speculation beyond the end papers of that book were frowned upon. At best, revealed religion dismisses myth as those charming lies breathed through silver that have no spiritual value, and at worst as a pagan path to hell fire.

AS ABOVE SO BELOW

Myth could never be gagged on the grounds that it was untrue. Truth depends upon integrity, upon perception through a rightness perceived in the holism of cosmic order. This may be summed up in the axiom expounded in the third century A.D. *Corpus Hermeticum,* the doctrine of Hermes: "As above, so below."[3]

In the Egyptian mysteries, to which the mysteries of ancient Israel owed no small debt, the god concerned with recording the integrity of a human soul against the measure of divine truth was Tehuti. But Truth itself was embodied in the goddess Maat, whose symbol was a feather against which each human heart was weighed.

Feathery winged beings, whether as aspects of the goddesses of ancient Egypt or the angels of Hebrew scripture, tend to denote beings who display cosmic principles. Before the Deuteronomic reforms of post-exilic Judaism, the angelic statues of the two Kerubim fashioned to enclose the Ark of the Covenant with the cosmic span of their wings denoted the facilitation of the reality of heaven in earth—the reality of "as above so below." Tradition, that embarrassing bedfellow of Hebrew canon law, assumed that one of the Kerubic statues was male and the other, female.

In this we begin to see what the Hebrew law extinguished. "As above, so below" presupposes a relationship, a union rather than a contract, between heaven and earth. Such a union depends upon what the mysteries call "polarity." The *Malkuth,* which is Israel on earth, is, as the Qabalists insist, betrothed to Yahweh. Heaven and earth gaze into each other's eyes like lovers and see themselves, the one in the other. Such is the polarity symbolized in the male and female Kerubim, who eternally, face to face, form the mercy seat of the covenant, the bonds of relationship between heaven and earth. Tradition also tells us that the Ark contained not ten contractual provisos chiseled onto cold, cynical stone, but four very human things. Two of these were not so much commandments as love letters. They were probably quite small, like the exquisite Egyptian foundation tablets of that time. Jesus Christ summed up their contents some two thousands years later: "Thou shalt love the Lord thy God with all thy heart, with all thy strength, and thy neighbor as thyself." [4] The two other trinkets of this love affair between heaven and earth were said to be Aaron's staff and the cup that had contained the sustaining manna of heaven. The cup of manna is somewhat like Ceridwen's womblike cauldron, and Aaron's rod (which "budded") is allied to it as a symbol of arousal. The ancient Hebrews who emerged from exile in the Egypt of Isis and Osiris expressed their love affair with heaven in very earthy terms. Yet the male and female Kerubim indicate the dynamic polarity by which heaven and earth may be as one. They are as two sides of a ladder, mighty pillars of love with the dynamics of that love strung as rungs to form the ladder between above and below, which Jacob saw at Bethel. All this was before theology found it prudent to be prudish and set distance between heaven and earth by neutering gods and angels. Until that time, we may heretically suppose, the child of that union of Kerubic Strong

Ones was Truth, displaying the essential traits of its archetypal cosmic parentage. For myth does not dish up lies, but rather indicates a truth born from the creative interaction between the archetypal world: the province of gods and myth "above," and the mundane world of humankind "below."

Early Hebrew scripture had attempted to explain this, and passing references in Genesis that escaped later censorship talk about the *Beni Elohim,* the angelic sons of gods mating with "the daughters of men." Latter-day Judeo-Christian commentators have fallen over themselves explaining away that polytheistic slip of the plural Elohim that means "gods" rather than the lone single god, Yahweh.

While gods, goddesses, and angelic beings (the distinctions are now both metaphysically and theologically blurred) operate for the most part on the archetypal "above" side of the business, human beings cut their godling teeth on the mundane, but no less necessary implementation of heavenly policy in the world below. As one eminent scientist put it, "There must be an outside for the inside to have meaning."[5]

In such a supposition the beings of heaven and earth are one teeming and sometimes mythically incestuous tribe, with the junior human branches of that tribe living and working on the factory floor. The whole purpose of the business is, however, *to create,* and the creativity of human nature and the supernature that it utilizes in its own being knows that creation works through what the mysteries call "polarity." Whether that polarity is between heaven and earth, light and dark, mind and matter, wave and particle, outside and inside, men and women, or even consenting Kerubim, that's the way things are. In the polarity of above and below, of "outside and inside," of myth and what we call reality, a mirror is fashioned in which heaven and earth see their mutual purpose. Like Alice and the unicorn, the inner and outer sides of creation establish a relationship based on mutual belief: a truth, established through the polarity between them.

The yardstick of that truth was, as we have seen, personified in early Egyptian myth by the goddess Maat. In the Canaanite mythology of what was to become Israel it was personified in the "priest of the Most High God," Melchizadek. The name Melchizadek is made up from two words: Melek, meaning "king," and Tsdeq, which is usually translated as "righteousness." Melchizadek is the archetype of the fully realized man, the priest-king who eternally mediates between heaven and earth, and the Tsdeq, which is implicit in his function, is that same realization of cosmic order in the polarity between earth and heaven that the Egyptians called Maat. In another of those half-edited fragments of myth from the Book of Genesis Melchizadek is called "king of Salem which is peace." This mythical coding brought in a number of concepts. In exoteric terms it referred to the high priest of the Canaanite god El Elyon, based at Salem, or Jerusalem, who met Abraham and his band of Hebrew immigrants when they came into Canaan in about 1600 B.C. Esoterically, this "king of Salem which is peace" indicated the peace and balance of a polarized relationship between heaven and earth, implicit in the Tsdeq in his name. This idea of the restoration of balance is emphasized by the fact that Melchizadek meets Abram (as he was originally called) immediately following Abram's defeat of the "kings of Edom whose kingdoms are unbalanced force." The meeting therefore marks the realization and restoration of balance, of peace between heaven and earth, the balance that is most vividly indicated in the Egyptian weighing of the human heart against the feather of Maat. Significantly, this weighing of the heart is in the hall of Osiris, the man-god, in which reintegration, cosmic order, and peace are restored largely through the efforts of his sister and mate, Isis.

In the Canaanite myth the same restoration and coming to terms with that order personified in Melchizadek are acknowledged in the symbolic gifts of bread and wine that Melchizadek gives to Abram, which may in a sense be compared to the heart and feather of the balance of Maat.

The peace, balance, and realization of truth as cosmic order implicit in these mythological characters and symbols grows from the resolution of the relationship, of polarity. Bread and wine, signifying flesh and blood, and thus body and spirit, become adopted by Christianity; they became the emblems of Christianity's own "High Priest of the order of Melchizadek," Jesus Christ, through whom the "above and below" is reconciled in every human being. The Hebrew heretic, St. Paul, inventor of what we now call Christianity, promises us in his letter to the Hebrews that he has much to say about Christ and Melchizadek, but time or censorship curtailed such elaboration. In any case, polarity, balance, and peace were not things that came naturally to Paul. He was cursed with a character that relished conflict and in his life and teaching assiduously sidestepped that most glorious human expression of polarity: the love between a man and a woman. Like the other monumental figure in the development of early Christianity, Augustine of Hippo, Paul's repressed sexuality found ready sanctuary in the lone and distant Yahweh, who had emerged in that reformed Judaism of the Deuteronomical puritans in 440 B.C. Through Paul and Augustine, Christ's God of Love was doomed to become a theological concept safely swaddled in sterile law.

The writings of the life of Christ, the Gospels, were written after the letters of St. Paul, and it goes without saying that those writers could not help but be influenced by this man who had converted a good portion of the known world to Jesus Christ. That conversion had of course been on Paul's own terms, which seem to have been other terms than those realized by St. James and those who had actually known Jesus. The Fathers of the early church were hard-pressed in the assembly of their own canonical writings to arrive at their "New Testament." The letters of Paul and his evangelical associates were an obvious inclusion, but the Fathers were spoilt for choice in the matter of gospels and hard-pressed by the Gnostics and others to arrive at a definitive statement of their new faith. Accordingly, they followed Paul and the earlier precedents of the Greek Hebrew Bible (the Septuagint), and suppressed or edited anything that strayed beyond those theological boundaries. This included anything that smacked of myth, not least because their Christianity had to celebrate, as they saw it, the historical incarnation of God on earth. The result, fixed in this hurriedly assembled temporal canon of a Palestine in turmoil some two thousand years ago, has given us an unsatisfactory spiritual heritage.

The mythical traditions of northern Israel from about 800 B.C., as we have seen in Genesis, talked to divinity as Elohim rather than Yahweh, "gods" rather than one god. Polytheistic myth made the divine a family, but the Yahwist monothesim that won the day made Him a single parent who, as time moved on from that frozen myth of 440 B.C., became a very distant parent, fenced off by law from his children. But mythology never intended such a distance. Its purpose was, and is, to draw heaven and earth nearer to each other by identifying evolving human beings with their divine lineage and purpose. Mythology needs gods who act like humans and humans who have the potential to act like gods, otherwise distant divinity must be assumed to regulate creation from its abstract throne with humankind left to consider itself as a cosmic aberration. There must be polarity, the dynamics of relationship through which creative potential can be realized. Christianity had the chance to address this, but failed.

Mythology is about potential, and the aspiration that realizes that potential is fed by desire. Above and below are linked by this mutual desire, this polarity, because mythical divinity needs its sexuality as much as the rest of creation. In the holism of being, the mythical gods do what humans do, except they do it better and on a more impressive scale—that was, so obviously, the way creation got started and was carried on—from the beasts of the field to the even more bestial human race, who were, after all, made in the image of God or "the gods."

But the Hebrews, suspicious from bitter experience of their pagan neighbors, needed a god who was "higher" and better than all that. Their god had to be the God of gods to ensure their survival. Accordingly, they removed the symbol of Asherah, their own goddess, from the Temple, and replaced it with one hard-faced, disdainful god who was beyond the mere flippancies of nature and human nature. The devout Hebrew soul passed from this world not to be gathered into the company of the gods like his pagan ancestors, but into the bosom of Abraham. The Qabalists later attempted to solve the problem of perceived isolation of divinity by their doctrine of Tsum Tsim, insisting that creation was held "within God." But this motherly metaphor failed to receive any expansion in mainstream Judaism. How could it? The canon had been opened and closed long since, and the loving symbolism of such an image was in any case incompatible with the God of Law.

A GOD OF LOVE?

The results of this aberration that divorced any intimate dialogue between above and below and left the people of Israel to talk to their god through their priestly lawyers seem to have been something that Jesus sought to address. As far as we can ascertain, He did so carefully, painstakingly using sane argument within the terms and traditions of Judaism to meet the law on its own ground. By self-sacrificing example He succeeded in fulfilling both the prophecies of the Hebrew canon and the mythology of the pagan faiths that Israel had long shunned.

Paganism had developed its own aberrations, turning love into lust and creativity into cruelty. Blood lust turned the Roman Coliseum into a quagmire of degradation and gore, and myth continued to be twisted to such degradation for another thousand years, until the blood ceased to flow down the pyramids of ancient South America. In mythological terms, beyond the confines of historical human time Jesus succeeded in reforging the polarity between heaven and earth and restoring the Tsdeq of Melchizadek. He might also have done so in terms of historical human time if it hadn't been for Christianity!

Christianity adopted its own canonical stance, and in its deification of Jesus it reverted to the Judaic isolation of the divine. The flesh and blood Jesus was forced to sit on the right hand of Yahweh, who had denied his followers anything but a minor role in the stewardship of creation, keeping them at arm's length from the divine purpose. The desire to be and do, in identification with humankind and so apparent in the life of Jesus, soon evaporated in canonical contrivance. The humanness that even the gods and goddesses of pagan myth were allowed was taken from Him, and the libido that affirms the being of every living creature was edited out of his story. While pagan myth allowed its divine beings to anticipate human libido, revealed religion made sure that its divine powers, including the newly acquired Jesus, were kept well away from anything smacking of human intimacy and sensuality. Christianity brought Jesus into the world psyche only to deny him human conception and intimate companionship, let alone a mate and children in adult life.

Revealed religion talks about divine love, but its lone god explicitly avoids that most intimate and human expression of love. The Adam Kadmon of revealed religion is, it seems, only very distantly "made in the image of God," and God is certainly not going to get involved in anything as messy as the creative essentials that he has initiated.

BAD TIMING

Unfortunately, with the exception of a few saints and theologians, in moving on from sensuality God appears to have left the rest of us behind! Somewhere along the way a dislocation has occurred in the creative chain of command, a dislocation that the theology of revealed religion calls "the Fall." The Fall introduces that tricky

concept and engrossing toy of theoretical physics: "time." Time
places humanity on tenterhooks while waiting for God to inter-
vene and overturn its inevitabilities, not least the inevitability of
death. Meanwhile, humankind, supposedly made in the image of
God, is commanded to live, love, multiply, and die, but the implication is that this is really an un-Godlike state of affairs, tolerated
only as a stopgap measure until some eternally postponed second
coming. What's more, we are persuaded to believe that come the
second coming we too shall suddenly abandon all our sensual and
emotional humanity for "pure" love. Being human is apparently an
impure state. All of this suggests that nature, and not least earthy
human nature, was a waste of time in the first place!

Even so, "Those whom God hath joined together, let no man
put asunder," for these distorted perceptions are and always have
been our own. Our spiritual impotence is self-inflicted and our
faults, theological and otherwise, are, as Shakespeare so wryly oberved,
not to be found in the mythical patterns of the stars, but in
ourselves.

To unravel this metaphysical mess, mythology persuades humanity to follow an Ariadne's thread back to the beginnings of it all.
There are of course many threads, and these are by now badly tangled or even broken. Nonetheless, we must try to untangle this
knotty bundle, and to do so we must find a beginning.

ISLANDS IN THE SEA OF EVERMORE

Hebrew, Egyptian, and indeed most creation myths begin in an insubstantial cosmic sea. This may be seen as the "sea" of space or the
amniotic fluid of a cosmic womb. The Egyptian perception of these
waters was the inertia of Nun which had arisen from Nu, "the watery one." Subsequently, the feminine aspect of Nu—Nuit—came
into being, but in the very beginning there was only Nu, waiting in
eternity "Before two things had being in this world." In Sumerian
myth, the divine Oannes arose from such a sea, and in the Hebrew

myths that were born from both of these, "Darkness was upon the face of the deep" before "the spirit of God moved upon the face of the waters."[6]

Into this state of eternal inertia before polarity came four masculine and four feminine gods, which the Greek-speaking Egyptians of the Ptolemaic period called the Ogdoad, or "group of eight." These four divine couples of precreation consisted, in the theology of Hermopolis, of Nun and Nuit (whose body was to become the Milky Way), Huh and Huhet, Kuk and Kauket, Amun and Amunet. The Ogdoad formed the latent potential of the cosmic sea and they stand in stark negative contrast to the better known dynamic gods and goddesses of later Egyptian myth. It was this contrast, this polarity of dynamic tension, that made later material creation inevitable. Other Egyptian creation myths supposed that Atum, father of the nine better known gods and goddesses of the Ennead, was alone in the state of Nu and brought the essence of creation into being through masturbation. His ejaculation may be translated in terms of modern astrophysics as the Big Bang!

One version of the lone Amun myth assumes that his masturbation, initiated by lonely desire, caused his hand to become his female consort Amunet. Much the same masturbatory scenario may be found in fragments of the Welsh Celtic myth of Arianrhod and Gwydion. In this, the Caer Gwydion, the Milky Way in the latent sea of space, appears to have been generated by Arianrhod masturbating her brother and lover Gwydion and then spinning his ejaculation on the silver wheel implied in her name (Arian-rhod) into the stellar constellations. The Egyptian and Welsh myths might lack the grace and style of the Hebrew creation with the face of Yahweh gliding over the waters, but they do have the sympathetic advantage of identifying the desire of divinity with human desire. In this they introduce, if belatedly, a second party to provide the necessary polarity that is so implicit in creation.

Whatever the creative technique of these primal gods in their quantum excitation of the potential of this latent fluid state, it is inevitable that sooner or later something mythically solid, an Otherworld island, will emerge from these unpredictable waters. In the Egyptian myths it is the ben ben stone; in the Hebrew myths a garden east of Eden; and in the Greek myths the Hesperides. In Celtic mythology these became islands of eternal youth, promise, and potential, frequently inhabited by giants. These island myths generally tend to be associated with flood myths and incorporate the fertile goddess/land motif with an island mound resembling an abdomen distended in pregnancy. They are mythological focii by which a folk soul finds its beginnings taking substance from the universal, amniotic sea that separates heaven and earth. Variations on this theme are almost infinite, not least the variation of the island of the Welsh Celtic goddess Ceridwen mentioned earlier. On this island in the middle of a lake, the womblike cauldron of the Goddess bubbles with the potential of creation.

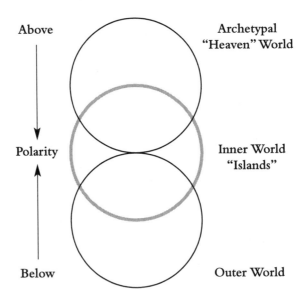

Polarity of Above and Below

Meanwhile, in the material outer world sacred places imitate such islands; for example, there are temples that are set upon rocks above the primordial waters, like the Jerusalem Temple set on the rock "at the center of the world" as an intentional recreation of the paradisal Garden of Eden on an island. The stylized outer decoration of that now lost temple shimmered in the sunlight to give the impression of waves lapping against its walls. The Temple of Isis was set on the island of Philae in the Nile, representing the point from where the life-giving Nile was seen to rise as Sirius, the star of Isis, announcing the annual, fertile renewal of inundation. For the Nile was seen as the earthly representation of the Milky Way, the sinuous body of Nuit winding across the ocean of space through which the Sun may know birth. Farther north, the pyramids of Giza imitate both the island ben ben and the fertile goddess, with their womb-like chambers entered through vagina-like corridors and their star-sighted shafts like fallopian tubes that join those symbolic wombs to the archetypal potential of the heavenly bodies. The burial chambers of northern Europe frequently carry much the same symbolism of womblike chambers approached through a narrow opening and have specific stellar/"starseed" orientation. In these less stylized, bucolic representations, the symbol of the island mound, the pregnant hump of the earth, is more obvious, and the surrounding ditches that were once filled with water emphasized these places as islands set apart in the waters of creation.

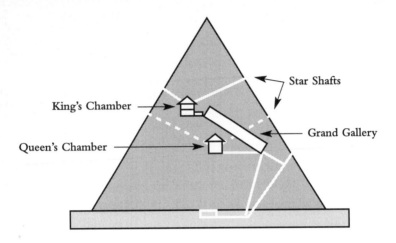

King's Chamber

Queen's Chamber

Star Shafts

Grand Gallery

The Great Pyramid

The mythology woven to these sacred places and what we know of the magical and religious activity attached to them prompts us to believe that they were seen as staging posts, half in this world and half in some underworld, set on the long road back, reaching beyond time to our eternal, paradisal beginnings. In that Edenic state, above and below are in balanced polarity and equilibrium. Maat and Tsdeq are operative. The further implication is that by finding our way back to such places of birth, such halfway houses in the chain of creation, we may know rebirth and in some way manage to rewind time to a point where we may perceive the purpose of creation and begin again.

Such is the mythology of *initiation,* a much abused word whose plain meaning is "to begin," but the essential mechanism of such beginnings is polarity. Nothing, as the mythograpers have told us, begins of its own accord. In the Egyptian myths the lone god soon finds that he cannot be alone if the creative process is to go forward; his urgent hand must become a goddess. Even in the edited Hebraic myth there is a polarity of sorts between Yahweh and the dark waters that he tastefully swoops over. In the Celtic myth of Ceridwen's island in the middle of Tegid Lake, the boy Gwion is reborn as Tal-

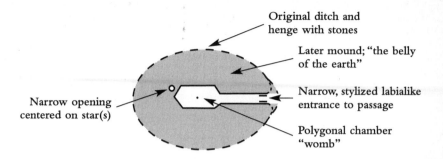

Bryn Celli Ddu Burial Chamber

iesin, but is required to polarize with the Goddess on a number of levels and through various modes of being before being taken into her womb to know a new, enlightened life. In the paradise east of Eden that becomes an island after the Fall, God is obliged to give his Adam an Eve, who gives the game away by asking the question posed by all myth, hovering at the edge of all beginnings, "what if?"

Such a question presupposes the initiation of some kind of dialogue. In other words, people who find themselves upon one of those inner islands or paradisal gardens of the prematerial world may, it seems, anticipate a creative dialogue, a relationship that in time confers a unique individual "polarity" with other orders of being.

FAERIES AT THE BOTTOM OF TIME'S GARDEN

The "what if" desire of every Amun, Taliesin, or Adam evokes the necessary consort who initiates our inner/outer/above/below polarity for the creative or recreative process to commence. Merlin, whom we shall meet later in the inner wilderness of Celydon, is joined, as his powers awaken, by his sister Gwenddydd. Little Gwion, whom we shall also meet again journeying to the island in the middle of Tegid Lake to become Taliesin, meets Ceridwen. In Tolkien's modern and very intuitive reworking of ancient myth, mortal Aragorn wanders in the faery woods of Rivendell musing on his destiny, and sees Arwen Evenstar. The original Garden of Eden myth gave Adam the same incidental encounter with Lilith before the Hebrew scribes decided that Eve was a more suitable and more easily blamable partner.

These desirable muses who obligingly materialize on our inner islands and the paradisal gardens of precreation to fulfill an initiatory dialogue—frequently with a more physical interaction implied—all fall into a certain category. In the Welsh Celtic myths that categorization is implicit in their names. The prefixes or suffixes "wyn," "wen," "gwyn," and "gwen" are all forms of the Welsh adjective that means "white." Thus Taliesin's "Cerid-wen," Merlin's "Gwen-ddydd," and curiously, either through intuition or conscious intention, Aragorn's "Ar-wen" are all white ladies. But these are by no means the virginal white ladies of some kindly inner convent. They hail from that inner kingdom that the Welsh myths called "Annwn" and that the Egyptians called the "Duat," and are envoys of another order of being. For by setting foot on those inner islands we turn back time to that mythical stage where paradisal creation first blossomed in the gardens of the gods. Accordingly, these beings of proto-creation shine with the power and wit of undiluted starlight, untarnished by what we think of as our Fall. These are the beings of Celtic faery, like the mighty *Tuatha de Dannan* of Irish myth. Not the Victorian faery spirits of tree and leaf, but the first spawn of the gods whose race precedes humanity, and who in turn mated, like the Beni Elohim of Genesis, with humankind. They stand as the oblique mythological ancestors of humankind like the Elven races of Tolkien's modern myth. They are the Annunaki, the immortals of Sumeria, from where mortal Abraham set forth to find Melchizadek in Canaan. They are the mythical Lemurians who founded lost Atlantis. Several attributes traditionally distinguish these faery beings from humankind: their immortality, their beauty and stature, and their ability in magic.

ABOUT MAGIC . . . AND SCIENCE

In the mythological world of "what if," nothing is written in stone and mechanisms are available to change things. This is a state that scientists might call "quantum indeterminism." One of those mechanisms for change is myth's fellow traveler: magic. In the inner worlds that myth and magic postulate, thought is a Cartesian, objective thing, as definite a tool as a hammer or a scalpel. However, science, having reached what it considers to be its rational adulthood, balks at coming to any conclusions about the interaction of mind and matter. Science is uncomfortable with such spooky stuff, even though Heisenberg demonstrated that the quantum worlds behind matter are, intentionally or otherwise, affected by the intrusion of human consciousness operating in the supposedly soulless, mechanistic world of particle physics.

Magic, meanwhile, is several incautious steps ahead. Most magicians hold that human consciousness is not only able to set foot upon such inner islands, but may be specifically directed to create and change outer material situations by doing so. Such direction is frequently given by the beings we have cited as faery women, Beni Elohim, and so on. Whatever the title and definition we lend to those beings, magic needs faeries at the bottom of its garden.

This represents the essential parting of the ways in the futile science versus magic debate. There may be constant wrangling about how and if incarnate human consciousness operates in Heisenberg's quantum worlds, but the existence of and discourse with other modes of consciousness and being is an absolute anathema to science. The new physics allows itself esoteric speculation about prematter and pre-time, but will not entertain any superstitious notions about prehuman consciousness. While it grudgingly maintains an uneasy truce with conventional religion, muttering that theology is not its field and allowing for God as another way of describing a *singularity,* it absolutely forbids the trespass of other intelligences, even discarnate human intelligences, into its quantum realms.

With the emergence of the insubstantial science of psychology, science felt itself able to stake its claim not only on the territory of nature but *of* human nature. In doing so it has consolidated itself as the unelected authority that dictates the bounds of human perception. Science has managed to reduce myth from a dynamic of human spiritual experience and purpose to mere wish fulfillment. Not infrequently it treats its exoteric public as if it were some elderly spinster, uneasy about ending her days with only herself to talk to. It concedes that dying can be a scary, lonely thing, and therefore allows that humans need a mythological paraphernalia that will provide comfort and assurance of ultimate immortality. Certainly, says science soothingly, such beings exist, but only in the mind and not in any independent state. Jungian psychology has explained them away as "archetypes of the unconscious" through which we may all have a personal Merlin, Osiris, or Isis. For science, spiritual experience and evolution is "all in the mind." For magic, it's all in the *polarity between minds*—our own human minds and those of other independent modes of being. But the intuition that stimulates inner relationships and the emotion that drives them refuse to be subject to such rational criteria. One cannot legislate for love. Science and magic, like science and religion, will probably never wholly agree, though from time to time they find themselves occupying the same quantum no man's land or the uncertain psychological territory of the collective unconscious.

But humanity whose blessing and curse is the ability to ask "what if?" inevitably wants to have its cake and eat it! It wants to be able to rationalize the unrational, it wants myth to be history, particles to have personality, and waves to have wizardry. It wants the square pegs of physics to fit into the round holes of magic, and the whole to form a neat holistic philosophy. The present literary vogue for the discovery of actual Gardens of Eden, sunken Atlantean islands, and so on is part of this seeking to prove that the inner worlds so ably charted in myth have actual existence.

THE ISLAND THAT NEVER WAS

There are as many Islands of Atlantis as there are mythologies, because Atlantis is of course that archetypal inner island where humanity rubs shoulders with other orders of being and seeks the roots of its origination. But we have to understand that Atlantis, like the Celtic Otherworld islands and the Edenic garden surrounded by waters, is all about early creation, not early civilization. It represents what myth represents, the quantum potential of an inner mode of being that precedes material existence and is thus the embryonic future rather than some long lost phase of the prehistoric past.

When Atlantis became the Eden of the Western Mystery tradition, it became an Eden where humanity didn't end up eating forbidden fruit from the Tree, but propagated a tree to accommodate its own appetites. Atlantis therefore presents a parable of those typical magical pitfalls—the hunger for power and the cultivation of pride. It demonstrates the profound distinction between the realization of selfhood and the cultivation of selfishness, between realizing one's part in service to cosmic order that the ancients called Maat and Tsdeq, and establishing an alternative order. It warns every magician, every seeker of the secrets behind nature, of the responsibilities they shouldered when they were initiated into the mysteries in the first place:

"What seek ye?" demands the Magus of the hapless initiate.

"To know," replies the initiate in faltering voice.

"Why so?" insists the Magus.

"I seek to know in order to serve," rasps the dry throated initiate.

As the legend generally has it, Atlantis was founded by the Lemurians. The Lemurians may be seen as the first beings of creation who knew an immortal, Godlike state, a paradisal state before the Fall. In this they may be compared to the Beni Elohim of Genesis or the High Elven beings of Tolkien's book *The Silmarillion.*[7] Their paradisal existence therefore equates with the faery beings of Celtic tradition or the Annunaki of Sumerian myth. They are essentially beings of angelic descent, "star born," beyond an earth or indeed a solar system that has potential rather than material existence at the time of their origination. But their business is to create, and in doing so to externalize the starry archetypal patterns of heaven in matter and in mankind.

To do this the Lemurians founded Atlantis, a group of islands in the so-called great western ocean. The fact that Atlantis is not a single island is frequently forgotten. Mythologically, Atlantis is a group of seven islands. "The great western ocean" is not the physical Atlantic, but the sea of space and the islands created by the Lemurians are the Sun and planets of our solar system. The largest of these islands is the central island of Ruta, which represents the Sun, or indeed the implanted star about which that solar system takes shape. The Lemurians are creating an archetypal framework of potential, a fluid mirror in which heaven may be reflected in physical existence. In this a number of things become apparent.

Atlantis is in the west because west is where the Sun returns to be hidden in the womb of deep starry space to join the other stars from which it originated. It returns to the starry faery kingdom, the underworld of paradisal islands so beloved of the Celts, where the cauldron of being bubbles with potential. This is the Annwn, which King Arthur visited with the bard Taliesin in the poem entitled *Preiddu Annwn*.[8] In this poem they travel in a white ship, Prydwen, and enter another realm of being that is sevenfold, or of seven Caers. These seven reflect the inner template of creation, a template drawn from the stars and especially from the visible seven stars of both Ursa Major and Ursa Minor that are the chief circumpolar stars. This same inner template occurs in magical and mythological systems the world over, as in the seven directions of the Hebrew Cube of Space and the seven *arrets* of the Egyptian Duat, because such sevenfold inner constructs anticipate the apparent structure of space/time in actual creation. We have sevenfold space in the four directions of the compass plus the threefold axis of above, center, and below, the seven days of the week, and, not least, the seven chakras, or points of inner and outer orientation, which yoga ascribes to the human form.

In this we may elaborate our inner map to indicate an Atlantean positioning that will certainly be familiar to students of Qabalah.

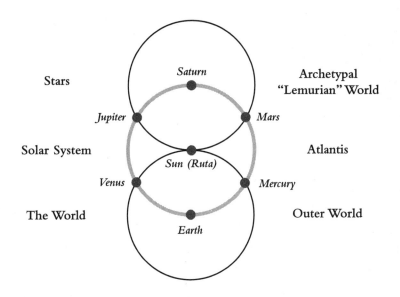

The Island That Never Was

Atlantis, as the mysteries describe it, never existed as a solid historical entity. The belief that it did so has arisen from the tendency of the ancients to twist myth and history together and speak of imaginative concepts as if they were actualities. Our ancestors spoke with an easy informality about their gods and goddesses as if these divine beings lived just down the road. Atlantis and similar mythological islands are about potential, especially the potential of men and women in equal and equitable stewardship of the multifaceted world we live in. For this potential, like the urgent optimism known at the start of a love affair, is where, between high heaven and deep earth, polarity magic finds and applies its power, the place where half mortal heroes are born. But, as in this mundane world, birth requires conception and conception requires desire. Desire is a realization of the potential for fulfillment, and myth pictures that potential in the context of a paradisal inner place. Its existence as an inner place set apart from the intrusion of normal human consciousness endowed it with a feeling of distance in space and time. But humankind, as the story of Adam and Eve is at pains to point out, is blessed with an innate curiosity; in fact, a curiosity that anticipates and thus invokes time. Placed in a situation that brims with potential, like Ceridwen's cauldron, Eve's "What if?" can only evoke a future beyond the eternal present. For all the disapproval of the Hebrew scribes and the subsequent Fall they claimed that Eve initiated, it is her question that fuels human evolution. Eve ponders myth's question, and the fact that she does so on that island between being and unbeing stirs the ready ethers of that Atlantean, Edenic, quantum world.

Eve's conceptual pondering gives the world its future, for the more that humankind seeks explanation and asks "what if" about the inner forces behind existence, then the closer those forces come to perception and actuation. That actuation may then unfold through the laws of quantum mechanics to flesh out the sevenfold archetypal template, the pattern of the stars that myth insists upon. We may further elaborate this in terms of Celtic mythology, or even in terms of physics, as the following illustration, taken from Mike Harris' book, *Awen*,[9] indicates.

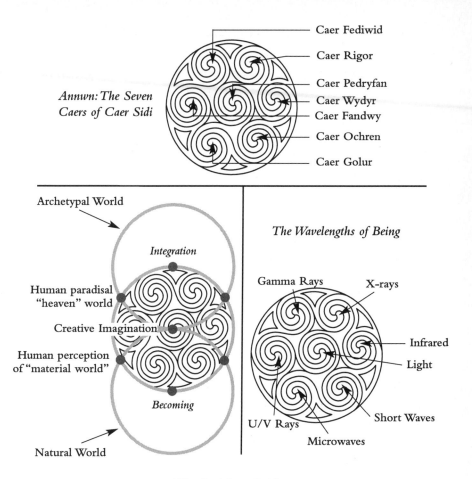

Annwn: The Seven
Caers of Caer Sidi

- Caer Fediwid
- Caer Rigor
- Caer Pedryfan
- Caer Wydyr
- Caer Fandwy
- Caer Ochren
- Caer Golur

Archetypal World

Integration

Human paradisal
"heaven" world

Creative Imagination

Human perception
of "material world"

Becoming

Natural World

The Wavelengths of Being

Gamma Rays   X-rays

Infrared

Light

U/V Rays   Short Waves

Microwaves

The Rainbow Bridge

Atlantis was mythologically born in volcanic fire, issuing up from beneath the sea. This symbolizes its emergence from the inner earth, a premise underworld in quantum dynamic fluidity moving to solidity. The symbolism, as with most myth, uses a suitable material metaphor, which in this case is the geological birth of the earth. Yet the stable solidity anticipated by the processes evoked in Atlantis was doomed to slide back into instability through fire and flood, a pattern that surfaces in many mythical parables. In every such case instability occurs because the archetypal Maat or Tsdeq, the star-bright, heavenly patterns of "above," become obliterated in the fog of human (or proto-human) free will in its anticipation of "below," and what starts as free will soon becomes willfulness.

LOVE UNDER WILL

The token of a God of Love is free will. A God of Love may not, by the very nature of love, compel. Indeed to do so, and to suspend free will, would cancel the polarity that enables divine self-expression. For if divine selfhood is to be fully realized, if Tsedq is to be fully expressed, then all its variations must be known. "For the 'inside' to have meaning there must be an 'outside.'" God is love, and may only know self-expression through love. It is upon these mythical inner islands where free will has its primal expression that a trysting place is found. The passion of such a trysting is in the polarity, the dynamic interaction of two individual, self-determining states of being, and, as in mundane human terms, equilibrium must be established. That equilibrium is reached through selflessness, not in the surrender of selfhood, but in its fulfillment. These are matters with which we shall deal in some detail when we examine the polarity of the mundane priest/priestess relationship.

In Atlantis, it is said, there was such a polarity, represented by the priesthood of the Sun Temple and the priestesses of the withdrawn Naradek Temple. The Sun Temple represented proto-human stewardship of an established solar system; the Naradek Temple represented archetypal inner empowerment associated with the patterns of the stars in the ebb and flow of the sea of space. It is said that while the Sun Temple, responsible for the consolidation of archetypal patterns, caused the demise of Atlantis, the Naradek Temple never fell. In other words, the essentially feminine receptivity to the Tsdeq of archetypal patterns remained aware of those patterns, while the Sun Temple, which had been charged with their implementation, began to orchestrate its own version of cosmic order.

The Lemurians who founded Atlantis to pursue the implementation of heaven in earth, eventually, it is said, realized that Atlantis was beyond redemption. They didn't really need to evoke mythological fire and flood to undo the sorry constructs that the Atlanteans had devised to indulge their pride. Those constructs were by their very nature unstable and volatile, for their contravention of cosmic law made their continued existence precarious. Willfulness and selfishness imposes its own exile. Just as the cauldron was broken and its island set beyond human perception, just as the Holy Grail was withdrawn into the upper ethers and the gates of Eden slammed shut, so Atlantis sank back into the anonymous, eternal sea.

But there were, however, survivors, for how else could myth write its story? Time may set beginnings and endings, but myth preserves the constant of eternity. When human consciousness begins again to search beyond its selfish self and ask the question, it is drawn in by those captivating threads, the folk memories of those who have journeyed to Atlantis and returned to tell the tale. Their tale is a love story, the romance of above and below. It is the story in which men and women may, through love, explore and expand the endless variations of true priesthood and stewardship of the God of Love. In the chapters that follow we shall see Eve's question posed in myth and lived in life. In doing so we shall return to those forgotten inner islands where our brothers and sisters of the ancient mysteries knew their own joys and setbacks in trying to realize the marriage of heaven and earth.

CHAPTER TWO

AKHENATEN, NEFERTITI, AND SUN MAGIC

THE TEMPLE OF THE SUN

Returning to Atlantis, we remember that the main focus of the "state" religion was the Sun, and that the central temple was the Sun Temple, which was located at the summit of the mountain of Ruta. Unlike the withdrawn temple of the Sea and Stars, the Sun Temple is said to have fallen both morally and physically, and thus was the epicenter of the forces that saw the end of Atlantis. The Temple of the Sea and Stars represented the survival and continuation of the pervading spirit of the Lemurian Age that preceded Atlantis. The beings of that Age were of a type whose nature was less individualized and whose bodies far less dense than those of the Atlantean and present Ages, living as they did in a world that had not yet taken its final fall into physicality. The work of the Sun Temple encapsulated all that was best—and worst—of the present human condition, where the awesome powers granted to humankind can be used in an angelic manner, or in the perverted wilfulness of an ego-driven desire for power. It is probably true to say that the redemption of the work originally undertaken by the fallen Sun Temple and its reinstatement at the center as a true reflection of the pure spiritual light of our Sun, both individually and at a planetary level, is symbolic of the quest of humankind.

But in many ways the Sun Temple remains to this day even more of an enigma than the Temple of the Sea and the Stars. What is Sun

Magic, when all is said and done? Although we are familiar with the idea of the influence of the planets upon our lives at an everyday astrological level (the proactive energy of Mars, for example), or working at a deeper level (found in the mysteries of Venus as the higher self of the earth), the star we know as the Sun as a magical or occult symbol presents something more difficult.

Two ancient Egyptian pharaohs of the Eighteenth Dynasty, Amenhotep III and his more famous son, Amenhotep IV, who later changed his name to Akhenaten, referred to the Sun as the Aten or Tjehen, the "Dazzling Sun Disc," and indeed we easily find ourselves "dazzled" by the Sun. We know that it represents our self, our central and unique identity. In Qabalist representation, for example, it stands at the center of the Tree of Life at Tiphareth, place of meeting of the upper and lower self, but in the sense that the Moon, or Venus, Mars, or Mercury, are "worked with" as occult powers, it represents something rather different. How do you "work with" the Sun? We are literally blinded by the Sun—and increasingly so in the present time. The disaster of the shrinking ozone layer makes us more aware of the dangers this star presents to us on earth as well as its life-sustaining properties.

SUN PRIEST, SUN PRIESTESS

Current commentators view Akhenaten as something of a heretic who attempted to impose a maverick monotheism in place of the pantheism that had served Egypt for thousands of years. We find it more useful and perhaps more accurate to postulate that what he actually tried to achieve was a remembering and renewal of humankind's connection with the Sun. In this he was more than ably supported by his priestess, his Great Royal Wife, Nefertiti. Nefertiti, as we shall see, was rather more than just a pretty face, and among the many magical partnerships, such as that of Solomon and Sheba, which have disappeared from the pages of history, Nefertiti's and Akhenaten's union was outstanding.

Akhenaten and Nefertiti were a couple whose extraordinary achievements continue to fascinate Egyptologists, theologians, and occultists alike. But as far as this book is concerned, what they offer in particular is an almost unique example of a man and a woman working in polarity at every level—that is to say physical, emotional, mental, and spiritual—and at the heart of the process of change that we have witnessed so far. All the evidence we have shows that they were happily married, raised a family of six daughters, and ruled with reasonable success over Egypt for a number of years. Most important, from our point of view, is that they managed to work equally as king and queen *and* priest and priestess in the Temples of the Sun, in whose mysteries they shared knowledge, belief, and ability. To achieve this successful mating on all levels is unusual—and what is more remarkable is that they were apparently equally successful in alternating the levels at which they worked, both evidently working actively and receptively on each plane. Each of them is depicted on the surviving bas reliefs as working actively in the temple, but it is obvious that each was also working upon the inner planes. Although Akhenaten is often shown wearing the white crown of upper Egypt, they are both portrayed as wearing the blue crown. Commonly known as the "war crown," it might be more accurate to think of it as indicating an active, positive mode rather than a battle mode as such, and Nefertiti, no less than her husband, is seen in active, positive mode in the reliefs that picture her smiting the enemies of the country. Smiting the enemy was a common stance for pharaohs to adopt in commemorative bas reliefs, whether or not they had actually done any smiting of enemies; it conveyed the impression of strength and firm rulership.

Their reign poses many intriguing questions, and although they were only rediscovered recently after having been effectively erased from history by their immediate successors, Akhenaten has since become the subject of some extraordinary interpretations: genetic abnormality, hormonal disorder, extreme physical deformity, mania,

Oedipal complex, homosexuality; you name it and he has been accused of it. Conversely, Nefertiti has somehow managed to remain untouched and apparently untouchable. We wonder at her beauty—but are left wondering. The impregnability of perfection acts as a protective barrier that has provided her with a defense more sure than any pharaoh's curse.

But if we look at their lives and work from an esoteric and magical point of view rather than from a historical or popular point of view, we must ask different questions. The esoteric point of view takes as a basic premise that when the time is right for a new influence to be made manifest in the physical world, then that new impulse will be initiated from the inner planes and brought about through the embodiment of new principles in the thoughts and actions of those capable of such work. In this way the template of Atlantis provides a continuing basis of new initiatives within the physical world, and there is no doubt that Akhenaten and Nefertiti were tapping into an order of things that far predated their own epoch. In fact, the entire Amarna Dynasty of pharaohs (that is, Amenhotep III, Akhenaten, Smenkhare, and Tutankhamun) proved to be one such time, although whether or not the work was at that time fully achieved and whether sufficient seeds were laid down for the future is a matter of debate. It may well be that they attempted too much too soon, or that the task of pulling the carpet out from under the feet of the vast hierarchy of priestly power at Karnak was simply not possible.

FROM KARNAK TO AMARNA

The building of the Karnak temple complex as a temple to Amun, "the Hidden One," had acquired colossal proportions during the progress of the Eighteenth Dynasty. Situated just to the north of the modern city of Luxor on the east bank of the Nile, it covers many thousands of acres. The "Great Harris Papyrus,"[1] which dates from the reign of Rameses III when the temple was already past the height of its influence, states that it was run by a staff of 86,000 people. It owned almost a quarter of all the arable land in Egypt and roughly two-thirds of all the temple land. Each successive pharaoh had outdone their predecessor in finding new ways of proving that size mattered. The result was that the religious purpose of the temple at Karnak was in danger of becoming engulfed in the weight of its own complexity and the aggrandizement of its builders. When a ritual ceremony has a cast of thousands, then the organization of numbers may become its own *raison d'etre*. Eighteenth Dynasty priest and modern visitor alike in Karnak's noise and confusion may find it hard to remember that its prime purpose was as a temple to a hidden god. In this city of thousands, no outsider, that is to say no one who was not of the priesthood, was ever admitted past its gates. Moreover, its chief deity was one whose very nature—"hidden"— was hardly one that appealed to the population at large who understandably preferred its gods to be a little more accessible. Significantly, of all the pantheon of Egyptian god/goddess forms, Amun remains the least known, the least used as a magical or religious image. Nothing is more likely to become a basis for corruption in religious or magical circles than the idea that the One God is incomprehensible to any but the priestly elite.

Although Akhenaten was brought up in the palace of Malkata, which lay on the west bank of the Nile at the foothills of the Theban mountains of the dead, soon after becoming pharaoh he took his family and followers to the north and built an entirely new city—now generally known as Amarna—halfway between Thebes and Memphis, or modern Cairo. Many miles from Karnak, he started afresh on virgin soil. Almost nothing now remains of this city, but in spite of the lengths to which the succeeding dynasty went in order to obliterate all record of his family, the prerequisites that ensured the survival of sufficient evidence of their work until the time was right for its significance to be made known, have been met. For example, we have the fascinating unsolved mystery of their apparent sudden disappearance, the confusion over possible candidates for Akhenaten's mummy, and his even more mysterious successor, Smenkhare. We have the absorbing mystery of the oddity of their sculptures and bas reliefs. We have the "Amarna letters," the correspondence between the royal family at Amarna and the near East, which give fascinating insights into the daily lives of these families. Above all, we have the magnificent sculptures of Nefertiti, who, through the miraculous survival of her portraits from the ruins of the city of Amarna, is universally acknowledged to have been the most beautiful woman in the world. These things all serve to ensure that they continue to stay alive in our consciousness, not fade away into the history books as another minor pharaoh and his wife.

As if this were not enough, Akhenaten, for some unknown reason, decided to build their city with building blocks that were smaller than usual, and although the city was abandoned and destroyed within a very few years of its construction, the sandstone blocks used to build it were small enough to be reused as "filling" when they were pilfered for some of the pylons of later temple buildings at Karnak. In this strange manner they were perfectly preserved until such time that technology advanced sufficiently to ensure that they could be "rebuilt" on computers like a ghostly jigsaw from the past, and have been reconstructed, without recourse to bricks and mortar, to show many hundreds of revelatory scenes of Akhenaten, Nefertiti, and family. And to make absolutely certain, the tomb of Akhenaten's son, Tutankhamun, remained unplundered until discovered within living memory by Howard Carter. It has revealed the most priceless and wonderful treasures of any that have ever been found. While the survival and discovery of ancient Egyptian artifacts is something of a lottery, there is also no doubt that at times, when necessary, there are other agencies at work, and the influence of inner hands is evident here.

So let us assume of Akhenaten and Nefertiti that their tasks and achievements were not the result of personal whim or genetic disorder. Let us first be sure that they were both of sound body and mind, living and working with arguably the most spiritually advanced people of the last five thousand years. More than this, they were a highly evolved partnership of priest and priestess, brought together as the most likely couple to bring about certain inner initiatives. When we realize that these initiatives had been slowly developing over the previous hundred years or so, we begin to see what Akhenaten and Nefertiti really achieved. There has been a tendency to see Akhenaten as a maverick whose strange ideas came out of nowhere and quickly died with him. It is probably more accurate, and certainly makes a lot more sense in esoteric terms, to pay closer attention to their immediate and illustrious ancestors, starting from the female pharaoh Hatshepsut. In fact, throughout the Eighteenth Dynasty there was a gradual separation between the priests of the hidden Amun at Karnak and the focus of the ruling pharaohs on an increasingly visible and externalized deity.

To put them briefly into their historical context, Akhenaten and Nefertiti reigned over Egypt toward the end of the Eighteenth Dynasty. It is likely that the equally famous Tutankhamun was Akhenaten's son, but after his reign the Eighteenth Dynasty soon came to an end and was to give way to the successful Ramesside kings of the Nineteenth Dynasty. It is difficult to fix any ancient Egyptian dates with any real accuracy because each of the pharaohs dated their reign not from any one fixed "Year Dot" as we are now able to do, but started counting anew every time from the first year of their own reign. However, current opinion tends to date Akhenaten and Nefertiti as having reigned in the mid 1300s B.C. (Other researchers, notably David Rohl, who shifts conventional dates forward in time, believes them to have reigned during the early 1100s B.C., which, interestingly, would make them contemporaneous with King David, founder of the City of Jerusalem.)[2]

AFTER HATSHEPSUT

Something very new appeared to be happening at the start of the Eighteenth Dynasty. Ahmose-Nefertari, wife of Amenhotep I, the Dynasty's founder who was later deified, took on the role of god's wife of Amun, a role she passed on with particular authority to the continuing line of very influential women throughout the Eighteenth Dynasty. Hatshepsut, sixth pharaoh of the Dynasty, was unusual even for a country whose attitude toward women had always been fairly enlightened. She not only declared herself pharaoh, but made it known that although she was born of a human mother, her father was Divine: the god Amun. In this she was one of a number of people throughout the ages, some of whom appear in the pages of this book, who claim to have been born from a Divine father and an earthly mother. One's response to this claim can range from unquestioning acceptance to cynical disbelief. Was it a genuine impulse from the inner planes or was it an all too human inflated ego at work? The attitude of these writers is one of interest and open-mindedness—by their fruits shall ye know them—and certainly Hatshepsut, who reigned against all odds for many years, seemed to have had something going for her. Whether or not she was actually the daughter of an earth mother and sky father, she was certainly the recipient of a strong inner impulse for change, and was able to carry it through into the mundane world.

Until the Twelfth Dynasty, the god Amun had been only one of the many minor local gods. His name simply meant "Invisible," or "The Hidden One." However, in a movement that was flourishing by the time of the Eighteenth Dynasty and climaxed in Hatshepsut's supposedly divine conception, his influence had grown and centered at Thebes, where he took on the attributes of all the Sun gods and became known across the land as "Amen-Ra." By combining his attributes of unmanifest power with the attributes of Ra, the god of the visible Sun, he was, in effect, now perceived as the one creative power, visible and invisible, which was the source of all life everywhere. There would seem to be little appreciable difference between Amen-Ra and our own "God."

Whatever the truth of Hatshepsut's origins, her relationship with Amun was such that during her reign are found the first recorded examples of a magical ritual, which appears to have been instrumental in bringing about a very close union with this most mysterious of gods, and which was evidence of the close understanding she had of the nature and power of Amun. As pharaoh she was in a unique position to transmit this to the people of Egypt. The ritual formed the private and intimate center of a ceremony that came to be known as the Opet Festival, which took place once a year toward the beginning of the season of the inundation. The statues of Amun, his wife, Mut (her name means "mother"), and their son, Khonsu ("messenger"), were brought out of their deeply protected and innermost temple and processed before the general public. The culmination of the ritual came about through an act of union that took place between Amun and the mother of the pharaoh within Amun's inner sanctuary. When this had been achieved, the pharaoh then entered the sanctuary to be reunited with his newborn light body or star body, known as his *ka*. Thus was he—or she—reborn. The ritual was obviously intended to achieve the closest possible union between an incarnate human—male or female—and the Godhead. As such, it became established as the culmination of the main religious ceremony of the Western world, and, in essence, there is probably little difference in what took place in the innermost temple of Amun at Thebes and what took place in the Holy of Holies in the tabernacle between the high priest and the God of the Hebrews.

THE BODY OF LIGHT

The concept of the ka is one that seems very far away from us now, and it is almost impossible to understand exactly what it meant to the ancient Egyptians. To our modern understanding, the ka is the body of light, the perfect template of our physical body that is held for us among the stars, in perpetuity, throughout our incarnations. Thus, the light body of Osiris was the constellation of Orion, and the light body of Isis was the star Sirius. The "fall," or separation from the body of light, is told in different ways in different mythologies and beliefs. To some it is represented by the descent of the light bringer, Lucifer, into the dense physicality of earth, where he serves as a constant reminder of what might be. To the ancient Egyptians the "fall" was symbolized by the separation of Nut and Geb, Sky Goddess and Earth God, who are fated to yearn without fulfillment for their lost state of oneness. The object of the Opet ritual was to enable the celebrant to reforge this union while still in the living body rather than wait until after death. In one sense there is nothing new here, and, as we have said, something of this order has formed the basis of the most advanced (Egyptian) magic. The pharaoh and some of the priesthood maintained a very close connection with their ka during their lifetimes, and the pharaoh was thus in a pivotal position to hold the collective force of this stellar energy in the balance of Maat and transmit its qualities to the populace. However, what was unusual in the Eighteenth Dynasty was the concept that the ka was apparently invested not in a star such as Orion or Sirius, but with the star we know as the Sun.

Amenhotep II, an earlier pharaoh of the Eighteenth Dynasty, appears to have been inspired by the wisdom of the Fourth Dynasty pharaohs Khufu and Khafre, who are primarily associated with the pyramids. He set up a stela in their honor on which is found the first recorded representation of the Aten Sun Disc. This small incident is symbolic of the increasing, if underlying, quest of the Eighteenth Dynasty pharaohs for the solar wisdom of an earlier age. It must be remembered that Khufu and Khafre had lived over a thousand years earlier and much of the significance of their work must have been lost. Their lifetimes were as far from the Amenhoteps as the Amenhoteps are from us. But it was apparently the Sphinx that was the particular source of their inner teaching: not only did Amenhotep II set up a temple dedicated to the Sphinx, but he erected a statue of himself between the paws of the Sphinx. The full meaning of the Sphinx has yet to be discovered, although many commentators have recently uncovered much of its significance. Suffice it to say that it appears to be by far the oldest construction in Egypt, much older than the pyramids, and has been rightly associated for many years as a source of hidden wisdom that may yet be discovered literally as a "Hall of Records," or simply as a focus for a teaching that comes from far beyond this place and time. While its physical origins are therefore something of a mystery, its continuing power and presence as a link of communication with the oldest wisdom available to humankind is as strong as it was five thousand or more years ago. Crouched upon the west bank of the Nile, its gaze is fixed upon the rising Sun in the east, set against the ever-changing background of the starry constellations caused by the turning of the wheel of the precession of the equinoxes, even as its physical form crumbles from the corrosive pollution of the modern city of Cairo at its feet.

It was Tutmosis IV, Akhenaten's grandfather, who made the most intimate connection with the Sphinx. Out hunting in the region of the Giza plateau, he fell asleep in its shade. At that time, indicative of the neglect of the monuments of the Giza plateau, the animal was almost entirely buried in sand. In his dream, at the moment of midday when the Sun was at its zenith, Tutmosis heard the voice of the Sphinx, who spoke like a father to his son, telling him that it was his task to uncover its buried body. In return Tutmosis would be made pharaoh of Egypt in spite of the fact that he had at least one older brother who was, of course, the natural heir to the throne. "For many years," said the Sphinx, "my face has been turned to you; my heart belongs to you, and you belong to me. Behold, I am in pain, and my body is ruined. . . . I have been waiting to have you do what is in my heart, for I know you are my son and protector."[3] Tutmosis did as he was asked and cleared the sand to reveal the full body of the Sphinx, placing a stela at its breast, which is still in existence—and he did indeed become the next pharaoh.

His son, Amenhotep III, was great even among pharaohs, and has well been called "The Sun King." It was said that he was conceived as a result of a mating between Tutmosis IV's wife Mutemweia and the god Amun in the manner described by the magical ritual of the Opet Festival. According to the inscriptions on the temple reliefs that show this event taking place, Mutemweia was sleeping one night when: "She awoke on account of the aroma of the god and cried out before him. . . . He went to her straight away, she rejoiced at the sight of his beauty, and love for him coursed through her body. The palace was flooded with the god's aroma. . . . 'How strong is your power! Your dew fills my body' and then the majesty of this god did all that he desired with her."[4] There is something about this description that comes across very convincingly. (A very similar description, as we shall see later, was given by the mother of Merlin after she had been visited in the night by a demon.) Increasingly identifying himself with the Sun, Amenhotep III was deified as the Sun god in the *sed* Festival of renewal, which he celebrated several times toward the end of his reign. He was also responsible, presumably as a result of the continuing veneration of the Sphinx, for the commissioning of hundreds of black quartzite statues of the lion-goddess, some of which can now be seen in the British Museum. But for our purposes the most interesting aspect of his reign was his increasing use of the Aten Sun Disc as a symbol, and it was Amenhotep III who created the first Aten priesthood and dedicated Aten temple at Heliopolis. By the time Akhenaten came to the throne, most of his innovations had already been carefully put into place over many years. We have seen that the clearing of the way for these changes had been working throughout the Eighteenth Dynasty—that is to say in the increased role of women in active priesthood and active service in the running of the country, and of the literal reemergence of the Sphinx as a voice of inspiration and inner direction. But above all of these was the externalization of the powers and hierarchy of the visible light of the Sun even while the Theban priesthood clung to Amun the Hidden One. All should have gone very well, and Akhenaten and Nefertiti evidently possessed great ability and originality. Let us look in detail at what exactly they were doing.

THE ATEN

The Aten itself, the Sun Disc, would appear at first sight to have been divorced by Akhenaten from all its previous associations with other deities, including all solar deities, both male and female. He was at particular pains to eradicate all depictions of Amun, presumably because of this particular god's associations with the darkness of the unseen and the consequent power this gave to the stranglehold of the Karnak priesthood. It is easy to assume that when Akhenaten replaced the worship of all other deities with the Aten Sun Disc, he expected to be worshipped as its embodiment. However, the many surviving depictions of Akhenaten and his family make it clear that this is not the case. We do not find in the Aten Sun Disc any qualities that readily put it in the category of "God" or "religion," especially in the sense in which the ancient Egyptians understood it. To them, the gods were the first and foremost example of polarity at work. Every goddess had a male partner, each couple had a child, and the stories of cosmic procreation and begetting were graphic in their detail. But the Aten was neither male nor female, and it didn't have any children; neither did it have any sign, or symbol, or associated animal or bird, nor any anthropomorphic representation whatsoever. There were no stories connected with it; it had no mythology. It apparently neither gave guidance nor protection; it could not be invoked in order to smite one's enemies; it had no humors. As a god or goddess it couldn't have had less going for it, and it is perhaps puzzling that Akhenaten should have abandoned his father's compromise of a successful relationship with the Sun Disc while at the same time maintaining a sufficient presence of the rest of the panoply of deities to keep the priesthood and the general public happy. The lack of anthropomorphic characteristics of the Aten meant that it was much more difficult for either Akhenaten or Nefertiti to embody any of its characteristics and mediate these to the country at large. But it would appear that he had no intention of trying, and while it would have been perfectly possible for him to have commissioned statues or temple reliefs of him wearing the Sun Disc as a headdress, and in this way embody the characteristics of the Aten to mediate them to temple users, there is no evidence at all that he ever attempted to do so.

In fact, almost every surviving statue of Akhenaten shows him in the conventional Osiris pose: holding the crook and flail, with arms crossed over his breast. This is by no means a coincidence, and we know from the innovatory style that is evidenced by the Amarna school that Akhenaten was not bound by convention. But Akhenaten and Nefertiti were attempting to bring the essence of religious worship out from the gloom of the temple sanctuaries into the full light of day and, simultaneously, to bring the focus of worship away from the exclusive, priestly, funerary cults of the afterlife and into the celebration of living creation in a manner that was available to all. The Osirian cult of the dead was not rejected, but transformed. When they moved from the palace of Malkata among the funerary temples of the Theban hills to the virgin territory that was to become Amarna, the boundaries of their new city were delineated with fourteen stelae. The number fourteen is, as we have seen, of great significance in the symbolism of many magical traditions. It will be remembered that in the earliest days of Egyptian history there was conflict in the skies between Osiris and his brother, Set. Set killed Osiris and dismembered his body, cutting it into fourteen parts that he then scattered about the land of the Egypt. Osiris' wife, Isis, mourned for her husband and travelled the length of the land in search of the pieces of his dismembered body. She found thirteen of them, and although the missing part was, unfortunately, his phallus, she was able to restore him to life sufficiently enough to become impregnated by his star-body. She later gave birth to their son Horus. The myth of the sacrificial death of the God, the bringing to life by the Goddess and the consequent birth of the son of light, became the fundamental symbol of the task of each pharaoh, who in this way became central to the maintenance of the connection between the risen Osiris, in Orion, and his people. By setting out the boundaries of his city by fourteen markers, the entire city of Amarna became symbolic of the dismembered body of Osiris and a talismanic representation, in earth below, of the template of the heavens above. We may guess then that the basis of some of the rituals undertaken within its temples, as had for so many years been the case, symbolized the rising of Osiris from the dead and the underworld, and his coming forth into day. But the essential difference was that whereas the star-body, or ka, of Isis was vested with the star Sirius, Nefertiti was not a priestess of Sirius—she was a priestess of the Sun, and it was therefore her powers that transformed the body of Osiris. It is therefore very significant to note that instead of giving birth to a Horus, the falcon-headed son of light, she gave birth to the symbol of the Sun—six children, all female.

Having ascertained what the Sun Disc is not, the problem is that we are apparently left with not very much. We could assume that Akhenaten's form of worship, if it was worship, consisted of a simple form of adoration that was not much more than you might see on the beach in summer. The imagination could happily create a picture of him as being pretty laid back; a gentle family man with hippy tendencies who wasn't into fighting and whose message was to relax, for the sunshine is great. To impute a simple appreciation of sunshine as the explanation for the motivation behind the work of this extraordinary pharaoh seems inadequate, and yet we run up against our initial question: what is Sun Magic? What does the Sun represent?

SUN MAGIC

In the absence of any other obvious information, we can only go back to the depictions of the Aten, and of the couple's relationship with it. Rather than interpret Akhenaten's insistence on the Sun to the exclusion of other gods/goddesses as evidence of ego-driven oppression, it is more fruitful to begin to understand his motivation. This seems to have been a positive encouragement to put aside the distancing effect of anthropomorphism. Indeed, it appears to assert that the light of the Sun was available to all, without any mediation by the pharaoh or his priests. This is a process akin to what has more recently been termed "the externalization of the hierarchy." To experience the light of the Sun, one has only (if living in Egypt!) to stand outside, although, as we shall see, the magic worked between Akhenaten and Nefertiti as priest and priestess went far beyond a simple worship of sunlight. And indeed, although he did build temples to the Aten, the fundamental difference from those of his predecessors was that they were roofless, open to the sunlight. Temple building of the previous period had been based on the ritual procession from wide, open courts, through the pillared hypostyle halls whose many columns represented the fields of rushes through which the traveller in the underworld of the Duat had to find his or her way, and then through progressively smaller pylons into smaller, darker courts, until eventually the single, unlit sanctuary (of Amun) was reached by the high priest alone, or the pharaoh. The most significant part of the Amarna iconography is the highly visible connection that is always made between the royal family and the Sun Disc. It is not a distant and impersonal round object in the sky worshipped from afar, but it makes a close, intimate connection with the people below by the long extension of its rays and the hand with which each ray ends; hands that interpenetrate the scene and reach out to touch the couple and their children, sometimes offering to them the ankh, the sign of eternal life. It is the relationship between Sun and human that is emphasized—the dynamics and qualities of the energy of the Sun as received by those on earth.

To the Egyptians of that time the hand was feminine, and we are reminded by this that the chief form of Sun worship, apart from that of the god Ra, who became subsumed with Amun, was through the goddess Hathor, the daughter of Ra. The Sun was seen as both male and female, according to its different functions and levels. One might say that the Sun is a symbol of all the things of God and Goddess. The central fire is love, the heat that flows from love is goodness, the light that accompanies its manifestation is the light of divine truth, or wisdom. The heat can nurture or destroy according to the greater needs of love. And so we find commonly depicted in temple bas reliefs the encompassing boat of Ra, in whose prow sits the daughter of wisdom and truth, Maat, while the nourishing goodness of the Sun is symbolized by the milk of the celestial cow Hathor and its destructive aspects by the fiery goddess Sehkmet. And so just as we find that Akhenaten was happy to continue with the prime symbolic function of Osiris, we also find that Nefertiti continued to rely upon the tradition of Hathor. This is confirmed by the many depictions of Nefertiti as priestess of the Sun worshipping in the manner of a Hathor priestess in the *Hwt Ben Ben* Sun Temple, which was reserved solely for women, as had always been the case in the rites of Hathor.

To we who look at these images the message is that the light, or the living spirit of the Sun, is literally *life,* and holds all living things equally. This is emphasized repeatedly by the depictions of the royal couple and their family in natural, informal, everyday poses that overturn centuries of the tradition in which the pharaoh and his family were shown only in formal, stylized positions. They are shown digging into plates of food; others are even shown vomiting. For the first and only time in ancient Egyptian art, the different effects of light and shadow are depicted. It is now very hard to appreciate these images in the manner in which they would have appeared at the time, but there is no doubt that they were intended to shock, just as they still shock, and to force people to confront their habitual conceptions of divinity and worship. How could the priest-hood and the populace continue to think of their pharaoh and his Great Royal Wife as being their chief intermediaries with the Divine when they not only looked "normal," but increasingly looked so unnatural as to be almost inhuman, let alone near-perfect? The unique style of art inspired by Akhenaten is so alien that it is tempting to attribute it literally to such an origin. The pointed head, slanted eyes, and androgynous form are the *sine qua non* of any self-respecting modern alien. But with the customary props of the abundant images and godforms with which the Egyptians clothed their temples taken away, nothing remained except the light itself, and it was this truth that Akhenaten wanted to convey.

It may well be that the famous statue of Akhenaten that shows him as androgynous is an indication of the nature of his and Nefertiti's true inner appearance. Although it succeeds in disturbing and in inviting questions, it undeniably holds a formidable authority that is belied by its inhuman appearance. Judged by conventional human terms of good looking, the representations fail on all accounts, but judged in the light of an earlier, prehuman existence, they might be a little more realistic. They are certainly a lot more than caricatures, and are arresting in a manner over and above any other Pharaonic depictions. Strangely, they do not repel; they are fascinating and ultimately benign. If we approach them from the standpoint that when Akhenaten inspired this particular style of art, he knew exactly what he was doing and why, then we will be more likely to come to an understanding of their purpose.

Had Akhenaten and Nefertiti's family survived to continue the Dynasty, then their rather extreme position would probably have been tempered with time and would have grown—or been diluted—into a tradition that was better documented and better incorporated into general temple and magical practice. As it is, the impression is that the weight of the magical and religious work in their city fell upon the shoulders of Akhenaten, Nefertiti, and the small number of the priesthood (Ramose, for example) who were attuned to the magic of the Aten and followed them from Thebes. Although the seeds of change had been planted through the previous hundred years or so, in any walk of life extreme and concentrated measures must be taken to achieve a real shift in the order of things.

THE BEAUTIFUL ONE COMES

Let us suppose that Nefertiti was indeed a "beautiful one" who came to earth, the ambassador or earthly representative of a power that was not of earthly origin. We can only wonder again at her origin, as she was not of royal birth, and it is curious that no one sought the kudos that would have come with claiming to be her parents. Her name, meaning "The Beautiful One Comes," was not a common one in Egypt, and the inevitable impression that she appeared as if from nowhere in order to take on a unique task is very appealing. It was as if the process of movement toward the recognition of the Sun, and sunlight as being the source of life above all other gods, had gone as far as it could through the work of the previous pharaohs, and this was the destiny of Akhenaten. What was needed now was the catalyst of one who embodied its principles to such an extent that they could be brought into physical manifestation and example. In this sense Nefertiti was an avatar of that New Age—as indeed she is of this present New Age. It is worth stating again that the equal partnership of king and queen acting also as priest and priestess is almost without parallel in recorded history.

It would seem that immediately after her birth Nefertiti was recognized as having particular qualities and was quickly taken into the royal family, where Tey, Ay's wife, became her wet nurse. There is a curious unearthliness about her. We see her sharing a normal family life and taking part in the duties of the state, but her voice is not one that readily expresses the commonplace. Her most famous sculpture, now in Berlin, shows such a perfect face that paradoxically it creates something that is a little removed from human—a little distance away from anyone we are ever likely to meet. Despite the perfection of feature and perfect symmetry—or perhaps because of it—the sculpture is unnerving in its remoteness, its sense of otherness, and of the absolute and single-minded determination it conveys. While "heartless" is not quite the right word, we get the impression that her motivation and driving force was not touched by anything we would recognize as human sentimentality. The other unnerving feature of this sculpture is that it only has one eye. The right eye is properly formed and made in realistic fashion from rock crystal, as was often the case, but the left eye is missing and the sculpture reveals no sign that it ever existed. (Some reproductions unfortunately are reversed.) As we have seen, she appeared to function as an equal to Akhenaten on a physical level within the world, but in the arresting symbolism of this missing left eye we are shown that while her right/masculine/outward eye looked clearly upon the physical world, her left/feminine/inner eye was equally sighted upon the inner worlds.

Another quartzite bust in the Cairo museum, although clearly unfinished, is brought alive by the fact that the artist has reddened her lips and outlined her eyes with a sweep of black paint. The head is unusually angled upward, and she gazes through strangely expressive blind eyes at a light that is beyond our recognition. She is gazing with an awareness that, paradoxically, would be lost by the depiction of her physical eyes. It is her inner sight that is paramount, and her total attunement to the energy of the unseen world that is her reality. To make contact with her we must raise our own rate of vibration to the level of that on which she fully exists, which is the level of pure spirit of which the Sun is the source and symbol—not only in its physical form but on the inner realities behind the form. She is a priestess of the Sun such as the world has not otherwise known. As to her physical appearance in her place of origin, it is up to us individually to make contact with her, if we will, and if she will.

Part of the purpose and work of Akhenaten and Nefertiti was to create a means of reaching the world of the spiritual Sun by circumventing the elaborate trappings of conventional religion and by demonstrating that through a full and dynamic relationship with the light you could exist in the light of the spiritual Sun even while existing on earth. This process is one that in the last few years has been "rediscovered" in the sense that it—or something very similar—is described and practiced in the process currently known as "Ascension." Although known for thousands of years by students of the occult, the process has recently been brought into more general awareness. By this process, through meditation and the tuning of the lower bodies, one may speed up the rate of their vibration and in effect raise the level of one's existence even while in incarnation. It is a process that on a personal level mirrors the process that eventually will affect the planetary being in the greater journey of the earth toward becoming a sacred planet. While these ideas are still received with as much resistance as was evidently shown by Akhenaten and Nefertiti's successors, the principle behind it is well-accepted. During the process of involution the created universe descended from pure energy into denser and denser form until it reached the nadir. Assuming that this point has been turned, the journey now is onward and upward back into the light, but it takes an active effort on the part of those at the bottom to get things moving and to overcome the attraction and inertia caused by physicality.

THE LANGUAGE OF THE SUN

If we seek to discover the essence of Nefertiti's achievements, then we need look no further than the sixfold form that she brought into earth: her family of six daughters, all of whom were born within a short space of time in her late teens and early twenties. In this we find her to have been the living embodiment of the feminine aspects of the Sun and an instrument of its form upon the earth. In their family of six daughters (no sons were born of her and it would appear that Akhenaten's son Tutankhamun was born of his second wife, Kiye), she brought to birth within the world the symbol of the Sun, whose sacred number is six: the feminine touch of the hand of the Sun's light, the six-sided manifestation of the Sun within the earth. We see this same form in the many six-sided symbols of the Sun, such as the six-rayed star, or the honeycomb, or the square of the Sun whose sides each add up to 666. Each of her daughters served in the temple from an early age, and in many reliefs we see them carrying a sistrum, an instrument whose inherent symbology and gentle sounds invoked and brought into earth the creative powers of the goddess Hathor, the goddess of the Sun from pre-Dynastic times. As we have seen in this chapter, Hathor's chief form was as a golden cow, and in this form her worship continued for many years in other times and other places. Although Nefertiti appears to have relinquished this image of Hathor, the goddess's other main symbol was the sistrum, a small, hand-held instrument carried exclusively, as far as we know, by priestesses of Hathor. It was made of copper or bronze, shaped like an ankh, and usually surmounted by the representation of Hathor in the form of a cow's head. The loop of the "ankh" usually had three or four crossbars to represent the different levels of creation. These were typically shaped like the fire-spitting goddess Uadjet, who was also seen at the brow of the pharaoh's crown. Threaded on the crossbars were copper discs, usually seven or nine. When shaken gently the instrument makes a soft rattling sound, which for magical and ritual purposes is very evocative indeed, forming a cushion of sound on which the levels of uncreate realities are briefly supported into manifestation.

A powerful image can be built by imagining Nefertiti and her six daughters standing under the blue sky of an open-roofed temple in the form of a seven-pointed star, or a six-pointed star with a central point, each gently shaking their sistrum, singing, and chanting in the manner evoked by the tarot image of the Sun: a child emerging newborn from the sunlight.

The religion of Akhenaten and Nefertiti was not a simple-minded worship of a distant impersonal spherical object in the sky, but was a highly evolved understanding of the power and quality of the light of the Sun—a quality better expressed by the Eastern concept of *prana*. They offered this as a technique for personal evolution. Their message was that the complex hierarchy of gods, goddesses, and priesthood was not necessary in this respect: the qualities of the sunlight were immanent and available to everyone—man, woman, and child. It may also have been the case that their conception of the ka did not follow the traditional teaching. It was previously the case that the ka, or body of light, was considered to be something from which you were separated during your life on earth unless you happened to be the pharaoh. But since the emphasis now was on the dynamic living relationship enjoyed between the light and the human body during incarnation, then it may have been the case that this was seen as a way of retaining the link with the body of light. Whatever the case may be, this message was publicly expressed through the example they set of a joyful and natural celebration of life on earth sustained by the sunlight. But there was rather more to their message than a sort of glorified sunbathing, because we also know from the artifacts found in the tomb of Akhenaten's son, Tutankhamun, that they possessed a very thorough scientific knowledge of its qualities and sacred numerology. We still know very little about the effect its various cycles, such as sunspot activity, have upon us, particularly upon our endocrine system.

The practice of Sun Magic does not have an easy history. We do not get the impression that Nefertiti was "Atlantean," even though the most renowned Sun Temple was the one that took shape in Atlantis. It is ultimately the perfection of the magic of the Sun that is both the downfall and the final achievement of humankind. Nefertiti is far more than the reincarnation of an Atlantean priestess, and we should remember that it was not the spiritual power of the Sun within its temple that fell, but the priesthood. The higher the power the greater the fall. Akhenaten and Nefertiti appear to have attempted to redeem the consequences of the fall of the Sun Temple by reinstating its magic in a pure and balanced manner, and it is fair to say that they made all reasonable attempts to reinstate the worship and magic of the Sun while avoiding one of the potential elements of corruption that goes with it by abolishing the elitism of a corrupt priesthood. In many ways their move from Thebes to Amarna accomplished this change, and although they took a few of the Theban priesthood with them, the essence of the magic from their new city was of the validity of the individual's experience. They were themselves the high priest and priestess of this new movement, but their insistence that they were also husband and wife, man and woman, living ordinary, everyday lives with their family, as did the poorest inhabitant of their land, was revolutionary. There is no evidence that either of them misused this power, nor that they were corrupted by it.

On the other hand, it is probably also true to say that the affairs of state were somewhat neglected during their period of rule. While the long and peaceful reign of Akhenaten's father, Amenhotep III, had brought about a prosperity and stability that gave them a certain amount of leeway to concentrate on what they had to do, things could not have gone on for too long in this way without Egypt becoming threatened. In the end, what really ruined things is that their reforms were too advanced, too different, too extreme for the general public, and that they had insufficient time to properly implement them. It would appear that their family was mostly wiped out by a plague that swept across Egypt and neighboring countries at that time. Four of their daughters died at an early age, and Akhenaten's sons, Smenkhkhare and Tutankhaten (later Tutankhamun), by his second wife, Kiya, also died at a comparatively early age, leaving no heirs. There is no reason to believe that Nefertiti did not also die from the same disease.

ESCAPE TO THE EMERALD ISLE

However, just as the final hours of the earlier Sun Temple witnessed the escape of a few of the priesthood who took to their boats and started afresh in another land, in a manner that is already familiar to us, their eldest daughter Meritaten gathered a group of friends, took to the boats, and sailed west. Many countries would have welcomed her, but she chose to go to Ireland. This surprising story is little-known, but clearly documented in an early chronicle called *Scotichronicon,*[5] a collection of earlier works that chart the early history of the Scottish nation, which was founded by a woman. Dating from 1435, it describes how a pharaoh's daughter, named Scota (this was presumed to be her name because she was the foundress of the Scots), and her husband, Gaythelos, or Gaedel Glas, a Phoenician, were fleeing Egypt because they had been advised by the gods of "certain plagues that were to come." The *Book of Leinster,*[6] which was written much earlier, around 1150, similarly refers to Scota, the daughter of an Egyptian pharaoh. Scota and Gaythelos are obviously not Egyptian names, but fortunately Bower names the father of Scota as Achenchres. This is none other than Akhenaten, Achencres being the Greek version of his name.

The full significance of this has yet to be understood. It is said that Meritaten's descendents eventually became the high kings of Ireland, whose seat was at Tara. Indeed, a necklace of Egyptian faience beads was found about the neck of a skeleton buried at Tara, which has been carbon-dated to 1350 B.C., the time of Akhenaten.[7] Some of her party who had lingered in Spain also eventually followed her to Ireland, perhaps led by a second "Scota," daughter of a much later pharaoh, Nectanebo. By this time her descendents were known as the Sons of Mil, or the Milesians, who, according to tradition, were the race who overcame the faery race of the Tuatha de Danaan. This would of course mean that the inhabitants of Ireland at the time of Meritaten were faery, not human.

In a final twist to this story, which brings us back full circle to the twentieth century and Dion Fortune's magical fraternity of the Inner Light, one of its early members, Christine Campbell Thomson, in her book *A Case for Reincarnation,*[8] discusses Meritaten. While she is very clear about many of her previous reincarnations, she says with some diffidence that although she has no personal memory of it, two or three people were quite convinced that she was a reincarnation of Meritaten and offered her this information quite unsolicited. She also mentions that she had discovered that Meritaten reincarnated almost immediately as the daughter of Tutankhamun (Tutankhamun's daughters, who were buried with him in fetal position, did not reach full term), then as the daughter of Seti I, "who pulled Moses from the bulrushes," and later still as the wife of Lazarus, the brother of Martha and Mary.

While we read this with interest and perhaps a pinch of salt, the greater implications of the destiny of Meritaten in these Western islands are profound, and take us into deeper waters than we can venture at present. This period of change and interchange between the faery race of the Tuatha de Danaan and the human race, represented by the descendents of Meritaten and the emigrants from the priesthood of Amarna, is pivotal in the history of these islands, and much remains to be revealed concerning this marriage of Egyptian magic with the wisdom of the faeries and the Druidic priesthood.

Ultimately, the Sun Magic of Akhenaten and Nefertiti is the simplest, the most high-reaching, yet the most difficult of all. You need nothing but the light. But the following visualization may help you to make contact with this priest and priestess of the Sun.

Journey to the Temple of the Sun

You stand alone within the precincts of a temple in the city of Akhenaten. The Nile is close at hand and you are aware of your utter dependence on it for each drop of water that supports the green fertility of this city. The temple is a temple to the Sun. It is open to the sky, which is a deep, cloudless blue. It is intensely hot, with the strong, dry heat of morning. You are dressed in a loose white linen robe. You are accustomed to the heat and it does not trouble you. The temple is large and rectangular, and the court in which you stand is enclosed on its four sides by a colonnade of square pillars. Upon each pillar is a faint bas relief of a female form, a priestess who raises her arms in salutation to the Sun. You can hear the faint sounds of birds; a chirping of sparrows who nestle into the dry sand to preen their feathers. But this is the only sound, and the air is poised and balanced with quietude. Many acts of high magic undertaken here have built an atmosphere of sanctity and mystery.

You wait, motionless, calm, stilling your thoughts and emotions. You become aware of the composition of the sunlight that shines within the temple. You close your eyes and breathe with gentleness and ease and allow yourself with each breath to become filled with the golden particles that float and dance upon the air until it is as if they become the molecules of your own body. You breathe the light through the pores of your skin. Your body dissolves into a dance of shining gold. You can no longer make a distinction between the physical limits of your body and the dance of the energy of life about you. Your solar plexus is charged and becomes a sphere of radiant and unfailing light and life. Your heart chakra is brought to light and life and love. You are part of the life of this Sun Temple and its work.

There begins to materialize a soft, faint sound, like the droning of bees. It is all around you; you cannot locate its source. It grows in intensity, now more like a soft, metallic jingling. A pattern develops. You listen, almost lazily, to a rhythm that emerges from the sound and then sinks back into the soft noise. It forms again, but in a different rhythm. You do not open your eyes, but you listen acutely as if you were catching the first sounds of creation, the first vibrations that move the grains of sand at your feet into brief, insubstantial images.

Pictures and shapes briefly build before your eyes, coming into form upon the sounds, and then vanish, as if sound and image were one. You see the shape of the sounds, you hear the colors, you become the dance that is creation, which is both inside and outside of you. You hold it: you are held by it.

Suddenly it is broken by the laughter of children. You hardly dare to open your eyes, but do so slowly so as not to break the spell. Within the temple precinct, six children, all girls, run out from the pillars. Each holds a sistrum, which you realize is the source of the sounds you heard. The children are golden with innocence and joy, and you cannot help but wonder if they are truly of this world. Although very young, they are perfectly self-absorbed and seem quite oblivious of you. They run to the center of the temple and stand in a circle. And then they begin to dance to an inner music and an inner conviction, circling and whirling with sureness and rhythm as if their steps were guided in a pattern or as if a template of perfection hung invisible upon the air. You see that a pattern is forming in the sand of the floor of the temple, not so much caused by the movement of their feet, but almost as if a reverberation was set up by their dancing and by the sounds of their sistra, which caused the sand to vibrate into a pattern. A complex pattern has built up upon the temple floor. You can see within the pattern a six-pointed star, but it is as if the lines of the pattern are still moving. The children disperse, dancing away into the shade between two of the columns at the side of the temple.

There is more laughter, and where the children have disappeared, a man appears. He is the pharaoh Akhenaten. He walks forward and stands upon the six-pointed star, facing you. You realize a moment of slight fear as you confront him. He is wearing a white kilt and golden sandals. Upon his head is a curved blue crown surmounted by the uraeus serpent. You are aware of the many preconceptions you have brought with you, and you know that he knows of them. In fact, it is hard to see him clearly, and a faint mist of garbled thoughtforms seems to float between you and this man. You wait until they have cleared, and until you feel confident that you can see him absolutely clearly. It is as if he invites you to look at him closely, at the details of his face—his eyes and his mouth—the few amulets he wears about his neck and wrists, until you have built in your mind's eye a full strong image of his appearance, which supercedes any previous images. You find that he is openhearted, but his authority and shining presence are unmistakable. You tell him your name. He speaks his name. You hear him speak it.

He turns away from you to face the other end of the temple, and invites you to walk forward and stand beside him at the center of the six-pointed star. You do so, and stand upon his right hand. The change in the atmosphere is noticeable, as if you have walked into an inner sanctuary. And you see that at the far end of the Sun Temple now stands his queen, Nefertiti, and their eldest daughter, Meritaten. Nefertiti's face is beautiful: awe-inspiring but formidable. Meritaten is youthful, exuberant. Between them sits a golden-maned lion, which crouches upon the sand like the sphinx, its forepaws stretched out before it. Nefertiti rests her hand upon the lion's mane. Then they both slowly raise their arms in the same gesture of salute to the Sun as appears on the pillars of the temple, and lift their faces up to its light. As they do so, the colonnade and wall of the temple behind her dissolves into light. All that remains is a cloudless blue mist. At the horizon is the deep blue of lapis lazuli, which blends into pure gold at the zenith. And behind them, as if descending from the very Sun itself, you see the many regents of the Sun, a glorious procession of men, women, and angels in which you may perceive Apollo, Sulis, Brigid, King David, King Arthur, Christ, and Raphael, the healing angel who stands in the Sun.

Take as much time as you need to receive this vision. When you are ready, allow the scenes to fade, ensuring that you have fully returned to this world.

CHAPTER THREE

THE LIFE AND DEATH
OF THE GODDESS

The Bible, compiled and largely rewritten with patriarchal hind-sight, is in no doubt that it was Eve's "what if?" that put the skids on human happiness. So it was that this Hebrew Pandora secured the doubtful distinction of dooming her race to be the first people to abandon the concept of a goddess. It was from this retrospective—Eve blaming, monotheistic—parentage that Christianity and Islam later grew to all but extinguish pagan religion. With the theocratic extinction of those precocious female deities, the concept of polarity as a sacred transaction between men and women, humankind and heaven, human nature and all nature, was lost. But the Goddess and her mythology did not go down without a fight.

The original roots of what was to become Judaism of course had no Eve of blame; she came much later, inserted to bolster a bitter theology that sought some archetypal scapegoat for the Babylonian exile. The editors of the Old Testament canon, the children of that exile, made sure not only that the woman was to blame for their current misfortune, but that she should carry retrospective blame from the roots of their rewritten history. But historically and mythologically, it really hadn't been like that!

EAST OF EDEN

The Hebrews saw the real beginning of their destiny in ancient Sumer. In this they were, as far as we can see, factually correct. The

Bible tells us that Abraham, then Abram, "father of many," the first of the Hebrew Patriarchs, came from Ur of the Chaldees.[1] While we are inclined to think of Abram as the product of a primitive world, the reference to Ur dismisses this. We can deduce that he probably left Ur some four thousand years ago, and at this time Sumer had long been a series of culturally advanced city states; the Egyptian pyramids, like the Sumerian Ziggurats, had been constructed and Jericho, that city of long biblical fame, had already been established for several thousands of years. Genesis tells us that Cain, Abraham's ancestor, having settled in the land of Nod and fathered Enoch, was "then building a city which he named Enoch after his son."[2]

CHILDREN OF THE ANNUNAKI

Sumerian myth deals essentially with the interaction of a divine race, the quarrelsome Annunaki, with humanity in general and Sumerian royalty in particular. This divine-human royal interaction, a common characteristic of most myth, may rightly be seen at a superficial level to enable the divine right of human kings. But kings as tribal fathers are, like Abraham, simply a personification of their race. At a deeper level, this marriage of heaven and earth, which provides the conceptual basis for polarity magic, indicates the way that individual men and women may bring heavenly, archetypal ideas to birth in the material world.

So it was with the Annunaki in ancient Sumer, and we are persuaded to consider their more junior membership as "children of gods" in the sense of the biblical Beni Elohim: that is, children of the cosmic originators. Thus, while they have immortal, Godlike qualities, they fulfill an intermediary role rather like the faery Tuatha de Danaan of Irish myth. In this they represent the final stage of invisible creation prior to human appearance, with easy access to the material world.

The Sumerian flood myth, like the biblical, Atlantean, and other flood myths that perhaps came from it, suggests that these Annunaki godlings, in creating humanity, were forced to wipe out their initial mistakes! Floods were certainly a fact of life for the ancient Sumerians, and the worst of these would have provided a ready linchpin with which to secure myth to apparent history. Sumerian writings tell us that the first eight kings of their people lived in perfect accord with the Annunaki as their earthly representatives, although the Annunaki, like the Beni Elohim of Genesis, seem to also spend time on earth in impressive, humanoid form. These are the Hebrew Nephilim, the giants of Genesis. Even so, the august presence of these divine beings could not guarantee the vagaries of human free will. As in Atlantis and elsewhere, things soon went awry. In the Sumerian myths the proto-humans are uncouth and noisy, whereas the biblical myth makes them sinful. The Atlantean myth makes them sinful and defiant, but whatever the divine reason, the earth has to be cleared of its initial, willful human population to provide a more trustworthy species with which these divine beings may interact.

The ideal way to clear the earth is to have a flood. This not only provides mass death and submerges the previous natural topography, it also allows for the survival of a chosen, boat-building few who can initiate a new race. In the Bible the chosen one is Noah and his family. In the original Sumerian myth it is Ziusudra, and in later Akkadian versions that feature Gilgamesh, the chosen one is Utnapishtim. The biblical and Sumerian myths are pretty much identical. In each case, the flood hero is tipped off by the gods in advance and instructed in the construction of a huge biological or zoological freighter so that continuity with the doomed earth is preserved, not only in its chosen human survivors, but in the stock of species or seed that they carry over the flood.

AFTER THE FLOOD

When the Sumerian holocaust has subsided and a new division of the human and divine status quo is instigated, the time comes for the earth to be restocked with a new humanoid species. The Annunaki all-mother, Tiamet, commands the making of mortal beings from blood and the residual clay from the flood. This her son Ea (or Enki) does, enlisting the help of his sister-wife Nin-Khursag, who had a "creation chamber" named Shi un-ti ("breath-air-life"). From this womblike contrivance she made fourteen humanoid fetuses, seven male and seven female. The seven male and seven female (the biblical "two-by-two" required for procreation) fetuses are then implanted in the wombs of those human women who have survived the deluge, allowing humanity to restart and provide a more suitable species through whom the eventual marriage of heaven and earth may be achieved.

ALL ABOUT EVE

The Old Testament provides us with a slightly rearranged version of the Sumerian myth. We have Eve in Enki's sister-wife, Nin Khursag, and perhaps in her other Sumerian name, Nin-ti, we have the "ti," which means "life," and/or the "ti," which means "rib," suggesting the Hebrew myth of her creation from Adam's rib. In Adam's name we have Hebrew words that suggest "blood" and "earth," and in this too we see the crossover with Sumerian myth, where proto-humanity is created by Enki and Nin Khursag from blood and alluvial clay, except that Adam is not the result of this gorey alchemy, but its initiator. Adam is, to all purposes, Enki. The problem with this of course is that it places Adam, Eve, and Eden after rather than before the flood, but in such mythical, primordial beginnings before and after are of little consequence. What is of more consequence perhaps is that Nin Khursag/Eve had a sister, Lilith, the femme fatale of patriarchal nightmare.

Aside from a spurious mention in the Book of Isaiah, Lilith is given short shrift by the Bible, although the medieval Jewish *Alphabet of Ben Sira* harks back to some ancient Hebrew traditions about her. These traditions figure a Lilith who was Adam's first wife, but on finding that she could not be equal to him uttered the Holy Name of God, deserted her husband, and flew away to be replaced by the docile Eve. Demonization by the Hebrews and canonization by modern day feminists inevitably followed! Yet Lilith represents a Sumerian archetype whose fundamental purpose misfired in the hands of the later scribes. In her insistence on a partnership of spiritual and temporal equality she represented what women should be, rather than what men wanted them to be. Consequently, as a woman scorned she resolved to play the bitter role assigned to her, feeding and festering upon the ill will that the folksoul assigned to her. For archetypes are more than mere psychological constructs. In very truth they have a life of their own and, as with human beings, the blighting of such a "life" may eventually produce a twisted soul. Lilith may in some very real sense have become the demon that the later interpreters made her. But it is men, not God, who have made her so, and it is men and women of good will and firm resolve who understand what polarity really means who shall one day remake her as God intended her to be. Meanwhile, she coils as the serpent about Eve's Edenic tree, whispering "what if" in her sister's ear. And her sister, having repeated the question and taken the fruit, unshackles human will and aspiration so that one day the marriage of heaven and earth may yet come to pass.

The end of Abraham's time in Sumer coincides with its decline. Eventually Abraham came to Canaan and met Melchizadek, the high priest of El Elyon, the "Most High God," who set Tsdeq, the mark of cosmic order, upon Abraham's unpredictable, nomadic world. We may assume that Abraham's Hebrews, as a scattering of disparate tribes, settled down with their memories alongside their Canaanite hosts. What we know of them suggests that by this time

their religious practices featured clan gods and goddess who were in
some way woven into ancestor worship. To what extent those ancestors were seen as the Annunaki, the divine ancestors of Sumer, we
may only guess. When famine threatened and fortune beckoned, the
Hebrew tribes of Canaan made their way into Egypt. Their priesthood may have gone down into Egypt to study in the magical and
occult disciplines that Egypt holds beyond all others (as has always
been the case). But it was perhaps also here that they received the
initial impetus for a monotheism, which was to all but extinguish
the Goddess, ironically, in the home of the most celebrated of all
goddesses: Isis.

EXODUS

During what is academically accepted as the biblical Hebrew
"bondage in Egypt," Tiye, a Mittani princess, married the pharaoh
Amenhotep III. The heir to the Egyptian throne, the "mose" born
from this union, was Amenhotep IV. Shortly after coming to the
throne, this pharaoh changed his name to Khuniatonu: "the incarnation of Aten," whom later Greek writers called Akhenaten and
whom history has labeled "the heretic pharaoh." His "heresy" has
been looked at afresh in chapter 2. After the demise of Akhenaten,
things soon reverted to the traditional polytheistic worship, and ancient Egyptian history took pains to disown its heretic by chiseling
his image from any bas relief that could be found depicting him.

The Bible, like all virtual history, tends to compress long historical
processes into single events, and this is particularly so with the sojourn of the Hebrews in Egypt and their "Exodus." What has come
down to us is a combination of history, myth, wish-fulfillment, and
politics. Hebrew settlement in Egypt under both sympathetic and
unsympathetic Egyptian administrations spans the totality of biblical
history right through to New Testament times and beyond. It may
have been that when Akhenaten fell from power to be replaced by a
pharaoh who was determined to stamp heresy on everything and

everybody sympathetic to Akhenaten's brief reign, that the Hebrews fell on hard times. Many, if not all, voted with their feet: perhaps not as the Bible suggests in one dramatic, sea-parting Exodus, but in a gradual, instinctive wandering back toward Canaan.

But the Canaan that they had left so many years before had moved on. The Canaan personified by Melchizadek of Salem who had welcomed Abraham in the Book of Genesis back in the eighteenth century B.C. is replaced in the Joshua account by a similar priest-king, Adonai Tsdeq, who, five hundred years on, is opposing the Hebrews. Times had changed! The wandering Hebrews were very much between pharaoh, a hard place (the wastes of Sinai) and a very unpromising land of Canaan. Unable to go back to Egypt or Canaan, they wandered the area broadly now known as Sinai for the metaphorical forty years.

ON SERABIT IN SINAI

It was perhaps during this time, left very much to their own devices and unappreciated by both Canaan and Egypt, that the Hebrews began to formulate their own innovative faith. The Egyptians had mining settlements in Sinai, but these were rarely garrisoned, and in Sinai, the Hebrews, out of sight and mind, and could do pretty much as they pleased. Even so, Sinai had considerable value for the Egyptians as a major source of precious metals and gems. Moreover, precious metals held not only monetary value but spiritual significance for the ancient Egyptians, as may be deduced from the temple of Hathor at the famous copper mines of *Serabit el Kadim.*

Serabit el Kadim is in all likelihood the place that the Bible calls Mount Sinai and Mount Horeb. The association of Moses with Serabit is intentionally or otherwise suggested in the biblically recorded tradition that the kin of Moses were *Kenites,* or smiths. *Serabit,* as an essential source of copper, had all the smelting and metal working facilities associated with smithcraft. But more than this, it is the Egyptian goddess Hathor, whose temple was situated there, who inadvertently validates the biblical record. Also, interestingly, a bust of the pharaoh Akhenaten's influential mother, Tiye, has been found at Serabit, and a stela from the later reign of Rameses I, which glorifies the Aten—perplexingly at a time when it is assumed that Akhenaten's Aten beliefs had been overthrown.

At first sight this seems to provide confusing and contradictory evidence. The whole biblically argued point of the Mosaic vision on Mount Serabit appears to be the consolidation of a divinity who is a single, commanding, male God with some rather strict rules to get across. Why, then, did Yahweh choose to speak to Moses at the site of a temple dedicated to a goddess known, among her other titles, as Mistress of the Vulva, whose rites were renowned for their laughter, music, dance, drunkenness, openly expressed sexuality, and leadership by women?

The temple of Hathor was well established, and as far as we know was the only temple in the whole of the Sinai peninsula during this period. The copper and turquoise mines necessitated a large community of workers and administrators, and Hathor, who had been the most popular of the panoply of Egyptian goddesses from at least the time of the Fourth Dynasty (2050 B.C.), was also one of the most "exportable." She was, above all, the great mother goddess in both the most earthy physical sense and in deeper ways that were concerned with the processes that occur at the moment of birth. She was the divine mother of every pharaoh and, indeed, of all Egyptians. Her name, meaning "The House of Horus," reveals the nature of her motherhood because, of course, the physical mother of Horus was the goddess Isis. Hathor's role was not so much concerned with the physical conception and birth process as with the care of the state of the soul of the newborn during both the process of birth into the physical world and the "coming forth by day" into the afterworld beyond the grave.

Although unusual for an Egyptian divinity, Hathor had seven aspects, personified and known by the unsurprising title of the Seven

Hathors. We may think of these seven goddesses as rather like the seven Faery Godmothers of European folk tales. They visited the soul at its moment of passage into a new life, each bringing a gift that had implications for the destiny of that soul. Each represents one of the seven planes of existence, that inner template of creation, and at the moment of birth each of these planes is, as it were, brought down from the fluidity of the subtle worlds and fixed into the solidity of the physical, or near-physical worlds within the subtle bodies of the newborn soul; a moment of transformation when the macroscosm becomes the microcosm. The name "House of Horus" (or "Mansion of Horus") also contains the idea that during the process of birth not only were the seven levels of cosmic order brought down into the bodies of the soul, but also that the complete human and divine ancestry of the soul was present to witness and contribute to the entrance of the soul into the physical world. It is said that the soul has full memory of its previous heavenly existence and of the reason for its incarnation until the moment it draws its first breath in the imprisoning flesh of the physical world and cries for the loss of the heavenly worlds it has come from. The newborn Hebrew nation certainly cried, and loudly.

THE SHINING

Hathor was also known as the Lady of the Sycamore. In Egyptian religion sycamore trees stood at the entrance to the Otherworld. In later times and in another country these trees became the two pillars at the entrance to the temple. But the most common form in which she appeared was as Goddess of the Sun, witnessed by her headdress of a golden Sun Disc enclosed by two cow's horns, and by her epithets of "Golden One" and "Cow of Gold." Biblical wording later managed to confuse the Hebrew word "*egla,*" meaning "a three year-old heifer," with "*egal,*" which implies a bull calf, thus avoiding the Hathor association. It is also quite likely that the biblical golden calf wasn't made of gold, but of copper, the metal that is sacred to every goddess of love, not least Hathor and her daughters of the classical future, Venus and Aphrodite. Where the terrain permitted, her rituals took place within a cave, where depictions of the golden cow were shown as if emerging from the interior of the earth. One such cave formed part of the temple at Serabit. It is said that when an initiate of her cult brought through much power, the horns of his or her headdress extended into beams of light. That strange repository of occult symbol, Rosslyn Chapel, contains a carving that depicts Moses with horns. The Egyptians sometimes called Hathor "Nubt," meaning "the golden one," and perceived her to be shining as *nub,* or gold. In this we may see that we are being surreptitiously offered the suggestion that the shining face of Moses when he descended from Mount Sinai may have been as a result of an encounter not with Yahweh, but with the goddess Hathor in her mountain shrine.

If we are to believe that Mount Serabit was the biblical Mount Sinai, and we have good reason to believe that it was, then the biblical account of what went on there seems, to say the least, unlikely. The making of the Golden calf by Aaron may well indicate the first clash between the Goddess and a single, commanding, male God. The God whom Moses tried to introduce to the Children of Israel when "Mount Sinai was all smoking because the Lord had down upon it in fire, the smoke went up like the smoke of a kiln, all the people were terrified and the sound of the trumpet grew ever louder."[3] The reference to a "kiln" (foundry) would seem, again, to verify the Serabit location. Moses takes the calf that Aaron has made, grinds it into powder, and, mixing it with water, makes the people gulp it down. He then rounds upon Aaron, who says that the people had asked for a sign and he had given it to them. The significance of the Serabit metallurgical happenings, of sacred tablets of stone (possibly ore), smoking kilns, and the images of the transformation of precious metals into goddess images, touch upon the beginnings of what came to be known as Alchemy, the spiritual transmutation of metals. Both Moses and Aaron, who were "learned in all the knowledge of all Egyptians" applied, each in their way, whatever they knew of Egyptian alchemical lore. We have no proof of this, but we read in the Book of Numbers that in the march from Kadesh Moses again falls back upon his metallurgical skills to make a bronze serpent as a standard for his army, thus bestowing the serpent power of, among other things, alchemical transformation upon them.

In the meantime, the veneration of the Hathor totem initiated by Aaron, and Moses' reaction to that veneration, place Moses in the unenviable situation of having to face down any opposition by asking "Who's with me, then?" The Bible inevitably says that the priestly Levites, the tribe of Aaron, rally to him. Moses then commands the Levites to slaughter all those who continue to deny his, and thus God's, authority. The Levites do so, which seems rather unfair in that Aaron, the principal Levite, encouraged their worship of the Hathor totem in the first place. But in the later Deuteronomic perception of the establishment of Judaism, nobody may stand against this new "nation of priests" and live, whether they are foreigners or, as in this instance, fellow Hebrews. Moses and monotheism win the day and after receiving two replacement tablets of stone from the Lord, Moses, Aaron, the tabernacle, and Ark (with the tablets and other items inside) make for Kadesh—a general mustering of forces in anticipation of a determined invasion of Canaan. In this latter regard, we may be in no doubt that they used the facilities at Serabit to not only forge the necessary sacred metalwork that the Covenant demanded, but, at the Lord's entreaty, to also arm themselves for the ethnic cleansing ahead!

As ever, the black/white, stop/go biblical record of events does not accord with either common sense or, except here and there, historic fact. The golden calf incident did not by any means mark the end of goddess worship in general or Hathor worship in its various versions in particular for a very long time to come. A golden calf was set up at Bethel ("The House of the Lord"), where no less a person than Jacob received his vision of the joining of heaven and earth, and Jeroboam set up another golden calf as a replacement object of veneration after the unspeakable loss of the Ark of the Covenant. This gives us a number of clues to the continued importance of goddess worship after Moses, and a more balanced picture of what actually happened at Serabit. Nonetheless, Serabit marks the starting point for a gradually changing world from which the great goddess Isis was doomed to all but disappear.

While Moses remains the essential protagonist of the story, his brother, Aaron, despite being the destined founder of Judaic priesthood, has his actions opened to question and his role diminished. Aaron's scriptural fate is, however, nothing to that of their big sister, Miriam, who stands as the founder of a line of heretical priestesses that stretches into the New Testament and beyond. It was, of course, unthinkable to the male scribes that a woman, in the mold of "that Eve," should have any spiritual prominence, but again, as with the goddess that she represented, occasional clues remain. The first such clue in the Exodus narrative is in chapter 15, when she is reluctantly cited as a prophet as she leads the Hebrew women in a victory dance after the divine defeat of the Egyptians at the Red Sea. She is there credited with singing the important invocation sometimes called "The Song of the Sea," and although the account credits the composition of this to Moses, most scholars agree that it was originally Miriam's, not Moses', song. We encounter this demotion again in the joint questioning by Miriam and Aaron of Moses's leadership, when they claim that, among other things, the Lord has spoken through them as much as through their "brother" Moses. The scriptural punishment for so questioning the great man is visited on Miriam, but not upon Aaron, who again seems to be retrospectively spared in view of his destined role of high priest of Israel. Miriam, however, has her skin turned white for seven days. One wonders, though, whether this was not so much a case of leprosy but the sign of ecstatic communion with the goddess Hathor. Certainly, if the vision of Mount Serabit was essentially concerned with the goddess Hathor, then it would be more likely for that feminine divinity to be mediated by Miriam, whose name probably derives from the Egyptian *Meri-Amun,* "beloved of Amun."

THE TREE AFLAME

In the biblical account of events at Mount Sinai, we are being persuaded to assume that the shining face of Moses, and perhaps Miriam, somehow result from a scorching encounter with the burning bush. But this burning bush, rather than being simply an immature display of divine pyrotechnics, is both a symbol of Asherah, Hathor, and of the Edenic tree from which Eve purloined the Fruit of Knowledge. It is also the "tree aflame" of later British Mystery tradition, and a very ancient symbol of the Axis Mundi symbol, which describes the alignment of earth to its pole star and hence the security and fertility of our world. It is Ygdrassil, the World Tree of Nordic and countless other myths. Such trees are traditionally located at earth navels, centers of the world where the allegorical navel represents the earth's umbilical attachment to heaven. It was beneath such a tree that Jacob had his vision of the marriage of heaven and earth at Bethel, where another golden calf was subsequently set up. Such trees and the goddess they represent are, however, intermediary. Like the ladder of Jacob's vision, they are set in a paradisal realm, an Eden of inner space over which some muselike reflection or image of the greater goddess presides. The Tree, sprouting up like an umbilical cord from the underworld womb of the earth to touch heaven, indicated the lineaments of the paradisal state. As we have seen, such inner territory set between heaven and earth has seven levels. On a journey through the land that the British Celts called Annwn, the Welsh bard Taliesin encounters "The horns aflame"[4] which peculiarly correspond to the cow horns employed to hold up the shining solar disc in the headdress of the goddess Hathor. In the cave shrine of Hathor, Moses, or more likely Miriam, had found a traditional way into the Duat, the Egyptian underworld, and in it had found the paradisal tree aflame and a sevenfold ladder of lights, the triple-aspected heaven that the Qabalists later came to know.

The tree was the symbol of Asherah, the Hebrew goddess. Among the articles that Moses is required to construct as a ritual object for the tent of meeting is the Menorah, the seven branched candlestick that is still an essential feature of Jewish sacred ritual. This stylized seven-branched tree aflame is a burning almond tree, geometrically constructed to indicate a mathematical combination of what we might call the "three about the One forming the seven."

The Menorah, along with the Ark of the Covenant and the Asherah, was to attest to the presence of the Goddess for a number of centuries, first in the moveable tabernacle of Moses, then in the bricks and mortar consolidation of Solomon's temple. Tabernacle and Temple were to become a stylized, Edenic garden, an area set apart between heaven and earth. At the absolute focus of this meeting place the presence of God in earth could be found over the Ark of the Covenant in the Holy of Holies: the "shining place," the Debir, corresponding to the house of gold in many Egyptian tombs where the deceased pharaoh came into his own as an "Osiris" god in man. In the Holy of Holies the Hebrew high priest, the descendent of Aaron the Levite, communed with divinity as Adam had in the garden. The presence of that divinity came to be called the *Shekinah,* and though the word is not mentioned in the earlier accounts of Tabernacle and Temple, its source is clear. Tradition coined the word *Sh'kinah,* "the one who dwells within." A Rabbi of the first century tells us that when the tabernacle was built the Shekinah descended to dwell with Israel, an idea later much developed in the Qabalistic Zohar. One cannot escape a "hint of Hathor" here, whose original Egyptian name, Het Hert, means "the house above," equating images of the Debir, the halfway house to heaven where the Shekinah was said to dwell. The Shekinah came to represent the feminine wisdom of Israel that Miriam had voiced. She was the Sophia, the Matronit, the wise virgin.

THE PROMISED LAND

After the Exodus eventually brought the Hebrews back to Canaan, Israel was ruled as a tribal confederacy by the Judges for some two hundred years. Then, in about 1040 B.C., the Philistine invasion came. We may never know why the Philistines were persuaded to invade the Hebrew tribal territories, only that they were a threat to the very existence of the Israelite tribal confederacy. The Ark of the Covenant, constructed by Moses in the wilderness as the focus of Hebrew belief, was taken to Shiloh to assure the assistance of Yahweh to defeat the Phillistines there, but the priests of the Ark were slain, Israel was defeated, and, not for the last time, the Ark captured. Against this background the prophet Samuel came to prominence and realized that strong leadership must be established if the Philistines were to be ejected. Eventually, reluctantly, he anointed Saul as the first king of Israel and thus Israel took the quantum leap from tribal confederacy to monarchy. With the establishment of monarchy came all the old pagan trappings of sovereignty. Indeed, the eighth chapter of the first book of Samuel warns of how the institution of monarchy will return Israel to the sovereignty-based paganism of her neighbors.

Before the formalization of monotheistic beliefs, the beliefs of "natural" or "pagan" religion reflected the archetypal processes of nature, fulfilled in human nature. At the heart of this was the concept of sovereignty. While time and circumstance adjusted and elaborated this premise, most ancient religion pivoted about the relationship of the sacred king and the Goddess. The priest-king, or tribal chieftain, was father of the tribe, and the Goddess, whether of sea, land, or stars, was its sustaining mother. The prosperity of the tribe, the growth of its crops, the health of its members, and the success of its warriors depended upon this right relationship of the king and the

Goddess of the land. From such premises grew the sacred kingship of Egypt, of our Bronze Age ancestors in northern Europe, and, even with Samuel's reservations, the sacral kingship of the Hebrews. It goes without saying that the Goddess emphasis in sacral kingship elevated rather than denounced the feminine role in spirituality. That denunciation, the blaming of Eve, the archetypal woman, was to come later.

In Egypt, the sacred kingship of the line of Osiris was empowered and restored by the goddess Isis. Even two thousand years later in Celtic Christian Wales, the old pre-Christian god, Math, was resurrected in the mythological Arthur, who was empowered by his goddess and faery queen, Gwenevere. Without the Goddess or her representative, known by the Israelites as the Shekinah, the interaction of humanity (whose foremost representative was the monarch) with the divine was considered to be impossible. So Israel made the uneasy transition from a tribal confederacy to a theocratic dynasty like that of Egypt and its other neighbors, even though the prophets held to the view that there could be no real king other than Yahweh, and anointed the kings with some reluctance.

THE TEMPLE

Even so, by the time of David a sacred dynasty was in place in ancient Israel, and with it many of those pagan philosophies that sacral kingship embodies, not least the idea of feminine empowerment. After David came Solomon, who fulfilled David's vision and built the first temple at Jerusalem. The Goddess was strongly present in all his accomplishments through the mediation of the queen of Sheba, who came to question Solomon and undoubtedly inspired and empowered him, although, as ever, her part in the story has been forgotten. The temple built by Solomon stood for the priest-kingship at the junction of heaven and earth fixed over the waters of chaos, and in it stood the Canannite and Egyptian symbols of the Goddess: the Asherah pole, the altar of incense with a horn at each corner, the Menorah, and, beyond them in the Debir (the Holy of Holies), the Ark of the Covenant, which the Philistines had since restored to Israel. The Ark was surmounted by the figures of two Kerubim, the angels of strength, carved in olive wood. The encircling wings of these two angelic sculptures, not unlike the outstretched wings of Egyptian goddess depictions, faced each other over the box-like Ark. The whole arrangement formed the Kapporeth, the Mercy Seat, the throne upon which the Shekinah, the motherly wisdom, the Sophia as the presence of heaven in earth, was seen to manifest.

Long before the Book of Genesis was written, the first Jerusalem temple represented the Edenic garden, the paradisal island at the center of the world, which rose as we have seen out of the primordial waters. Indeed, the horned altar of incense imitated the horned corners of the ziggurats of ancient Sumer. As the biblical account makes clear, no expense was spared in the building of the first Jerusalem temple. Solomon ranged far and wide beyond the borders of Israel to secure help, materials, and presumably ideas to build the temple. The sort of ideas that he adopted may be seen in the Song of Songs: "I charge you daughters of Jerusalem, by the spirits and the goddesses of the fields. Do not rouse her, do not disturb my love until she is ready," and, "Open to me my sister my dearest, my dove my perfect one, for my head is drenched with dew, my locks with the moisture of the night."[5]

The Song of Songs may be regarded as a collection of erotic poetry or, in a more esoteric context, as the liturgy of the kind of polarity magic that was celebrated in the Isis and Osiris mythology of ancient Egypt, and the Asherah myths of Canaan. Indeed, it has been noted by academics that it displays the intensity and style "of ancient Egyptian love poetry." This is probably why, centuries later, in the consolidation of the Old Testament canon, many rabbis thought the Song of Songs to be unsuitable for inclusion in Israel's sacred writings at all. The association of such pagan delights with Solomon and the first temple may, however, be further emphasized by the artifacts that Solomon placed within it. As we have said, among these were the bronze serpent, the Asherah, and the Menorah. The temple Asherah was probably a stylized wooden staff, not unlike the rod of Aaron, which tradition had placed in the Ark of the Covenant, for the tree was one of Asherah's totemic symbols. Other early Hebrew temples also had representations of her and, in fact, there appears to have been an Asherah cult equal to the early Yahwehism. In early Hebrew religion the feminine aspect was celebrated rather than vilified. That vilification came later.

Like the temples of Egypt, Solomon's temple also reflected a sacred geometry of line and number that indicated, many centuries before Pythagoras, patterns of polarity that imposed divine order over the primordial, chaotic flood. In this pattern of Tsedq, of cosmic order set in earth, we return to the Jerusalem priest-king of the Canaanites, Melchizadek. For Melchizadek does not stand alone. Esoteric tradition says that he brought a number of sacred influences from Venus, and in this is encapsulated the polarity between the archetypal priest-king and the Goddess, who may be variously named Venus, Asherah, or Hathor. When St. Paul said that he had much to say of Melchizadek, he meant it. Not only would his full explanation of Melchizadek have revealed the goddess to whom the great one had been polarized, but would also have answered a number of questions about the Christ, the anointed king whom he was comparing to Melchizadek. Sadly, the promised explanation is lost to us and others who realized the importance of this, just as the heretical Melchizadekians who worshipped at Hebron are also forgotten. But this means that the Bible as we have it erroneously presents both Melchizadek and Jesus Christ as standing alone. These are puzzle pieces that must await detailed consideration in a later chapter.

The very focus of the temple, the Holy of Holies, was the part of the paradisal garden, where Adam and Eve had spoken to God. The bronze serpent was that archangelic serpent that had typified the transmission of divine wisdom through Lilith, the first Sophia. In fact, the rock upon which the Jerusalem temple was built was said to be held within the jaws of the serpent Mahon. The Menorah represented the Tree of Life within the garden, as well as Jacob's tree and the burning bush of Moses. But Asherah's tree totem cast, as did the Aaronic staff and serpent of bronze, too blatant a finger of accusation on the dismissal of Lilith and the blaming of Eve, and the days of all these sacred things were numbered.

The mercy seat, or Kapporeth, from which an essentially feminine spirit of divine wisdom addressed the high priest, was thus formed by the Ark of the Covenant overshadowed by the Kerubic wings. It was the wings of Isis that beat life-giving air into the lungs of the dead Osiris. Even as Isis breathed life and divinity into Osiris, so the high priest knew the divine breath of the Sophia, the Goddess of Wisdom, upon his face, the breath which uttered the words "I am." We should also note in passing that the essential symbol of Isis was a throne, a mercy seat, often shown as part of her headdress.

Solomon's reign was the golden age of Israel, accepting of the goddess worship that is implicit in sacral kingship. But what was acceptable in Solomon's reign was soon to become heresy. After his death the kingdom divided between Judah and Israel and became weakened. In its weakness it became prey to aggressive neighbors who had been held at bay by the late monarch's wealth and diplomacy, and some three hundred years after Solomon's death a weakened Judah eventually came under Assyrian domination. To get out from under this Hezakiah instituted certain religious reforms that were to have far reaching effects, effects that have shaped the religious and cultural outlook of Western civilization up to the present day. In about 700 B.C. he removed the Asherah, the bronze serpent, and the Menorah from the temple. This act removed once and for all any outward sign of acceptance of the Goddess, and thereafter placed the absolute stamp of patriarchy on Judaism. It is at this juncture that the Goddess, summed up in the archetypal Eve and all the concepts of priestesshood and polarity magic that attached to her, commences her gradual withdrawal into those shadowlands of heresy. The Judaism that had known the presence of God as a tangible thing that empowered sacred kingship in the mythology of Melchizadek began to be something that became less and less tangible. By the time of Josiah, the law, the Torah, became the abiding religious yardstick in the place of unpredictable religious experience.

But the reforms that had seemed to deliver Judah from the hands of her pagan enemies did not maintain her security for long. A hundred years after the death of Hezekiah, the Jerusalem temple was destroyed and the majority of Jews were deported to Babylon. Judah had become part of a changing world, where the sovereignty of little nations had little chance against the flexed muscle of emerging history. These changes eventually engulfed the oldest and mightiest of the Middle Eastern kingdoms. Egypt herself, the model for all theocratic dynasties, had ceased to be the dominant empire in the Middle East some hundred and fifty years before the reign of Solomon. She had continued under various pharaohs who perpetuated belief in sacral kingship, but in 525 B.C. fell briefly to Persian domination. After some hundred years she again gained independence, but the die was cast and the native dynasties of Egypt were soon to become supplanted by the nobility of Greece (the Ptolemies) and, subsequently, Rome. It may be said with both justification and irony that Cleopatra the Seventh was the last high priestess of Isis who, like her Hebrew colleague Eve, voluntarily submitted herself to the serpent's bite. And forty years after the death of the last priest-king of the Canannites and Jews, Jesus Christ, the third incarnation of the Jerusalem temple ceased to exist. Only its foundations and the western wall now remain.

The story of Jesus Christ and of the three Marys associated with him who were to carry the ancient torch of Miriam under the cold stare of later Christian censorship must await a later chapter. Suffice it to say that when the temple that Jesus Christ had predicted would fall finally fell, it marked the advancement rather than the decline of the patriarchal Judeo-Christian faith. The evangelical shoots of St. Paul's Christianity sprang out of the wreckage of the temple from which he had in earlier years been ejected. Judaism kept its council and survived in some surprising ways. It was not long before the monotheistic Judeo-Christian faith that Rome had sought to contain and whose temple she had demolished, adopted Christianity as her own. In that adoption the Goddess became disinherited; the marriage of heaven and earth ceased to be a love affair and descended into a theological brawl.

We conclude this chapter with a magical working that endeavors to recreate the Temple as it was originally known—except that in this instance the feminine powers have been restored. For reasons that become evident, it should be undertaken by two men and two women. For those accustomed to ritual magic, this is a simple "four-hander," with officers sitting at the quarters and with ritual movements and accoutrements made clear in the text. For those less used to this work, we hope that, by a measured and imaginative reading of it, both men and women will take this journey into the heart of the Temple.

THE TABERNACLE AND THE ARK

East: Brethren, we are met this day to build the tabernacle of the Most High God. May the thoughts of Almighty God, blessed be He, attend our building.

[East rises.]
East: In the east, Raphael.

[Lights quarter candles.]
West: In the west, Gabriel.

[Lights quarter candles.]
South: In the south, Michael.

[Lights quarter candles.]
North: In the north, Auriel.

[Lights quarter candles.]

East: In the beginning before heaven and earth took form, the Almighty, blessed be He, created the seven.

[East rises with Menorah and holds aloft, circumambulates, then sets Menorah at center.]

West: *[Standing with lighted taper]* First He created the Torah. And she was his truth, written with black fire upon white fire.

[West goes to center and lights central candle of menorah; returns to west.]

South: *[Stands.]* Second he created the throne.

[South lights one candle of Menorah.]

North: *[Stands]* And on the one side He set Paradise.

[Lights third candle of Menorah.]

South: *[Stands]* And on the other Sheol.

[Lights fourth candle on Menorah.]

North: *[Stands]* Then before Him he set the sanctuary.

[Lights fifth candle of Menorah.]

West: *[Stands]* Therefore, within that sanctuary He made the altar.

[Lights sixth candle on Menorah.]

East: *[Stands]* And upon that altar set a jewel. And graven in fire upon that jewel was the name of the Messiah. *[Lights seventh candle, saying]:* Behold I lay a stone in Zion, a cornerstone, chosen and precious, and like living cornerstones, be yourselves built into a tabernacle, a house of the spirit.

South: And that Spirit was the Torah, the beloved one of God.

North: And God took counsel with the Torah, asking her how creation might enshrine His truth and what creatures might have stewardship of it.

West: And she counselled Him thus. A king should have his court, but shall those courtiers obey my laws?

East: And He sayeth unto her. All shall be forgiven before it is begun. And men shall come to the temple to atone for their sins, and a Messiah shall be sent among them to bring them salvation.

South: Then the twenty-two letters of His holy name, graven in fire upon His crown, descended, each with their petition to be the first sound of creation. And God granted the petition of Beth, and thus her sound was the first of all sounds.

All Officers: *[Intone with three notes]* BER . . . AHHH . . . HITH.

West: Berashith! In the beginning! God created the heavens and the earth.

South: Seven heavens for the first seven holy things.

[North lights the seven lights of the eastern circle, while east and west intone the seven notes.]
North: And seven earths in which they may be realized.

[South lights seven lights of western circle, while east and west intone the seven notes.]
East: The fourteen thoughts of the Almighty, in whose mind every heaven and every earth is contained. The fourteen courts of angels and of men as the Torah had appointed.

West: The fourteen parts of the body of the king of kings.

South: So were the rounds of heaven and the rounds of earth set forth. And each round spanned seven in its radius and twenty-two in its circumference. In these things are set the mysteries of the building of the tabernacle.

North: For where the circles of all heavens and all earths met, God set a garden, to the east of Eden. Then in the garden He set the Tree of Life.

East: And a river flowed out of Eden to water the garden, and it branched into four streams.

[West takes up chalice and sprinkles water at east.]
East: The name of the first stream was Pishon.

[West goes to south and sprinkles water.]
South: And the name of the second stream was Gihon.

[West goes to north and sprinkles water.]
North: And the third stream was called Tigris.

[West returns to west and sprinkles.]
West: The fourth river is called Euphrates.

[West sits.]
East: And God said it is not good for man to be alone and formed all the creatures out of the earth that the man might name them.

[East goes to west.]
South: But there was no partner for the man. So while the man slept, the Lord God made a woman from clay.

[East raises west to her feet.]
North: Lilith she was called, and equal to Adam in beauty and power.

South: Yet the scribes tell us that Lilith went forth from the garden and from Adam, because she would rather be exiled than be subservient to her husband.

[West turns her back on east.]
North: So came mischief from the mouths of the scribes, setting emnity between man and woman. For they set Adam to be before the woman they called Eve, saying that she was made from his rib. Then they placed upon their Eve the blame for leading Adam into disobedience and sin.

South: Thus were the purposes of God twisted by the minds of men, and the spirit of the Torah forsaken.

[West remains facing west, east turns away and returns to east; both then sit.]

East: So did the dreamtime pass, and men hardened their hearts to the will of God.

West: And the Almighty caused the four rivers to rise up and the world was covered by a great flood.

[West takes water to center and pours out, then returns to station.]

South: Then the old ones, whom we call Noah and his kin, entered the boat of a million years and took with them things that were raised above the flood. And with them was Melchizadek, he who is without mother or father, without beginning of days or end of life, but who abideth a priest continually.

North: And it was said of old that Melchizadek had with him the sacred head of Adam. That was the essence of the first unfallen Adam, of humankind made in the image of God before time was.

[North holds up bread and wine.]

East: Then when the great deluge subsided, Melchizadek set that essence at the center, where heaven and earth were met.

[North places bread and wine at center.]

East: And there the Canaanites built the first temple. This was the temple where El Elyon, the one we call Melchizadek, mediated between humankind and the Most High God.

West: Then Abraham and his people arose from the land of Ur and entered Canann and Melchizadek; the priest-king came out and met Abraham.

[East and west rise and come to the center; east takes up bread and wine.]

South: And Melchizadek gave unto Abraham and his people bread and wine. For these are the symbols of the covenant between God and humankind.

[East gives bread and wine to west, which west elevates, while east elevates Menorah.]

North: These are the elements of the great high priesthood under God in fulfillment of the true Torah.

[East and west intone AHHHHIAAHHH, then lower bread, wine, and Menorah, placing them at the center and returning to places.]

East: The years passed and the children of Abraham went down into Egypt and bondage, until Moses led them forth in the long journey back to the sacred land.

West: And in their journey Moses spoke with God as Adam had done and was charged by God to write the precepts of the Torah on tablets of stone.

South: Thus did the children of Abraham recall their priesthood to the Most High God and built the tent of meeting, the tabernacle, in which they recalled the garden where Adam and Eve had walked in the cool of the day and spoken with God.

North: In this tent of meeting were placed the Menorah, the Shewbread, the cauldron of Bronze, and the Ark. And the Ark, the mercy seat that contained the tablets of the Torah, was at the holiest place in the tabernacle, where only the high priest may go.

East: So was the tabernacle, the temple of the children of Abraham, established in the wilderness, a spiritual Eden in the desert, until these holy things should find their true home at the center of the Promised Land.

South: In due time the children of Abraham came to that Promised Land, and after many trials David was anointed their sacred king. And David would have built that temple, but the prophets, fearful of the power of a priest-king, would not have it so.

West: Then, in due time, Solomon, son of David, became king, and began to build the temple in stone upon the rock that his father had appointed at the heart of the Promised Land in Jerusalem—the rock upon which the Canannites of old had built the temple of Melchizadek. Thus, in that Holy place on the rock where David had spoken to the Lord was begun the first temple of the children of Abraham.

North: Then Solomon brought gold from Ophir and cedar from Lebanon and built the house of the Lord. Thus, where Melchizadek had set the essence of Adam after the flood, Solomon set his temple at the center of the world. For this was the garden of God, set upon a rock in the midst of the waters of chaos, even the rock held within the mouth of the serpent Mahon.

East: Brethren, let us set forth in vision and enter that holy place as it once was. So in the deep of night we come secretly to that temple, set upon the mighty rock that was called the threshing floor of Araunah the Jebusite. Within that towering rock, be aware of the waters that surge deep within the earth, the stirrings of the serpent. We ascend the steps and enter the outer courtyard, where all may pass without let or hindrance. The sky above is sprinkled with stars. Be aware of the great constellation of Uru Anna, a name meaning "the light of heaven," overhead. This is the constellation we now know as Orion, with the three stars of the hunters belt relating to the threefold construction of this temple. Beyond Orion is Auriga, the celestial chariot of the Lord. To the right is the mighty constellation of Taurus, with the seven sisters of the Pleiades clustering on his shoulder. These are the seven lights that weave the destinies and form of human priesthood under God. To the south, on our left, is Sirius, the star of Isis. The courtyard is vivid with starlight. We see the palace buildings on either side, and in the south, beneath the starlight of Sirius, the quarters of the daughter of pharoah, Solomon's wife. Before us a low balustrade is broken by a flight of steps. We ascend the steps to the inner courtyard where the great bulk of the temple itself looms above us. As we do so a figure appears in the starlit gloom and bars our way. As we look the figure seems to grow in size until his head seems to be crowned with the three stars of Orion's belt. His aura extends like mighty wings, vibrating with awesome strength. His eyes scan each of us, eyes that flicker with the light of heaven. We cast our eyes down and are afraid. In his hand is the sword of Orion, alive with red and white fire.

South: And the angel of the threshold of the temple arose and said: "My sword is upon thee, keep faith with these mysteries."

West: Look into your hearts brethren, seek the knowledge of the heart, and ask of your innermost self if you are worthy to enter this sacred place. For this is a place where the gate of heaven stands ajar. Know, therefore, that you are here to serve these mysteries, not of your own willfulness but by the grace of God. Therefore, in God's grace, remember. Remember a time before time when we were mighty in our innocence as spirits before the throne. *[Pause]* "Not in forgetfulness, nor in utter nakedness, but in trailing clouds of glory do we come from God, who is our home."

North: Speak these words in your heart, without fear, and pass through in joy. Otherwise, for the sake of thy soul, turn aside. For if you know not your true home in God, it would be easier for a camel to pass through the eye of a needle than for unfaithfulness to enter here. Yet in knowing ourselves we may choose to turn aside and in this there is no dishonor, only sadness.

East: Therefore, those who shall pass through shall see the inner court etched in starlight. The bulk of the temple is before us, yet in front of it stands the bronze altar of sacrifice. Come to that altar and cast your human fear upon it, and it shall be burnt away in the fire of God's love. For perfect love casteth out fear, so that all that remains is fear of the Lord. And that fear of the Lord is love. "Greater love hath no man than this, that he lay down his life for his friends."

West: Beyond the altar are the ten steps that lead up to the temple itself, the house of the Lord. These ten steps represent what the

Misnah knows as the ten degrees of holiness. These are the ten circles of sanctity that extend like ripples from the rock cast into the waters. So they extend from this holiest place ever outward tenfold to the ends of the earth.

South: On either side of the ten steps, soaring up into the stars, are the great bronze pillars Jachin and Boaz, said by some to represent the pillar of fire and the pillar of cloud by which God led the wandering Israelites. They are decorated with chainwork and pomegranites, further symbolizing the polarity and fertility vested in sacral kingship.

North: Passing between the pillars we encounter a pair of massive doors made of cypress wood. The doors swing open and we enter the Ulam, the temple vestibule. It is empty. Ahead of us stand another pair of cypress doors, which we reverently approach. "Now enter then His gates with praise." The second set of great doors swing open and we enter the Hekal, the sanctuary.

East: The Hekal is a long hall, lit now by the seven lights of the Menorah. Starlight filters in from the five narrow windows set high up on either side. There is a smell of incense in the air. In the gloom we see the walls shimmering. They are panelled with polished cedar wood set with jewels, depicting images of creation, vegetation, palm trees, and among these the mighty angels who underpin creation, the Cherubim. At the far end of the Hekal stands the Asherah, the image of the Goddess, and also the Bronze serpent, each on either side of the Menorah. In front of these stands the altar and the table of shewbread. At the far end of the sanctuary, a further flight of ten steps again lead upward. At the top of these steps is the great curtain, the veil, embroidered with exotic fruits and foliage. Here is the entrance to the Debir, the Holy of Holies, where only the high priest may enter and then only once a year, to speak with the real presence of God, the Shekinah. Here is the entrance to the garden at the center of the world and the gate of heaven.

West: So we stand in the sanctuary, in the place where only the priests may be, the place forbidden to women. Yet here we are gathered, men and women, at the very gates of Eden, descendants of Adam and Eve, at the threshold of our beginnings. For beyond this place is set the mercy seat, where our merciful God reaches out to us, careless of the theology and taboos of human priesthood. In this we no longer stand in the temple built by the hands of Solomon and Hiram, but in the eternal temple not built with hands and set upon the rock of faith.

South: We look around this great hall, this porchway of Eden. The great curtain ahead of us stirs in some otherworldly breeze. The walls shimmer in the gloom, voices seem to whisper to us, and as we watch, the carvings upon the walls seem to move. The palm trees and grasses are waving gently in that ethereal breeze and the great figures of the Cherubim seem to take on life and movement.

North: We become aware that the Cherubim depicted upon the walls encircle us. But these are not the guardian figures of the threshold, for they hold in their hands not swords but branches of palm. Listen with your heart and hear them speak.

East: We who are from the beginning salute you. We who hold the foundation of all that is, greet you. In the deeps of the four great rivers are the rocks, and set upon the rocks are the numbers, and held within the numbers are the words. Hear the words of the spirit of the Torah incarnate, hear her words. And as we hear her words we look up and upon the steps of the sanctuary, above the seven lights before the Holy of Holies, and we see the image of a young woman, hear the words of the star of the great sea, hear the words of Mara, temple virgin and weaver of the great curtain.

West: When I was in this temple and received my food from an angel, there appeared to me one in the likeness of an angel, but his face was incomprehensible. And straightway the veil of the temple was rent *[east and west rise and come to center with scripts],* and there was an earthquake and I fell upon the ground *[west kneels]* but he put his hand beneath me and raised me up *[east does so]*.

East: Hail thou who art highly favored.

West: And he smote upon the right hand, and bread appeared, and he set it upon the altar of the temple and did eat. Then he gave to me also *[east does so]*. Then he smote upon the left hand and there came a great cup of wine. And he set it upon the altar of the temple and did drink, then gave it to me also *[east does so]*. Then he said to me:

East: Yet three years and I shall send word unto thee and thou shalt conceive a son and through him shall all creation be saved. Peace be unto thee my beloved, and peace be with you continually.

[East takes up bread and wine and holds them out at waist level; west takes up Menorah and holds above her head.]

South: We see before us the Virgin standing with the great high priest before the Holy of Holies. The king of peace and the queen of peace. And in the sacred things that they hold between them see a triangle of white fire appear. Look into this triangle of fire and see beyond the veil. Look into the Holy of Holies, the place in the garden where Adam and Eve ate from the Holy Tree. See them of equal stature in the grace of God, and in that same grace, see the angel of the Presence feed them from that Tree of knowledge, which is love.

North: Once in a time, before all time, before men called her Eve, Lilith she was named by the Son of the Morning. And she was the Evenstar, the gem from the crown of the Most High. Therefore, purge yourselves O sons of men, seal your lips O scribes, and know her as she truly was in the beginning. For she shall bring forth children who shall be sons and daughters of comfort in the age that is to come. Virgo, Isis, Mighty Mother, so shall these Cherubim hold forth their palms, and hail thee. "Blessed is she in the name of the Lord, Hosanna in the Highest."

[East and west lower arms and taking Menorah and chalice and bread return to their stations.]

East: Now the vision is passed, and we are in the sanctuary of the temple, and alone. The carvings upon the walls of the Hekal are static, the jewels glint in the candlelight. We make our way back toward the vestibule, then pause and turn, looking for a moment back toward the veil. It is torn in two, and we are aware of sunlight filtering through from the Holy of Holies into the sanctuary. Somewhere from the depths of temple a woman's voice is saying words from the Song of Solomon.

West: Rise up my love, my fair one, and come away, for lo the winter is past, the rains are over and gone. The flowers appear in the countryside. The time is coming when the birds shall sing and the voice of the turtle dove shall be heard in the land.

East: Lord, now lettest thou thy servants depart in peace. For our eyes hath seen thy salvation. We come out into the courtyard in the sunshine. The Holy Land is spread out below and around us like a garden filled with the sounds of bees and the cooing of doves. And in the morning Sun that garden stretches away to the ends of the earth . . . and the beginnings of heaven. Beneath it are the rocks, and within the rocks are the words, and within the words are the names.

[Stands and extinguishes quarter lights.]
East: In the east, Raphael.

West: *[Stands]* In the west, Gabriel.

South: *[Stands]* In the south, Michael.

North: *[Stands]* In the north, Auriel.

East: The peace of the Lord be with you. Let us depart in peace. Amen.

CHAPTER FOUR

THE PRIEST KING AND THE TEMPLE WEAVER

We are mindful of the fact that this chapter may be indifferently skimmed over by dedicated pagans and give rise to a gritting of the teeth by conventional Christians. But what this chapter and the chapter that follows try to demonstrate is that what was really going on in the Christian story was the most ambitious piece of polarity magic, for want of a much better expression, ever attempted then or since. It was, in fact, not only magic—in that it was a working dialogue with the inner worlds—but also mysticism, in that it was a dialogue with the Divine. The mysteries are inconsequential if they cannot apply themselves, over however immense a time scale, to making changes in the world and its inhabitants. Whether pagan devotees of the mysteries empathize with the Judeo-Christian tradition or not, they have to face up to the fact that for better or worse Christianity profoundly affected each and every folk soul that it touched, inwardly and outwardly, and continues to do so. To conventional Christians we would say that it is our view that holy scripture deliberately invites honest and sincere challenge. Like Job, we are encouraged to wrestle with our angel and test the strength of our convictions. The age of dogma is passed, so the reader must believe or disbelieve as he or she will.

Christian scripture is like the proverbial iceberg. What you see is not necessarily what you get, for beneath its synoptic surface lie many contradictions, historical inaccuracies, and a profound sense that there are too many loose ends. But there is also a wealth of magical gems to be dug by those who know how to look for them. Sensible biblical scholarship and informed esoteric insight have realized this for a very long time, although the general public was largely indifferent to or unaware of any alternative New Testament interpretation until the publication of *The Holy Blood and the Holy Grail,* in 1982.[1] This book alerted the public to the fact that the New Testament story might not have been as cut-and-dried as institutional religion had claimed. There are Christian traditions fragmentally scattered here and there, not only in apocryphal and recorded heresy, but also in fervent denials and affirmations. In that the story of Jesus was inextricably bound to the political machinations of His day, the word conspiracy is regrettably unavoidable.

THE ANOINTED ONE

The story of Jesus Christ is initially the story of ancient dreams. It is the story of possibilities spilling from the ample cauldron of myth to drip into the alembic of human history. The Bible contains many "anointing" references. These are applied essentially to kings, although probably after the fall of the monarchy priests were also anointed. In the fourth chapter of Zachariah, the high priest and the king are referred to as the "two anointed ones," although the actual term *māšîah* was avoided in this instance because there could only be one "Messiah," one priest-king. Ideally, a Messiah would be of the lineage of David, in order that he would be in rightful succession to the original warrior king and also in priestly succession through the line of Aaron, the brother of Moses. But this messianic office was by no means unique to Judaism. The priest-king role was common to many ancient cultures, with the monarch being seen as the son or daughter of a god or goddess and thus naturally combining the roles of high priest or priestess, and sovereign. This divine right of a monarch to be both head of state and head of state religion persists, if only in token, in the British monarchy to this day. The present anointed queen is technically both head of state and head of the Church of England. Her divine right to be both is alluded to on the nation's coinage, which is inscribed "D. G. REG," short for Deo Gracia Regina ("by the grace of God Queen"). This diluted remnant of the ancient belief in divinely ordained sovereignty embodying both temporal and spiritual power reminds us that it was once considered essential that a nation should be governed through a direct link with the Divine.

In ancient Sumer, from which Abraham had come, the original kings were seen to have descended from the Annunaki, the divine race. In the Egypt from which Moses had brought the Hebrews home, pharaoh had been not only king but high priest to his people. At about the same time in the northern European Bronze Age we see much the same belief. The Celtic myths, which appear to reflect these earlier Bronze Age beliefs, insist on the chieftain-king mating with and mediating divinity. Thus, Arthur takes Gwenevere as his queen, for her original Welsh name, "white shadow," tells us that she was a being of the immortal race of faery, a princess of the inner realm of Annwn and a representative of the Goddess. In this she was intended both to validate and empower Arthur's sovereignty. She was able to do this by virtue of being from the inner formative worlds, which in some senses are between the archetypal angelic worlds and material actuality. Such a faery queen was therefore able to mediate archetypal cosmic order (the Hebrew Tsdeq) to her human sovereign mate so that his kingdom could be governed in line with divine principle.

The early Hebrew concept of a priest-king Messiah was in essence very much the same as this, even if a polarity with the empowering feminine was seen in a somewhat different way. The priest-king who mediates Tsdeq was, as we have seen, implicit in the Canaanite archetype of Melchizadek, which the early Hebrews readily adopted. St. Paul's reference to Jesus as "the great high priest after the order of Melchizadek"[2] confirms that the early Christians saw their Christ, as Melchizadek had been, "priest of the Most High God" and "King of Salem (Jerusalem) which is peace."[3] He had been anointed so by Mary of Magdala, as we shall later discuss. From the Holy of Holies of the temple, which symbolized Eden, the Messiah, the anointed priest-king would come to preside and set Tsedq, the archetypal principle of heaven, in earth.

This was what had been expected of Jesus during His lifetime. Indeed, it was that seemingly failed expectation that prompted Pilate's grim jibe of having "King of the Jews" set over the cross. The Jewish temple authorities found such an inscription blasphemous, even a bad joke. They objected, only to be met with Pilate's legendary rejoinder "I have written what I have written." It was important to Pilate that he made sure that any other would-be "Messiahs" knew what to expect. He couldn't afford to have a messianic uprising that tried to eject either his own occupying forces or the hated Herod Antipas, whom his superiors in Rome had installed as puppet king. About half a century later the gospel writers couldn't resist noting this (albeit negative) acknowledgment of Jesus as the Messiah, the "King of the Jews," and of weaving a further messianic assertion into the account of Jesus' execution. For having noted that Jesus was seen as the Messiah and was executed for this, the gospel writers record that the centurion supervising the execution remarked: "Surely this man was the Son of God."

OF ANGELS AND MEN

The archangel Michael was the patron saint of Israel, and his name means "like unto God." Humankind are created, angelic beings are begotten. The difference between the two is that begotten angelic beings reflect the precise will of God, while created creatures like human beings patently fail to do so. Angels mediate Tsdeq, the divine plan that humans in their better moments only aspire to. Certainly the angelic spark, often inaccurately called the divine spark, is within every human being, but the exercise of human free will inevitably dims its sparkle! In Paul's remarks about Melchizadek we see that telling phrase "Thou art my son, today have I begotten thee."[4] Paul's "Son of God," his Messiah who is a priest and king in the succession of Melchizadek, is "begotten" and thus divinely conceived and angelically conscious, for he reflects the Tsdeq of the divine mind, the will of God. As a Son of God He becomes incarnate through the mediation of the archangel Michael so that He too shall be "like unto God," for Michael is the intermediary mirror, reflecting the image of God in the Melchizadek office, and the incarnation of Melchizadek is the Messiah.

The early Jewish Christians of Egypt understood all of this, but their "Gospel of the Hebrews," written before the other gospels, is long lost. The only fragments that we have are quotations from it by the early Fathers. One such quotation reads:

> When Christ wished to come upon the earth to men, the Good Father summoned a mighty power in heaven which is called Michael and entrusted Christ to the care thereof. And the power came into the world and was called Mary, and Christ was in her womb seven months.[5]

In this we see an interaction between heaven and earth with the archangel Michael, the patron saint of Israel, as that essential intermediary. His mediation is facilitated by a Jacob's Ladder set between God and Israel, which Qabalists will recognize as the Tree of Life. At the summit of this Tree is the triune Godhead who reveals Himself in creation by descending through the subsequent seven spheres (called *sephiroth*) of the Tree, hence Mary's "seven month" pregnancy. The Qabalist Tree of Life therefore delineates the "ladder of lights" between heaven and earth, which the spirit of God progresses down to incarnate in the Messiah. The Qabalist teachings of the *Merkabah,* the "Chariot Throne," explain how that metaphysical ladder may be utilized by the Messiah. Jacob's vision at Bethel was a vision of the Tree of Life. Ezekiel's vision was a vision of the Merkabah, and Merkabah mysticism was at the core of the Judaic mysteries from the time of Solomon's temple. Fragments alluding to it are to be found in the Essene "Dead Sea Scrolls," but until the middle ages its teachings as such were only transmitted orally between initiates. Indeed, the Mishnah states that liturgical use of the chariot throne symbolism is forbidden, and that no "wise man" should share his knowledge of the Merkabah with one of lesser knowledge. This was essentially because Merkabah indicated the secret way by which a Messiah, an anointed Son of God, may be simultaneously present in both heaven and earth and Tsdeq restored. Therefore, Merkabah was considered to be the "secret ingredient" of the divine plan, and that plan's completion was in the incarnate Messiah upon the chariot throne, the *Kapporeth* or "Mercy Seat" set in the Holy of Holies.

The stages of that interaction between the One God, through His archangelic thoughtform of Michael, his eternal immortal priest Melchizedek, and His incarnate Messiah, were seen as stages of the courtship that anticipated the mystical marriage of God and Israel, heaven and earth. In this, Israel as the Qabalist "Malkuth" ("kingdom") is frequently described as "the bride." This is the ultimate piece of polarity magic.

The Tree, therefore, mapped out the form of the restoration of Tsdeq, of "earth as it is in heaven," and the Chariot Throne the means whereby this should be accomplished. With this restoration of the paradisal state through the priest-king Messiah, the angelic spark within humankind would in some sense be revived. Thus, the angelic impulse initiated through the archangel Michael would reconcile men and angels, and return things to that first Edenic era when the Beni Elohim, the sons of the gods, descended to consort with the daughters of men. We might also assume "the daughters of gods" consorted with the "sons of men," as angels are not confined by the limitations of gender!

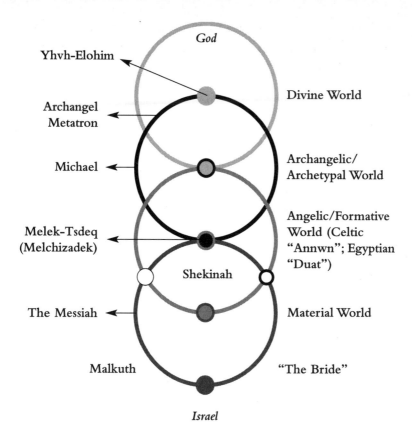

Yhvh-Elohim

Archangel
Metatron

Michael

Melek-Tsdeq
(Melchizadek)

The Messiah

Malkuth

God

Divine World

Archangelic/
Archetypal World

Angelic/Formative
World (Celtic
"Annwn"; Egyptian
"Duat")

Shekinah

Material World

"The Bride"

Israel

Merkabah: The Descent of the Chariot Throne

THE GODDESS IN THE GARDEN

On the one hand the priest-king represented Israel to God, and on the other he represented the Son of God to Israel. In his ritual in the Edenic garden, which was the Holy of Holies at the gate between heaven and earth, the Messiah became the intermediary for both parties in the marriage of heaven and earth. In this we remember the garden imagery of the gospels. The major instances of Christ demonstrating both His mortality (submitting to arrest and consequent execution) and His immortality (resurrection from the tomb) take place in a garden. The gospel garden is symbolically the Edenic garden that the Holy of Holies was meant to represent. Israel was God's destined bride, and God, through his "Son," was her destined bridegroom.

Yet to so represent Israel, the priest-king had to be empowered and validated by a priestess-queen. She would be the Israel who would anoint the priest-king to represent her. Inevitably, the revisionists eradicated her role, yet in the Solomonic temple rites that are preserved in the Song of Songs, again set in a garden, the bride sings:

> The fountain in my garden is a spring of running water,
> Pouring down from Lebanon.
> Awake north wind and come south wind
> Blow upon my garden that its perfumes may come forth
> That my beloved may come to his garden
> And enjoy its rare fruits.

To which the bridegroom replies:

> I have come to my garden my sister and bride
> And have plucked my myrrh and my spices
> I have eaten my honey and syrup
> And have drunk my milk and wine
> Eat, friends, and drink until you are drunk with love.[6]

So does the archangelic impulse in Miriam-Mary induce the spirit of the Messiah to set his path toward the Edenic garden of the world, where in the person of another Miriam-Mary she will anoint Him. For she is the Tree in the garden, she is the woman who asks "what if?" just as Eve had done. She is Israel, who in her heart of hearts is as eager for her God as He is for her. She is young, yet she is old, for she is the Isis of many names—and is in a sense as old as the garden of the world itself, for she *is* the Tree of Life.

In all of this we see the Shekinah, the feminine power that is the alter ego of "the bride," giving power and validation to the rightful Messiah. The Asherah Pole became his rod or scepter, signifying the validation of his sovereignty and priesthood. As the Celtic heroes (who were to become Arthurian knights) were armed and thus validated by their mothers who represented the Goddess, the priest-kings were in early times anointed and validated by a priestess who represented the Shekinah. Thus, the Hathor of love who had nurtured them became the Hathor of blood who armed and empowered them, even as Miriam the Blessed Virgin nurtured the Christ child and Miriam of Magdala had anointed Him. In acknowledgment of this almost forgotten validation of a Messiah as warrior, priest, and king, the high priests of the second temple would sprinkle the blood of sacrificed animals upon the veil, which was, in effect, the portal of the dweller within, the Shekinah who had so long before been the Hathor of blood.

While the Asherah pole represented the trunk of a tree, the Menorah, the seven branched candlestick, represented a whole tree, indeed, an almond tree aflame. Each representation in some senses embraced both her fertility and mediation roles. The straight pole, the phallic rod, implied her ability to initiate fertility. This symbolism may be seen in many mythologies where it relates to the axis mundi, the pole that joins the center of earth and station of the earthly king to the pole star at the center of the heavens. In other words, there is a desire implicit in the king's alignment with the archetypal patterns of the stars by which his rule shall reflect Tsdeq, the patterns of cosmic order in earth. In actuality, this stellar alignment of the king's scepter-phallus as the axis mundi relates to the earth's tilt and the precession of the equinoxes, and thus the turn of the seasons through which fertility in earth is initiated.

Menorah

Under these symbols, the priestess, the "Miriam," the bride who was both desire and the initiatrix of desire, invited the bridegroom into her paradisal garden. The ancient catechism of such rites surviving in the Song of Songs is a litany of sacred sexuality. It is the litany of what the western mysteries know as a rite of polarity magic that is celebrated between a priest and priestess, and it leaves us in no doubt that these rites are expressed in a very physical way:

> I have stripped off my dress, must I put it on again?
> I have washed my feet, must I soil them again?
> When my beloved slipped his hand through the latch hole,
> My bowels stirred within me.
> When I arose to open for my beloved
> My hands dripped with myrrh
> The liquid myrrh from my fingers
> Ran over the knobs of the bolt
> With my own hands I opened to my love.[7]

But the Edenic dream time expressed in such rites in Solomon's time was soon to come to an end. With the division and weakening of the kingdom after Solomon's death, the sacred role of the king began to decline. In Hezekiah's reign, the Asherah staff and the seven branched Menorah were removed from the temple. Later came the destruction of the temple itself, and exile. The garden was closed until four hundred years later one Joshua bar Joseph, whom history came to call Jesus Christ, began His ministry and spoke in parables about wise and foolish virgins waiting for the bridegroom.

MAGICAL MATING

It has been something of an open secret among a number of pseudo-Templar mystery lodges for a very long time that Jesus was deliberately, humanly, conceived to fill the Messianic role. The gospels certainly don't shrink from promoting Him as the deliberately conceived Messiah; the only difference is that the Sanhedrin decided to give the Almighty and the Blessed Virgin a little help in that conception. Christian dogma notwithstanding, experience indicates that the Almighty tends to *work through,* rather than override, the processes of nature, including, especially, human nature. The idea of the deliberate conception of such a miraculous child was, as we have seen, an accepted part of the magical procedure of the high-priesthood.

Magical procedures have always existed by which a priest and priestess may conceive a child under ritual conditions to induce a high soul into incarnation to physically embody an (angelic) archetype. Procedures also exist by which a human being may mate directly with a partner from another order of being to incarnate a divine-human hybrid. Such remain, for obvious reasons, among the most secret procedures in the armory of Western magic, and are rarely used. One or two modern magicians have touched upon the subject in print. Aleister Crowley, albeit for the wrong reasons, was fascinated enough by it to write his novel *Moonchild.*[8] It is a tenet of magic that the most profound mysteries are best conveyed in fiction—which is subsequently adopted as myth. The seriousness with which Crowley took this particular subject may be seen not only by its delivery as fiction, but by his outrage upon finding that two of his disciples attempted to ritually conceive such a magical "Moon" child.

The principles of magical mating to incarnate a soul from another order of being may also be deduced from Dion Fortune's *Esoteric Philosophy of Love and Marriage.*[9] The publication of this book caused Moina Mathers, then the head of the Hermetic Order of the Golden Dawn, to admonish Dion Fortune (and some say eject her from the Order) for this disclosure of magical secrets. Reading between the lines we may understand why! Dion Fortune and her successor, Margaret Lumley Brown, did a great deal of mediumistic delving into the myth of Atlantis. As we have already seen, Atlantis represents proto-creation rather than early civilization; it is that inner, formative place between the worlds and represents an Edenic state. According to Gareth Knight, who provided a commentary upon much of the mediumistic material gleaned by Dion Fortune and Margaret Lumley Brown, the most powerful of the Atlantean magic consisted of magical mating. This included not only mating to provide suitable physical-etheric vehicles that could be ensouled by inner beings who embodied a force or archetype, but also involved direct intimacy with beings from higher planes of existence. We are again reminded of the Beni Elohim—"the sons of gods resorting to the daughters of men"—or, if one cares to cite Adam's encounter with Lilith, daughters of gods with the sons of men.

THE ANNUNCIATION

We are reminded again of that extract from the lost Gospel of the Hebrews telling us that:

> When Christ wished to come upon the earth to men, the Good Father summoned a mighty power in heaven which is called Michael and entrusted Christ to the care thereof. And the power came into the world and was called Mary, and Christ was in her womb seven months.[10]

The Annunciation according to The Questions of Bartholomew[11] is Christian (as opposed to Gnostic) apocrypha. While extant texts date from the third century, it is very likely that it was originally written much earlier (as is so often the case). As the name implies, the narrative is instigated by Bartholomew, the new apostle after the death and resurrection of Jesus. Bartholomew asks the Virgin Mary about the Annunciation. In this Gospel it is Mary who is at the center of the "new twelve." Jesus has risen from the dead and only incidentally appears to admonish Mary when she seems to giving away too many secrets. Mary asks the disciples to gather around her in a circle and utters twenty-two words—the emanation of the name of God through the Hebrew alphabet—then proceeds to give her account of what happened at the event that later came to be described as the Annunciation. The twenty-two utterances indicate a comparatively early Qabalistic awareness. Yet we may also see in this a representation of the incarnate Isis, who as Isis the woman was nonetheless "lady of the words of power." But let us hear what the Blessed Virgin has to say in her own words, or at least those that she was recorded as saying:

> When I abode in the temple of God and received my food from an angel, on a certain day there appeared to me one in the likeness of an angel, but his face was incomprehensible and he did not have in his hand bread or cup, as did the angel which came to me aforetime. And straightway the veil of the temple was rent and there was a very great earthquake and I fell upon the earth for I was not able to endure the sight of him. But he put his hand beneath me and raised me up and I looked up into heaven and there came a cloud of dew and sprinkled me from head to feet, and he wiped me with his robe. And said unto me "hail thou that are highly favored, the chosen vessel, grace inexhaustible." And he smote his garment upon the right hand and there came a very great loaf and he set it upon the altar of the temple and did eat of it first himself and then gave also unto me. And I beheld and saw the bread and the cup whole as they were. And he said unto me "yet three years and I will send my word unto thee and thou shalt conceive my son. And through him shall the

whole creation be saved. Peace be unto you my beloved and
my peace shall be with you continually." And when he had
said so he vanished away from mine eyes and the temple was
restored as it had been before.[12]

At face value this looks like Luke's Annunciation story, but some
of the differences are profound. Even so, the text wasn't, as far as we
know, considered to be heretical. Mary says that she was living in
the temple. She was visited regularly by an angel who brought her
food. Then one day a man *in the likeness of an angel*—that is to say,
not her usual angel—appears and gives her bread and wine, which
he also takes. He then tells her that he will appear again to her, or
send word to her, and she will conceive his son. The appearance of
the man who looks like an angel and who wants Mary to have his
son is attended by an earthquake, and the veil of the temple is torn
asunder (a dramatic effect that the orthodox gospels reserve for the
crucifixion). Before Mary can say more about this to the disciples,
the risen Christ appears and admonishes her.

This annunciation, set in the temple and incorporating an im-
promptu Eucharist, poses some hard questions for the fundamentals
of Christian theology and history. This isn't the only apocryphal
gospel to record that Mary lived in the temple. But if she was there
she would never have been allowed to be beyond the outer Court
of Women, and certainly wouldn't have been in the temple building
itself, unless someone smuggled her in. Assorted apocryhpha suggests that she was in the temple as a child, from the age of three, but
was removed when she reached puberty, and betrothed to Joseph. It
seems that after this she returned to weave the temple curtain, and
this was the time when she saw the man who looked like an angel.

Once a year, at Yom Kippur, when the high priest entered the
Debir, he cast aside his priestly robes and put on a plain white robe
to be "as an angel" for his annual audience with the Lord. This may
have been what Mary saw, in which case we have a man looking
like an angel who, in spite of "magically" making himself and the

bread and wine appear and disappear, tells her that she will become the father of his child. But a further problem occurs in that this appearance before the veil would have been in the *Hekal,* which only the priests could enter. The bread and wine also appear to be a problem in that they are not particularly related to Yom Kippur. The obvious conclusion is that this is a later bit of Christian eucharistic interpolation. Yet in those ancient Canaanite myths adopted by early Judaism, the bread and wine had significance. Melchizadek brings bread and wine to Abraham as the chosen first enter the Promised Land. Later, David cites Melchizadek to make himself a "Messiah," a priest-king, and Paul attaches the same Melkchizadek archetype to Jesus. We may also see something of Melchizadek "The king of Salem which is peace" in the blessing that the "angel" gives to Mary: "Peace be unto thee my beloved and my peace shall be with thee continually."[13] The Annunciation is, after all, the anticipation of that Messiah, a second Melchizadek, expressed later in orthodox scripture in the sacred bread and wine of the first Melchizadek. Mary's angelically robed visitor would appear to be somebody fulfilling the priestly office of Melchizadek, and in doing so, the visitor breaks all the rules. It is difficult to imagine now how heinous a crime it was for a girl past puberty and thus regularly menstruating to be anywhere in the temple beyond the outer Court of Women. But there would be little point in an annunciation to a prepubescent child! So either somebody in the temple hierarchy had the confidence to risk death and initiate these preliminaries of sacred sexuality at the heart of Judaism, or it was an accepted, if secret, part of the role of the priesthood.

It is recorded that it fell to one of the priests named Zacharias, supposedly the same priestly Zacharias who was the father of John the Baptist, to pray for guidance in the practical arrangements. The divine advice he received was to get a group of distinguished widowers to each bring a rod or staff to the temple, and to whomever the Lord gave a sign should take Mary as his betrothed. While a

Freudian interpretation of this advice seems inescapable, we should recall that a pole was the symbol of the Solomonic temple goddess Asherah, and that it is central to the priestly mythology of Aaron, brother of Miriam, and later, to the Joseph of Arimathea legend. When, as we are told, the dove that symbolized the Holy Spirit alighted from the staff and settled on Joseph's head, we can see that this is as much an "annunciation" for Joseph as it is for Mary, and precedes her own annunciation! We should note that Joseph is a rich Jerusalem widower, not the humble Nazareth carpenter that customary mistranslation has made him.

This is, of course, the same symbolism used when Christ is baptized in Jordan and acknowledged as the "Son of God." The idea of Sons of God being those in whom the Spirit of God is active, is equally applied to mortals and angels throughout the Bible. It appears to indicate the state of *Elohenu,* which is the immanence of the Elohim mediated through an angelic overshadowing. After this overshadowing, Joseph the widower and Mary became betrothed. This suggests that whether by mortal or divine design, Joseph is definitely "chosen." Having been betrothed, Mary then returns to the temple to be selected as a weaver and receives her Annunciation. The thread that she weaves is the purple thread, the color of royalty, for the new temple curtain.

And indeed at about this time Herod the Great would have been coming to the conclusion of his rebuilding and refurbishing of the temple. Josephus describes the refurbishing:

> . . . the entrance doors which with their lintels were equal in height to the temple itself, he adorned with multicolored hangings with purple colors and with inwoven designs of pillars.[14]

Bartholomew doesn't mention that Mary, though residing in the temple, is there as a weaver. But he does mention that when "the man who looks like an angel comes to her, the veil is rent and the earth moves." One may surmise from this an occasion during the

refurbishing of the temple when the old curtain was either intentionally or otherwise torn. Such a "rending of the veil" may like so
many other things have been taken out of context by later writers,
and may have been enlisted by Bartholomew as it was by the gospel
writers when they came to paint their dramatic background to the
crucifixion. The "earthquake" may have arisen from a similar mundane occurrence thanks more to Herod's builders than to any sign
from heaven. As Josephus tells us:

> After removing the old foundations, he (Herod) laid down
> others and upon these he erected the temple which was a
> hundred cubits in length and twenty more in height, but in
> the course of time this dropped as the foundations sub-
> sided.[15]

In all of this we begin to see practical as well as metaphysical
plausibility in Bartholomew's account. But of all the questions of
Batholomew we must return to the most intriguing one of all: "the
man who looked like an angel."

At the time of Jesus, the Melchizadek mythos still had special relevance for two groups: the Essenes and the Sadducees. As with so
many New Testament words, we must search behind the Greek ap-
proximation to find the original Aramaic. In this case we find that
the word "Sadducee," meaning the followers of *Saduc,* is the Greek
adaptation of the followers of Tsdeq. The Sadducees were, like the
Essenes, "Zadokites," who held the mysterious Zadok the priest in
great reverence. This was, of course, none other than the
Melchizadek-like figure who had anointed Solomon. In this they
still held to the "royal cult" of the Messiah as understood in the days
of Solomon's temple. While in general terms the Essenes viewed the
Sadducees as Herodian-Roman quislings who had "sold out," a
number of exceptions stand out. Joseph of Arimathea and Nicode-
mus, both Sadducees and members of the powerful Sanhedrin, are
obvious examples, but more subtle examples may be found in Jesus'
family. While a number of attempts have been made to show that

Jesus was an Essene, there can be little doubt that he was a Sadducee, or at least from a Sadducee family.

We must also note the matter of Jesus's brother, "James the Righteous," or, to give his Jewish name, "Jacob Tsdeq." We are told that James preached at the temple in Jerusalem, and the early Christian fathers tell us that he wore the high priest's miter. According to the church historian Eusebius, "He alone was permitted to enter the holy place, for his garments were of wool not of linen."[16] This astounding statement suggests that Jesus' brother James, a devout Zadokite, acted as high priest and was accorded access to the Holy of Holies, wearing the white wool that made him "as an angel." And while the canonical gospels tell us that James was not a follower of his brother until after the resurrection, the apocryphal Gospel of Thomas tells us that "The disciples said to Jesus 'we know that you will depart from us, who is to be our leader?' Jesus said unto them 'Wherever you are, go to James the Righteous, for whose sake heaven and earth came into being.'"[17]

The Christian story as the once and for all marriage of the eternal with the temporal was intended to change the course of earthly evolution. It probably did, perhaps not in ways that its contemporary human instigators anticipated, but in ways that others had foreseen many ages before. After the crucifixion it may well have seemed to those involved that all was lost: that the royal cult of Melchizadek, the ancient dream dreamed in Canaan, was not to survive. But another green and pleasant land was made ready, and its preparation had been long in the making.

A CELTIC INTERLUDE

The Welsh bard Taliesin, an initiate bard in the Roman Catholic Wales of A.D. 1200, makes what seem to be a series of absurd boasts in a text that has come down to us as the "Hanes Taliesin."[18] But by taking two of his statements in the "Hanes Taliesin" we find corroboration of all that we have so far suggested. Taliesin states:

1. "My original country is the place of the Cherubim."

The place of the Cherubim is, of course, the Debir of the Temple of Jerusalem or of the earlier tabernacle, the Holy of Holies where once a year the high priest symbolically entered Eden to communicate with the Shekinah, the divine feminine presence that resided over the Ark of the Covenant.

The bald simplicity of his statement hides an extraordinary claim. Not only does it indicate a close knowledge of the esoteric law of a very different religion, but it also suggests that his true "country," that is to say, the place with which he most identifies, the true place of his origin rather than the country in which he was presently in incarnation, was one that lay at the very heart of Judaic belief. That this was where he "was coming from."

2. "I have been in Canaan when Absalom was slain."

He confirms and enlarges this statement by offering a piece of little-known Judaic history. Absalom, third son of King David, challenged his father for the kingship, or, as David attempted to make it, the priest-kingship. Like his father, Absalom was anointed at Hebron. In the second book of Samuel, Absalom says, "If the Lord brings me back to Jerusalem I will become a worshipper of the Lord at Hebron."[19] And it is at Hebron that the people flocked to Absalom, before his father defeated and killed him.

Although we are no longer aware of the entire significance of Absalom's rebellion against his father, it is evident that it was known to Taliesin, who is, in effect, mourning the death of Absalom and the consequent loss of the holy place of Hebron. However, a suggestion as to the meaning of the event is given in the Talmud, which records that when David was forced to abandon Hebron, where he had been anointed as King, a heretical group called the *Melchizadekians* arose and insisted that such a move was a sacrilegious act. As far as they were concerned, David's abandonment of Hebron was a belittling of the priestly part of his office. David doubtless saw the change from

Hebron to Jerusalem as a sensible logistical move—but tradition (and one in which Taliesin clearly was part) didn't agree with him.

What was special about Hebron? To start with, it was the place at which the head of Adam was reputedly buried. The exact location was said to be the cave of Machpelah, which later also became the tomb of Abraham and Sarah. An early Christian legend appears to connect this latter information to the Melchizadek mythos in that it describes how, before the flood, Melchizadek took the head of Adam onto Noah's Ark and, when the flood had subsided, buried it "at the centre of the world." Such a place was Hebron. In ancient times it was seen as one of a series of earth navels, oracular shrines where the umbilical cord of earth was seen to be joined to heaven, where a priest-king of the Most High God would naturally establish himself. In fact, Hebron shares the same latitude as the predynastic Egyptian city of Behdet, which was taken to be the northern point of the centerline of Egypt. Similar geodetic and oracular shrines like Sardis and Delphi shared successive latitudes to the North.

3. "I conveyed awen to the deeps of Hebron."

This is perhaps the most extraordinary of all Taliesins's statements, and pivotal to our argument. As we have described, "Awen" is the name given in Celtic language to the inner inspiration, the unceasing flow of creativity that wells up from within and is held by those of the angelic faery race who bear its name of "white."

In that the Awen, like the Edenic river, flows from and enables the Edenic state, this is a further insistence that Hebron and its mythology are the true place of Tsedq. But what takes this statement even further is that Taliesin is claiming *responsibility* for taking the essence of the pre-Celtic Faery world and the underworld inspiration of the Awen, and controlling its flow at a level that occurs before physicality so that it will find an outlet of expression at the very heart of the Judaic priest-king tradition. His statement evokes potent images of vast, slow movements, events that take place within the deep waters of the pre-physical world beyond the confines of space and time, and movements that he claims to be capable of manipulating.

We may put this in terms that we introduced in chapter 1, and suggest that Taliesin can therefore be seen to be acting as a priest of the Atlantean Temple of the Sea and Stars; a priest of the withdrawn temple that witnessed the rise and fall of many a Sun Temple, but continued its work at the deeper levels of creation in which many thousands of years may pass before an event is brought to fruition. And in this case he can also be said to have witnessed the events at Glastonbury, in England's green and pleasant land where the Holy Child walked with Joseph; for Hebron, then Jerusalem, and finally Glastonbury are each an island in the sea, where the Temple of the Sun periodically reemerges to house the anointed priest-king.

> 4. "I have been at the crucifixion of the merciful son of God,"
> and "I have been with Mary Magdalene in the firmament."

In this sequential change from the Old to the New Testament, both of these statements suddenly take the anointed king of the old Hebron-Melchizadek mythology and place him at the side of Mary Magdalene (a heresy to which we shall soon return!) with the stellar associations of "in the firmament." Again we see Taliesin operating beyond the confines of time and space—and stating without equivocation that Mary Magdalene was the one who worked with him at this level.

But why should the Welsh Taliesin bards of the Middle Ages ever concern themselves with such things, and where did they get them from?

The Taliesin bards—for there were many who took this name—were well versed in the lore of sacral kingship, and much of the Taliesin material deals with another sacred king mythos, that of the British Bronze Age, and not least the paradisal tenure of the severed head of Bran and of inner islands in Annwn. At the hands of the bards the pagan magical cauldron that had been guarded by Bran became the Holy Grail guarded by Bron or Hebron. The inner province of the Celtic Annwn was already comparable with the Hebrew ideas of Eden, where Adam the intended priest-king of all humankind, had ruled.

The master of the dream of the earthly Messiah is Melchizadek. Yet, as we shall see, there may be no Melchizadek without a Miriam. Melchizadek may open the gate of heaven, but without a Miriam there is no gate. This is the essential truth that orthodox post-exilic Judaism and Christianity alike failed to grasp.

GIVING MEANING TO THE MEANING

All this is, or should be, of more than academic interest! You may, for example, wish to sit quietly, light a candle, perhaps even burn some incense, then close your eyes and visualize the following inner journey:

You are standing on a rock plateau at night. The air is warm and the stars glitter in the night sky, where the Great Bear shakes her tail out over the Valley of Kidron below you. Across the valley the Mount of Olives rises over Gethsemane, and to the right the line of the white road running away to Bethany stands out in the light of the Moon. Behind you is the new wall not long completed by Herod's builders, rearing up to enclose the temple precincts, and within that wall, slightly to the left, is the arch of the Shusan Gate, which leads through Solomon's Portico into the Court of Gentiles.

You turn through the unguarded gate and make your way into the great expanse of this outer courtyard. Nobody is to be seen, for the gentle night has wrapped itself about this holy place and its pilgrims. Ahead and to your left is another enclosure raised up above the great plaza in which you stand. You walk toward it, your feet patting on the temple rock. The walls rear up, and before you is another gate and steps leading up and into that inner enclosure. This gate is called the Beautiful Gate and leads up into the Court of Women. There is a guard on this gate, but he is unaware of your passing, and you rise up the steps to find yourself in a much smaller enclosure, perhaps no more than twenty-five yards wide on either side. Ahead of you, you see more steps leading to other courts, but beyond this, rising up against the night sky, the great bulk of the temple seems to float like a raft in the sea of stars. You pass quickly and unhindered up through the Court of Israelites and into the Court of Priests, where the great altar of sacrifice stands. And looming over the altar is the temple itself. The meeting place, the Tree of Life, the ladder of lights that joins earth to heaven and heaven to earth. Here is the House of the Lord that Solomon built with wood from the cedar tree and from the olive tree, and stone and gold from the roots of the earth.

Before the temple stand two great pillars of bronze, crowned with the likeness of lilies; these are the pillars of cloud and fire that led the chosen through the wilderness, the pillars of the polarity that lead each living thing from the womb of the Holy Thought into the Eden of its being. And the pillar on the right is called Jachim, and the pillar on the left is called Boaz, the mystical stanchions of a great doorway that leads to higher things. For this is the gate between the material and the formative worlds. You pass through that gate, overhung with weavings in which the bright purple momentarily is caught in the light of the Full Moon and find yourself in the *Ulam,* the vestibule of this holy place.

Beyond the Ulam is the *Hekal,* the sanctuary, which you enter through great, silent doors to find yourself in a place of dim ethereal light, yet of great light for those with eyes to see. The air is heavy with incense and holiness. The walls are of beaten gold highlighting the images wrought upon them of trees and flowers and angelic beings that mark this place as the outer court of heaven. These images seem to have movement in the warm light that flickers from the far end of this long sanctuary hall. For there is the great candelabra of gold, the Menorah of seven lights, standing as it had stood centuries before in Solomon's time. Beside it stands the altar of incense, and beside that the speckled pole of the Asherah.

You stand and look about you, absorbing the images encased in shadow and sanctity. Above all, you look to see the great embroidered curtain, with seven steps before it that separate this sanctuary from the inner sanctuary of the *Debir,* the Holy of Holies.

Then you hear the sound. It is a subdued urgent whisper, and for a moment the hairs on the back of your neck rise. Then you see her, a still figure, kneeling before the Asherah pole with her back to you, head and shoulders shrouded in a long white veil and cloak. She is unaware of you and continues her urgent whispered prayer in Hebrew. You stand very still, aware of the devotion in the young and urgent voice. You cannot make out or understand what she is saying, but you are aware of the atmosphere of the sanctuary vibrating to her prayers.

Then suddenly, above the rise and fall of her sweet litany, there is a deep, echoing rumble and the sound of grinding of stone. The building shakes for a moment, the seven lights of the Menorah flicker, and there is a tearing noise, like a loud scream. Strips of the great curtain fall in tatters and reveal an opening into the Holy of Holies. The figure of a man stands there in white robes, his face indistinguishable.

He makes his way slowly down the seven steps, and comes to the kneeling woman, then gently reaches down and brings her to her feet. He says something to her in Hebrew, raises his right hand, then lowers it, and a loaf of bread is in his hand. He breaks the bread, eats some of it, then gives some to her. Then he raises his right hand, brings it down, and he is holding a chalice from which he sups then gives to her. He says something to her, embraces her and is gone.

You stare into the dimness. The curtain is again intact, with the young woman kneeling before it. Then slowly her head turns and she looks at you. Something seems to shrink in your soul, and you lower your eyes and then quietly leave the sanctuary.

You make your way back through the courtyards, moving swiftly through the gates. At the outer Shusan gate you begin to make your way down into the valley of Kidron under the stars. As you walk, the scene and the smells of that place seem to fade and you become aware of your feet set firmly upon the floor of your room in this time and place. You open your eyes and think on what you have seen, and know that you may return again to meditate upon these things.

CHAPTER FIVE

THE PRIESTESS FROM MAGDALA

The Blessed Virgin Mary, having been central to the early narrative of the life of Jesus, tends to move to the middle distance after the wedding at Cana. Many of the miracles cited in the New Testament have to be looked at in context, and at Cana it is the wedding itself rather than the miracle of turning water into wine that is of importance. The deeper focus of the miracle signifies the change from one state to another, which marriage is, and a change that Jesus makes at His mother's instigation. The imagery of marriage as the marriage of heaven to earth is, as we have seen, used extensively throughout the Old and New Testaments. We may be persuaded that we are dealing with a heavily abridged, not to mention censored, version of events in the account given in John's gospel. In his curiously truncated Cana narrative he obviously wants us to know that this is a crucial event in the life of Jesus, as may be seen from the profound statements in scraps of dialogue.

When told by His mother that the wine is running out, for example, Jesus cuts her short with the retort: "My hour has not yet come."[1] We can only guess at what He means, but He is surely indicating that whatever event is being celebrated at this wedding it is ultimately of less significance to Him than another that will follow. Nevertheless, John tells us that Cana was the first occasion upon which Jesus "revealed His glory."[2] A chapter later we are nudged back to the incident with "Once again He returned to Cana in

Galilee where He turned the water into wine"[3] and as has been pointed out by others, Jesus certainly acts as if He were the bridegroom at this wedding.

Whether or not Cana was the scene of Jesus's own wedding, it would be inconceivable that a young Jewish man of Jesus's times would remain single for long. If Jesus had for any reason departed from this normal behavior, then this, rather than his marriage, would certainly have been matter for comment. Couples did not choose partners then, they were chosen for them by their parents as a matter of course, and at Cana we sense a certain "pushiness" by Jesus's mother. Indeed, if Jesus was the Rabbi that the scriptures cite Him to have been, it would have been *de rigeur* for him to have had a wife and to have raised children to the glory of God. If, moreover, He was from a wealthy family, as we believe that He was, it would have been perfectly acceptable for Him to have had several wives.

Until this matter is addressed we are encumbered by a theology that wants us to believe in a Messiah, a God made fully flesh, who experienced all human life—almost. As ever, we are faced not with "man made in the image of God" as much as God incarnate having to conform to the image of what man would like to be. The image that the church foisted on Jesus was the image of a Jewish Benedictine monk. Certainly, we have an Osiris-like man-god, all the better for being a historical reality, but this Osiris, against all historical and mythological odds, is neutered from the start and doomed to stand unmated to any Isis. Like the Welsh poet Meirion Evans, we may wonder: "What shall we do with the pansy Christ who hangs high on the walls of the memory's vestries?"[4]

The temperament of St. Paul and of the early Fathers of the church, like the sexually repressed Augustine of Hippo, didn't help, and would seem to provide a *prima facie* reason for the church's unmarried Jesus. The essentially patriarchal stance of the Judaism of those times (which the gentile Fathers thought they knew) would seem to be another reason. But if Jesus had had a wife or wives, it seems reasonable that there would at least have been a cursory mention (as other biblical women were mentioned). If, however, that mention ran the risk of betraying any spiritual status, any complementary role to that of the Messiah, then the wife of Jesus would have got short shrift. The New Testament is presenting Jesus as God incarnate, and monotheism could not countenance a potential "Mrs. God incarnate" without feeling itself tumbling into that awful pagan abyss of gods and goddesses.

THE OTHER MIRIAM

But when ordinary human nature challenges theology, a heresy isn't very far away! The question is not so much "was He married?" but "to whom was He married?" and unless the gospels have completely submerged some unknown woman from his life and times, Mary, or (significantly) Miriam of Magdala, which was her original Jewish name, would initially seem to be the most obvious candidate.

Miriam of Magdala probably came from a town about fifteen miles from Cana, Magdala ("the town of doves"). She is considered by conventional scholarship to be from aristocratic stock in as much as she appears to have been one of the major financial supporters of Jesus's ministry. In spite of this, she is frequently shunned by apostles and gospel writers alike. In many respects she is not typically Jewish, and we cannot assume that she was of orthodox Jewish faith. Many of Jewish blood living in Palestine then, as now, were not practicing Jews. The area of northern Galilee that Mary came from was historically a haven of heresy and religious dissent. Such dissent may be suggested by the gospel record that Jesus drove seven devils out of her, but this may have been a convenient assumption and misrepresentation of the facts, as we shall see later. Her apparent wealth may be attested to in that we may be reasonably sure that it was she who anointed Him with the precious ointment of spikenard. The ointment would have cost most ordinary Palestinians a year's wages, a fact that

Judas, apparently objecting to her wasting expensive ointment, uses to conceal the real reason for his outrage: the ceremony itself.

But in this action, Mary of Magdala is throwing away more than money—she is initiating the sequence of events that lead to the loss of His life. For it is because of this anointing that Judas makes his initial approach to the priestly authorities about a reward for "information leading to." We may assume that Judas is not acting out of a purely pecuniary motive. He is not aware of the conspiracy to set Jesus on the throne of David. He can accept Jesus the rabbi, even Jesus the prophet, but Jesus being anointed as Son of the Most High, and at the hands of a *priestess* was, for Judas, the ultimate blasphemy. It has remained the ultimate blasphemy for almost every Christian believer ever since. But history has its obligation to myth. The life of Jesus and those around Him must work out that primordial pattern of betrayal and sacrifice and, ironically, the fact that history cannot but help itself to do so presents the essential argument for the "divinity" of Jesus.

The early Christians were well aware of this interaction of history and myth. They accepted that Miriam of Magdala held a pivotal role in all of this, but they hesitated to explain the specifics—or perhaps did not fully understand them—and therefore blurred her role in the gospels. The later Roman church had no such qualms. Saint Mary of Egypt had been a reformed whore, so why not Mary of Magdala? So they preached the legend that Mary of Magdala was a reformed whore. True, you couldn't find it your Bible, but they "knew"—and it tied up all those embarrassing loose ends.

With the mythical loose ends neatly tucked away, everything fell into place. In Genesis, Adam was the victim as a result of the precocious action of Eve. In the Christian tradition, Christ was the second redeemed and redeeming Adam. Ipso facto, he becomes the victim by allowing himself to be openly anointed as a king by Mary Magdalene, for it is immediately after this, indeed because of it, that an outraged Judas reports Him to the priestly authorities. The Magdalene therefore facilitates her man's downfall just as Eve had done by taking the initiative. Everything falls into place with "T'was not I Lord, t'was the woman." So while the tradition of Mary Magdalene as the tart with the heart has no biblical or apocryphal basis, being a loose woman gives her the right mythical potential.

THE SACRED WHORE

Making the Magdalene a prostitute provided the image of a sexual trap into which the Messiah, unlike lesser sacred kings, did not fall. This averted speculation about a sexually active Jesus: a Jesus with a wife. But another possibility arises from the "sacred whore" tradition. If Miriam of Magdala had not been his wife but, as with most sacred kings, his *hieros gamos,* she would have fulfilled a sacred sexual role. In other words, she would have been the empowering queen priestess to Jesus's priest-king, fulfilling the Goddess role of sacred mate to her God made flesh. From this perspective, the early writers would have been inclined to identify her with the priestesses of the pagan mystery cults who practiced sacred prostitution.

The irony of this is, of course, that Jesus Himself appears to have been brought into incarnation by much the same techniques of polarity magic and sacred sex employed in those temples. The results of such rites that induced the birth of archetypal beings tended to be seen as "immaculate conceptions" and "virgin births." Unlike later Christian thought, these terms were not intended to naively suggest that no sexual activity or gynecological change had taken place. The virginity of the priestess was not physiological but spiritual in that, as was the case with Jesus's mother, the priestess had no named consort and employed her human sexuality purely as representative of the Goddess to be the vehicle for the birth of a god.

YOU CAN'T KEEP A GOOD HERESY DOWN

Whether or not Miriam of Magdala did fulfill the *hieros gamos* role, heresy and history place her very close to Jesus indeed. While the synoptic gospels refuse to tell us the identity of the woman who anointed Jesus, St. John tells us that it was Mary—not Mary of Bethany, as is so often assumed, but simply "Mary," and that it was "at Bethany." It may in any case be that Mary of Bethany and Mary Magdalene were one and the same. Possibly Mary of Magdala is the unmarried Mary, while Mary of Bethany is the same woman after she becomes part of Jesus' household. There certainly appears to be a curious ambivalence in the biblical gospels as to the true role of Mary Magdalene in Jesus' life. There is no doubt from the frequent number of occasions in which she is described as being with Christ, and the fact that of the several named women among his followers she is almost always named first, that the gospel writers felt compelled to acknowledge that "something was going on." But one gets the impression that they themselves did not know exactly what it was. It is as if they knew that they had to report the existence of Mary Magdalene, that to omit her entirely from the story would in some way not be acceptable, even though they did not know what they were describing. If, however, she was a member of an inner esoteric order of priesthood, then that would explain their ambivalence. Certainly the use of the phrase "the Magdalene" hints at the existence of a title rather than simply the name of a place, as in, for example, "Mary of Bethany," or the name of a husband, as in "Mary Cleopas."

The very early church called her "Apostola Apostolorum," the "Apostle's Apostle," a name that suggests that part of her role was to interpret and mediate Christ's message to the male apostles. It would certainly seem that she knew far more of His real identity and purpose than they did, and that she had a level of knowledge and understanding that far exceeded theirs. In fact, the twelve men appear to understand remarkably little of what He says, and one is tempted to wonder why He picked such dullards—or if perhaps his "real" followers were an inner group whose names and existence were not recorded. It is the Magdelene who stays the course when Peter "the Rock" and the rest of the men have crumbled and fled.

According to the concluding chapter of Matthew's gospel, "Mary of Magdala and the other Mary" are not only the first to see the empty tomb, but the first to be angelically commanded to go and tell the rest of the apostles, and on their way to do so are the first to encounter the risen Jesus.[5] In Mark's gospel all this is experienced by Mary of Magdala alone.[6] As with the anointing, such an honor and responsibility falls naturally to the Apostola Apostalorum, yet the New Testament cannot bring itself to number her or the other women who followed Jesus among the apostles who later became celebrants in the early Church. While focusing on the especial place of Mary Magdalene in Jesus's life, we should not forget that all the early evidence shows Him to have had an extraordinarily egalitarian attitude to all women and, briefly, offered them a liberation from their restrictive Jewish domesticity.

The gospels give us only two brief episodes that reveal anything of the nature of the priest-priestess relationship between Jesus and the Magdalene: the anointing, and the casting out of the seven devils. As we have seen, the anointing of Jesus with spikenard is an action that simultaneously confirms his status as sacred priest-king and initiates his sacrificial death. Implicit in this ceremony is the inescapable recognition—Christ's and our own—that Mary Magdalene was able to confer this status upon him by virtue of her own authority. And yet it remains puzzling as to why the event apparently took place in public (or at least within a small domestic group rather than a secret, and therefore unrecorded, temple ceremony) in the household at Bethany and in the presence of Mary of Bethany (assuming her to be another Mary), Martha, and Lazarus. But, assuming the existence of such a "pagan" priesthood in which a woman was honored as an initiatrix, perhaps we should not be surprised at the apparently humble and domestic setting in which such mysteries could remain hidden in an otherwise hostile environment. The same situation exists today in contemporary pagan religion.

It is in Mark's gospel that we read the oddly placed comment that: "when Jesus was risen early the first day of the week, he appeared first to Mary Magdalene, out of whom he had cast seven devils."[7] Clearly some great change had taken place within her that had been initiated by Jesus, but the presence of the number "seven" alerts us to the idea that this may not have been a matter of demonic possession. It may well have been an intense spiritual or visionary experience, an opening up of the seven levels of perception, an initiation or an experience of enlightenment, and the curious positioning of this piece of information makes us ask whether indeed the event took place *during* Christ's period in the tomb.

The apocryphal gospels have no time for such subtleties and ride roughshod over the reticence of the New Testament canon. The Gnostic Gospel of Mary confirms her authoritative role and has her pulling things together after the crucifixion. Like her ancient namesake Miriam, the sister of Moses, she rallies the faithful and later becomes featured, again as her namesake, as a source of wisdom.

The apocryphal Gospel of Philip, like the Pistis Sophia, emphasizes the feminine wisdom figure, the Miriam figure, in the life of Jesus, and, finding love and wisdom rolled into one, doesn't mince its words: "As for the wisdom who is called 'the barren' she is mother of the angels. And the companion of the Saviour is Mary Magdalene. But Christ loved her more than all the disciples and used to kiss her often on the mouth. The rest of the disciples were offended by it and expressed disapproval. They said to Him 'Why do you love her more than all of us?' The Saviour answered and said to them 'Why do I not love you like her? When a blind man and one who sees are both together in darkness, they are no different from one another. When the light comes then he who sees will see the light and he who is blinded will remain in darkness.' "[8]

While these passages have been interpreted as proof that the Magdalene was the wife of Jesus, it would seem to us that this sort of questioning from the male disciples would not be at all appropriate if she *was* His wife. If she was His wife it would not make sense for them to object that He loved her more than other women, or for them to object to the fact that He kissed her on the mouth—it would only be right and proper behavior on His part. The disciples would only have "disapproved" of His behavior if He was showing that He had a close physical relationship with a woman who was *not* his wife—and this points with inevitability to the conclusion that the Magdalene was his priestess, in which case the men's resentment of a relationship which excluded them from His inner confidences and teaching rings only too true.

We must of course be aware that, just as the New Testament gospel writers were writing to an agenda, so were other writers, not least the "Philip" of this Gnostic gospel. As to the supposedly factual nature of what is said, we have to realize that it is borrowed from tradition, having probably been written during the third century. Predictably, it is condemned by Epiphanius, one of the Palestinian church Fathers of that time who was a convert from Judaism and a noted heresy hunter. He roundly condemned "the Gnostics of Egypt," protesting that "they produce a gospel forged in the name of Philip the holy disciple."[9] Forgery or not, we see Epiphanius acknowledging that the Messiah had come in Jesus, but unable to allow a mere woman to be set above the men of Christ's spiritual entourage. In fact, the Gospel of Philip was probably written in Syria, but Epiphanius obviously has a thing about what we might call "the Egyptian connection" and the heresies that attended it.

Such heresies also called her "Mary Lucifer" or "Mary the light bringer." This was before the later medieval church demonized the name Lucifer, and when she shared the title with Bishop Lucifer of Calgari, staunchest of champions against heresy with his followers prizing their title of "Luciferians." In the early church, "Lucifer" was a spiritual accolade! Meanwhile, we return to the Gospel of Mary, from the Nag Hammadi Scrolls, to hear Peter acknowledging that Jesus had a relationship with the Magdalene that surpassed that of their own: "Sister we know that the Saviour loved you more than the rest of women. Tell us the words of the Saviour that you re-member—which you know but we do not, nor have we heard them."[10] She readily tells them of what Jesus has said to her, but her wisdom evidently fell on stony ground, for Andrew's reply was that he did not believe that the Saviour had said any of it. "For certainly these teachings are strange ideas."[11]

The Nag Hammadi texts, found in Upper Egypt, are regarded as being, for the most part, Christian, albeit Gnostic-Christian. In view of the usual ascetic and abstemious character of Gnosticism, they have no reason to promote a "mated" Jesus. The archaeological evidence indicates that they were hurriedly concealed by a heretical Christian monastic community, perhaps in about A.D. 200. This was about the time that the Christian canon was being finalized and, as we have seen from Clement of Alexandria, noncanonical works were being suppressed. Upper Egypt, far distant from Alexandria, was the home of a good deal of outmoded and unorthodox religion and philosophy. The Nag Hammadi community may well have been a remnant of the first church—that of Ethiopia and Egypt founded by St. Mark of suppressed "secret gospel" fame. Intriguingly, they shared their isolation with the temple of Isis at Philae, which was still operative when the Nag Hammadi Scrolls were buried and was not overrun until much later, and by a very different brand of Christians!

Before the canon was finalized and censored, it appears that several groups subsequently dubbed as heretical took it for granted that Mary of Magdala was in some sense the partner of Christ and first among the apostles. The austere patriarchal stance known to the later established church replaced Christ's true purpose, which had more to do with the Sacred King concept of antiquity, including that of the ancient Solomonic temple cult. Another version of the Gospel of Philip bases its teaching around the concept of the Holy of Holies as the bridal chamber. Again we are reminded of the

Solomonic Song of Songs, with its bridal chamber and Edenic garden symbolism, and the female empowerment of the priest-king. In this we return to the ancient royal cult of Solomon, so beloved of the Sadducees, and to the Song of Songs, remembering that Miriam of Magdala anointed Jesus with oil of spikenard, and that she allegedly came from Magdala, the town of doves.

The bride (queen/priestess) says:

> While the king reclines on his couch
> My *spikenard* gives forth its scent.
> My beloved is for me is a bunch of myrrh
> As he lies on my breast . . .

To which the king/bridegroom replies:

> How beautiful you are my dearest,
> O how beautiful,
> Your eyes are like *doves.*

And:

> *My dove* that hides in the holes in cliffs
> . . . let me see your face, let me hear your voice.

And:

> Open to me my sister my dearest,
> *My dove* my perfect one.

A further passage from the Song of Songs merits consideration:

> My love had turned away and gone by
> My heart sank when he turned his back
> I sought him but I did not find him
> I called him but he did not answer . . .
> The watchman going the rounds of the city met me . . .
> If you find my beloved will you not tell me?[12]

Compare Miriam of Magdala's remarks related in John's gospel at the Gethsemane tomb: "They have taken my Lord away and I do not know where they have laid Him." And: "If it is you sir who have removed Him, tell me where you have laid Him and I will take Him away."[13]

There seems little doubt that the early gentile church made the connection between Miriam and Magdala and the bride of the Song of Songs, and this is well substantiated by the cult of the Black Madonna, which grew up in the south of France, where the Magdalene was said to have gone after the death of Jesus. The bride in the Song of Songs, Solomon's queen tells us: "I am black but comely O ye daughters of Jerusalem."[14]

As we have seen, scholars point out that the Song of Songs is very similar to the liturgy of Egyptian polarity rites, particularly those associated with Isis and Nephthys. The Osirian theme is seen in the king and lover being lost, searched for by his priestess queen and restored. It is a sacred king and his empowering queen playing out a god/goddess rite, and pagan references abound.

What is clear is that we are bequeathed a picture that has as much validity—yet no resemblance—to accepted Christian scripture and doctrine. At times that bequest may be seen in its muted way in Celtic Christianity, not least with its Pagan/Christian Brigid mythos and its practice of allowing women to serve at the Mass as *Conhospitae*. That, in turn, rubbed shoulders with the Celtic mystery schools of the initiate bards, whose Welsh branch was to give miraculous birth to the Arthurian legends. Later the Magdalene appeared fleetingly in such British folk contexts as Maid Marian, consort to the esoterically named Robin and co-leader of an outlawed faction, supposedly during the heyday of the Templars.

Yet the picture was, for a time, most vivid in France, where Miriam of Magdala was said to have fled. It was eventually perhaps a picture too vivid for its own good. For a time its Song of Songs resonated through the Trouvees and the cult of Courtly Love, but the Trouvees had dangerous bedfellows such as the Templars and Cathars, and the Moorish Jews, whose Qabalah understood these things. Through the Templars, Marianism made its respectable way in Cistercian monasticism. But the Templars were too powerful and the Cathars were too close to the Gnosis to remain unmolested. With the encouragement of a Templar-scorned French king, the Church of Rome screamed "heresy," and Cathars and Templars felt the rack and pyre of the ineptly named Holy Inquisition. The Inquisition made sure that few traces of any irregular Christianity remained.

THE ORDER OF MIRIAM

The Holy Inquisition has long had its teeth showing, and now, as the Congregation for the Doctrine of the Faith, confines itself to matters of ecclesiastical discipline. Perhaps the time has come to see what the implications are of the Magdalene, Miriam of Magdala, being so bound to Jesus in the fulfillment of the ancient priest-king mythology.

As we have observed, early Israel inherited much more than is admitted of the Egyptian and Canaanite mysteries. These imports were readily integrated into the first temple of Solomon. They then appear to have been carried over by various factions into the second temple, through and beyond the lifetime of Christ until the destruction of the temple in 70 A.D. Thereafter they continued a patchy, often shadowy, existence through various so-called heretical and mystery cults.

However, the majority of these cults insisted on a heretical understanding of the Judeo-Christian tradition. They had anticipated the coming of the Messiah, the great priest-king. He was the mighty angel Michael, Son of the One God EHYEH, whose physical presence at the paradisal junction of heaven and earth was mediated by Melchizadek. For them Melchizadek then stepped from myth into history in the person of the incarnate Messiah, Jesus the Christ, who would return creation to an Edenic state of Tsdeq. From this marriage of heaven and earth, God's human children on earth could fashion creation to be as it is in heaven. Thus would

EHYEH's labor of love be completed, and He and creation fully know each other as true lovers do, each seeing themselves in the eyes of the beloved and knowing absolute union.

This was all very well for conventional religion except for one or two details. Implicit in this was the specter of an equal feminine, and therefore of an equal feminine priesthood. Furthermore, it was all a bit close and personal, seeming to replace the formality of hierarchical male contact with divinity. A male priesthood gets a male God because "He" becomes the image of what they want to be. The Patriarchy, unable even to come to terms with even its own feminine traits, found an intimate approach to God all very touchy feely and disconcerting. They didn't understand ancient esoteric Judaism and where it had come from, and they certainly didn't understand the spiritual dynamics of polarity magic. Their superficial understanding was, however, that anything that involved gods *and* goddesses and priests *and* priestesses was degenerate paganism.

But priestesses there had to be, and they had been there from the beginning, representing the feminine of triune divinity. They represented what Israel aspired to be: "Miriam," the beloved of Amun, the one God whom the Hebrews came to call ADONAI, "The Lord," whose presence was set before creation by the archangel Michael. Ultimately, it would be the task of one of these Miriams, as the beloved of God, to give birth to the son of God.

The Order of Miriam, if we may call it that, continued (and perhaps still continues) as an heretical adjunct to orthodox Christianity, albeit under other names. One such name may be the "Brigids" of the Celtic church. Brigid is called "Mary of the Gael," and appears in many guises, pagan and Christian. Her feast is the Celtic season of Imbolc in February, which she shares with Isis. Yet she has three aspects, and like Isis and her two sisters, Hathor and Nepthys, forms a "triadic" feminine power. An identical triad of "Miriams" appear as the "three Marys" of the New Testament: Mary the Virgin, Mary of Magdala, and Mary Cleopas.

Brigid's name means "The High One," and we are reminded of the titles of both Miriam of Magdala and Miriam the Blessed Virgin. The latter was addressed by the angel as "most favored one," and the former as "Apostle of Apostles." In her mythological pagan guise Brigid was the daughter of the Dagda, the chief of the Tuatha de Danaan. While we may approximately equate the Tuatha de Danaan with the Hebrew Beni Elohim, the elder "faery" race were said to be upon the earth before humankind. As both a daughter of the Dagda and a mortal Christian saint, we are left with the suggestion that Brigid was perhaps seen as the product of another of those couplings between the angelic–elohim–faery realms and humankind. Such an "immaculate conception" would place her, as Mary of the Gael, on a par with the Blessed Virgin Mary, and indeed in Celtic myth she takes the role of foster mother to Christ. This fostering takes place at Glastonbury, where her chapel was said to be at Beckary. Yet before its dedication to Brigid, the Beckary site was held to be sacred to the Magdalene.

While we shall be dealing with the intricacies of the Celtic mysteries in the next chapter, it is from correspondences such as this that we are able to perceive with greater clarity the role and influence of Miriam of Magdala and the line of priestesses that she was part of. Brigid set the cloak of the Sun about the shoulders of the Christ child even as Miriam of Magdala anointed Him. The three stages of the triple feminine power, like that of Isis and her sisters, all at their various stages bring the Son of God to His priest-kingship in earth. For every Melchizadek there must be a Hebrew Miriam or a Celtic Brigid. The original Miriam of the Exodus acted as foster mother to her baby brother Moses, being Nephthys to his Horus. She then went on to be one of the priestly triad with Moses and Aaron; she was Hathor to the Hebrews who built the golden calf at Serabit, and mother Isis, who succored fledgling Israel on her wisdom. She had been Sarah to Abraham, and, though seemingly barren, miraculously produced Isaac by divine intervention at the ripe old age of ninety!

After Eve, she was considered the original Hebrew mother of nations, and was buried at Machpelah, the Hathor shrine of Melchizedek at the Edenic center of the world.

The Miriams in the life of Christ are twice threefold. There is the Virgin Mary who gives birth to him, and Mary of Magdala who is the priestess who empowers Him. In a more profound sense she is the lady wisdom, the Sophia who informs his Messianic office. Then there is Mary the wife of Cleopas, who is the sister of the Virgin Mary and Jesus's aunt. In some sense she represents the Israel of the world.

These are the essential three Miriams, but there are others. We find reference to Mary of Bethany, Mary Salome, and Mary Jacobi. We can assume perhaps that some of these other Miriams are one and the same in that the gospel and apocryphal collators of the story used different "Mary" suffixes. Depending on their personal perspective, differing commentators would call one of the Mary's "Mary this" or "Mary that," just as one friend may call a man Jack Williams and another may refer to him as John Williams.

In the cult of Isis, there was as we have seen a bright Isis and a dark Isis. In the confusing cult of Mary/Miriam we also see the bright Madonna, Mary the Virgin, suckling her child in almost identical statues to those from ancient Egypt, which show the bright Isis suckling Horus. In the dark cave of Hathor, we leave the mother aside and confront the sacred whore. She is the initiatrix who is the dark Isis and the black Madonna who is Miriam of Magdala.

As Sarah had been Asherah in her shrine at Melchizedek's cave of Machpelah, so Miriam had come out of the Egypt of Isis to stand before Hathor's shrine on Serabit. Each embodied the lady wisdom, virgin, sacred whore, and mother to a nation. Behind them walked Ruth and Judith, and the Queen of Sheba. When the time was ready for the ultimate consummation of history and myth, the three Miriams came into the world. Like Melchizedek and Christ they were mated yet unmated, and themselves conceived by the descent of heaven through the inner worlds into earth. They came like Isis and her sisters, or like the three persons of Brigid, to answer the urgency and desire of heaven. They are of this world yet not of this world, for every Miriam is the consort of every Melchizadek, and one may not exist without the other.

They may be called "The Order of Miriam" or "The Order of Brigid," as indeed they have been in the Celtic lands. The wisdom they bring to conception, birth, and power within the world is Tsdeq, whose secret name is love. When this comes to its fulfillment, each woman will be a Miriam, the lover of God, even as each man shall be a Melchizadek, her "Michael" made in the image of God. Then shall each look into the eyes of the other and see heaven in earth and earth in heaven, and the bride and the groom shall be as one. For even as Miriam of Egypt looked into the cave of Hathor, Miriam from Magdala looked into the yawning tomb of Gethsemane and saw not a dead man, but an angel.

FROM READING TO REALIZATION

The priestess of Magdala passed from myth into history, and then on into legend. And even now we have yet to fully grasp any of this. To do so, however, is not merely to solve a historical or theological puzzle, it is to come to terms with the reality of love. Before we set these things aside as mere historical curios, we should remember that men and women down the centuries were prepared to face death and torture to come to this realization. What we inherit from those Christian heretics is a conviction that the way must be found to marry earth to heaven and heaven to earth. It is therefore incumbent upon those of us who believe this to try to do something about it.

The power of thought can bring about profound changes, and much can be achieved simply by ensuring that every time we visualize Christ we also visualize the Magdalene standing at His side. Further than this, men and women could do worse than to start by reading The Song of Songs to each other. As time goes on the images will build and become stronger, for they are already invested with an ancient power and life of their own. They are certainly erotic, yet all the better for that, as long as the eroticism is seen as a prelude to loving union. From sitting and reading by candlelight with a little incense, this sacred rite may then progress to the employment of the scents, sacred oils, and gestures mentioned in the text. In time the reading may be built into a full rite, where sensuality and sexual magnetism become the outer structure of an inner and more profound realization that is the temple not built with hands. What therefore begins with the personal becomes the universal, and what becomes the universal then proceeds to become the archetypal. If and when this happens, men and women will be doing a greater service to the marriage of heaven and earth than even they may ever know. For Jesus will not have been anointed without cause and Miriam will not have gone to the Gethsemane tomb in vain.

CHAPTER SIX

TALIESIN, CERIDWEN, AND THE MYSTERIES OF BRITAIN

The Celts did not invent the British Mystery Tradition, for the most part they inherited it. When the European tribes, which the Greeks had named *Keltoi,* began to wander into the British Isles from about 600 B.C., there were already about a million people living in main-land Britain. Some of this population were the descendants of the people who arrived in Britain at the beginning of what we call the Bronze Age, some fourteen hundred years before the Celts. They, in turn, had augmented the Neolithic people who had become Britain's first agriculturists from around 5000 B.C.

Unlike the ancient civilizations of Sumer and Egypt, historical and mythological information is sparse. While the Celtic loremas-ters, the Druids, appear to have used a cryptographic language that we now call *Ogam,* surviving examples tell us little. However, as Robert Graves indicated in his book *The White Goddess,*[1] the mys-tery teachings behind the Druidic "Tree Ogam" did survive well into the time of the medieval bards and can be found woven like some esoteric code into their written poetry, as in the *Cad Goddeu,* "The Battle of the Trees." But the first "proper" writings about the native British are in Latin, and date from Cesar's invasion of Celtic Britain in 55 B.C. With the subsequent Romanization of Britain and then the influx of Christianity, occasional commentaries con-tinued in clerical Latin. But as far as we know, no British writing by and about the British themselves in their native tongue appeared until A.D. 600, and by this time the Romans were long gone. These writings, set in a language now called late Brythonic (a far ancestor of Welsh), are the *Canu Aneirin,* or "Song of Aneirin."[2] They were written by a priest called Aneirin, and include a poem called *Y Gododdin* to mourn the fallen after the battle of Catreath. In this we get our first glimpse of the towering figures of British myth: Arthur, Taliesin, and Merlin.

The fact that native writing came so late does not, however, imply that before this time the British were uncultured or backward. Neither does it suggest, as some would like to believe, that the early Celts and the Bronze Age folk before them were a strange mystical breed who communicated through obscure shamanic symbols. The Bronze Age certainly showed that the ancient Britons could operate internationally. Contrary to popular belief they were not an isolated civilization over the back fence of the known world, and as we begin to unravel the Celtic and Bronze Age mysteries of Britain we will see that there are striking similarities between Egyptian and ancient British mystery lore and the interpretation of that lore in sacred structures. But none of this became a matter of contemporary record, because those "records" were flesh and blood, and the principal loremasters of the Celts, the Druids—and possibly the Bronze Age priests who preceded them—were, to all intents and purposes, walking books.

Nobody knows exactly when primitive Christianity first came to Britain, but it was long before either the mission of Augustine or the Roman adoption of Christianity at the beginning of the fourth century. Whatever the actual date, we have good reason to assume that Christianity reached the demoralized Celts of western Britain some time before the end of the first century. The British Celts appear, surprisingly, to have taken this new faith in their stride. What survived of Druidism in mainland Britain seems to have readily adapted its pagan triadic gods and goddesses to a sort of Christian compliance. Some of the early Celtic Saints were undoubtedly pagan Celtic gods and goddesses, or converted Druids representing their cults. We see this in the legends of the goddess Brigid, who, as we have noted earlier, became a Celtic Christian Saint while retaining much of her earlier mythology. Celtic Christianity was, at least at its inception, Christianity on its own Celtic terms, and, ironically, it was because of this that much of the pre-Christian native mythology was preserved. For Celtic Christianity, while retaining what can best be described as "Druid attitude," nonetheless got into that essentially Christian habit of writing things down—and eventually in the native language.

THE BARDS

Since the Celtic languages were designed to be recited rather than written, poetry became the essential vehicle for the transmission of wisdom. The Druids became replaced by bards, and bardic linguistic subtlety became a very useful way to transmit mystery teachings, especially when Celtic Christianity became submerged by the less liberal Christianity of Rome. Subtlety became even more necessary when the Welsh bards bridled against Norman England.

At this time ancient ideas of sovereignty came to the fore, employing much of the sacred king lore of Bronze Age times some two thousand years earlier. It is mostly from this time that we inherit material that gives us a panoramic, if slightly fragmented, view of the "Celtic" mysteries from their Neolithic and Bronze Age inception to contemporary practice. This practice was confined to initiate bards, in spite of the fact that by this time Wales was, technically at least, a Roman Catholic country. We sense in their endeavors and those of their Irish colleagues an urgency to transmit and preserve their lore before its demise in the face of Roman Christianity and Norman dominance.

There were two distinct types of bards operating in Wales at the time. The first of these were the court bards, who by then had largely become political consultants aligned to various chieftains.

Then there were the more independent bards who preserved the mystery tradition. These were the Awenyddion ("the ones inspired by the Awen"), who frequently wrote under the name of "Taliesin," the mythical, archetypal bard of the Celtic mysteries. We may be sure that Taliesin, whose name means "Radiant Brow," was a bardic title rather than the name of one bard, unless that one bard lived for some six hundred years and wrote in a wide variety of poetic styles; a magical feat indeed.

But it is to all those "Taliesins" that we owe the preservation of the Celtic mysteries. Something of their riddles, touching upon the roots of the Melchizadek tradition, has already been quoted in chapter 4. It was the Taliesin bards who resurrected a pagan sacred king called Math and renamed him Arthur, and who eventually wrote the books of poetic myth that collectively came to be called the *Mabinogi*. Perhaps one was a Welsh cleric living in Norman England whom we now call Geoffrey of Monmouth. For it was Geoffrey of Monmouth who, in trying to promote the idea of the archetypal initiate bard, gave us Merlin.

THE STORY OF TALIESIN

Geoffrey's account of Merlin in *The History of the Kings of Britain*[3] and the *Vita Merlini*[4] would better have been titled *The Life and Times of a Taliesin Bard,* for we may see that many of the characteristics and feats that Geoffrey attributes to Merlin were also cited for the archetypal Taliesin. Merlin's story is one that we shall deal with at length later, but for now it is Taliesin with whom we are principally concerned, for it is from Taliesin that we hear what the British mysteries were all about.

The "Hanes Taliesin," or "History of Taliesin," did not appear in writing until several hundred years after Geoffrey of Monmouth. This "history," while written down in the thirteenth century, goes back to a mythology that was already perhaps three thousand years old. It was the old cauldron myth, the myth of the womb of being, the myth of a cauldron that could both mold and transform physical reality. It was the myth of the womb of the Goddess whose amniotic fluid, the Awen, fed the potential of all being. Through the sipping of this sacred nectar the archetypal Taliesin came to be, and from the cauldron itself came that fabulous vessel of both pagan and Christian heritage, the Holy Grail.

The archetypal Taliesin had started life much like the rest of us. He was a youth named Gwion who was looking for a job, who had wandered over the Berwyn Mountains from Llanfair Caereinion. He came down, so the myth tells us, into the valley of the Upper Dee, around what is now called Bala. This part of North Wales on the old border between Meirionydd and Flintshire is an ancient area of Bronze Age mystery practice. The flanks of the valley and the surrounding high moorlands are littered with burial cists and small stone circles. The focus of the area and the source of the river Dee is Llyn Tegid, which tourists know as Bala Lake. The lake is a flooded glacial ravine of considerable depth; indeed, it is something of a Welsh Loch Ness, complete with its own monster, its primordial flood myth . . . and its resident goddess.

That goddess, who transformed the youth Gwion into the arch bard Taliesin, was later employed as the Lady of the Lake to furnish Arthur with *Caledfwlch,* the sword of destiny that came to be called Excalibur. But the original goddess of the lake was Ceridwen. Ceridwen lived on an island in the middle of the lake, although there was never an actual island there. As we saw in chapter 1, this was a common inner world metaphor, like the islands of Avalon and the Hesperides. The lake itself signified the flowing out of Awen from the inner depths of creation, which were called "Annwn" ("the deep"). Lakes and springs provided a ready thoroughfare between Annwn and the material world for inner world beings. Such beings may be found throughout Welsh folklore under the generic name "Graig Annwn" ("wives from the deep"). The word "wives" suggests, as many folktales make clear, that these beings from the

Celtic underworld came into the material world to mate with humankind. Again we are presented with the old Beni Elohim theme, except that here they are essentially "daughters of the Gods," or in other terminology, faery.

Ceridwen was the Underworld goddess, and in a sense the collective expression of all such faery women. When Gwion was employed by Ceridwen, he was summoned to the island in the middle of Llyn Tegid by her, and thus into the precincts of Annwn, where Ceridwen's cauldron was poised. For from that island, on the borderline between the inner and outer worlds, the Awen could flow out into the material world. Gwion's task was to heat the cauldron, which, as we shall see, is an allusion to "raising the inner fire." Thus he is persuaded to employ the heat of his own sexuality in his approach to the "cauldron," which is the womb of Ceridwen. The image conjured in the intimacy between Ceridwen and Gwion is an ancient one, the image of the mature woman, a "Mrs. Robinson" of myth, initiating the youth into the mysteries of sex. But in this instance the mature woman was the Goddess of the Underworld, and the sexual imagery of their meeting is the mere prelude to something a good deal more mysterious than that youthful awe in the power of a woman's body.

It was said that Ceridwen constructed the cauldron to compensate her son Agfaddu for his extreme ugliness. Her child, indeed children, for she also had a beautiful daughter, Creirwy, are of course proto-humanity. Meanwhile, Gwion tends her cauldron and feeds the fire beneath it, but there is no sign of Ceridwen, who is presumably off somewhere gathering ingredients to enhance the already bubbling brew. Ceridwen is either dormant or absent, until suddenly a drop of the Awen spits from the brew and scalds Gwion's fingers. He licks his fingers three times, and then things begin to happen, for he has tasted the forbidden brew of Annwn. There is a great cry from the cauldron, and it splits in two. At the same time, Gwion, having tasted the brew, is able to see the embryonic future and indeed the creative matrix for all things that shall take material being, for all these things are held within the quantum potential of the brew, the Awen.

Seeing the near future, Gwion realizes that Ceridwen knows that he, a mere mortal, has tasted the brew, and that she intends to kill him, for in some senses he has broken the evolutionary rules by instigating his own rebirth before his time. Looking for a means to escape her, Gwion utilizes an appropriate animal form to make his escape and becomes a hare. Ceridwen, mistress of the cauldron, is aware of his transformation, so she turns herself into a greyhound and pursues him. Gwion therefore changes himself into a fish and dives into the lake, whereupon Ceridwen becomes an otter. Leaving the water, Gwion becomes a bird and takes to the air, but Ceridwen changes herself into a hawk. The hapless Gwion flutters about looking for a further way to escape as Ceridwen the hawk begins her deadly dive. Below him he sees a threshing floor covered with grain, so flying down to it he changes himself into a grain of wheat, hoping to avoid detection among the millions of other grains. Ceridwen follows him down to the threshing floor and transforms herself into a hen, pecking patiently away at the grains, until eventually she swallows Gwion. Having done so she returns to human form and realizes that she is pregnant with the seed that was Gwion.

Eventually the child is born, or rather reborn, and having previously been prepared to kill him for his precocity, Ceridwen now finds herself unable to murder her own child. She therefore lets fate take a hand and, placing the child in a bag, she takes him to the sea and casts him adrift, like Moses. The bag is eventually washed up in the Dovey estuary, where Prince Elphin is netting salmon on May Eve. The bag is caught in Elphin's net, and he opens it. The child inside who tells him that he is a bard and has been in the bag for forty years, and that his name is Taliesin. From this point on the child who was Gwion grows in Elphin's care and becomes the greatest of all bards.

The simplicity of the myth belies its esoteric depths and its formula as an advanced rite of initiation. Like all such rites, it is a profound piece of polarity magic on many levels, but in its initial action we are left in no doubt that the earthy double-entendres of its symbolism show that the impetus of Taliesin's initiation by Ceridwen is provided by sexual dynamics.

Taliesin is, in effect, romancing the Goddess. First he fires up the cauldron of her fecundity and its gynecological juices, the Awen, are stimulated. His fingers are dampened by this stimulation and the cauldron divides with an orgasmic cry. Ceridwen is now fully aroused and takes the initiative, and the two meet as a series of complementary and polarized creatures driven through various instinctual animal states that correspond to the elements, not least the elements as they are reflected in human psychological states. The elemental sequence is from the fire beneath the cauldron to pursuit over the earth, then to pursuit in water, and, as both take wing, to pursuit in air, until Gwion is consumed by the Goddess and drawn back into her womb to be reborn. His seed is in her, but it is the seed of himself.

The first of the animal forms that Gwion adopts is also interesting, containing, as so many bardic tales do, a number of layers of meaning often disguised in puns. The form of the hare naturally suggests an appropriate animal form for speedy escape, but it is more than this. The female hare is sacred to many Underworld goddesses, for it has a unique gynecological feature. The female hare has the ability to achieve a secondary pregnancy while already pregnant, which is an apt motif not only for the startling fecundity of nature but for birth and rebirth. Indeed, initiates of the mysteries have down the ages invariably attracted the expression "the twice born." The hare is thus a symbol of the powers of the initiatory cauldron, and Gwion's initial transformation to a hare is intended to alert us to the fact that his sudden ability to see the future signifies such an initiation. From this we see why hares were often sacrificed and their entrails examined in divination rites that the embryonic future, the vision of the Awen, may be discerned.

After Ceridwen has given rebirth to Gwion, there is a further period of gestation in the bag that she fashions, which floats in the amniotic sea salt until it is opened and its embryonic bard delivered by a prince during the fire festival of Beltane. The child who was Gwion is eventually reborn as Taliesin the Bard. The name Taliesin is usually taken to mean "radiant brow," although "rainbow brow" would be more appropriate, even though the Welsh word for rainbow is *enfys*. For the rainbow is the "Caer," the outer reflection of Ceridwen's inner Annwn. It is, after all, the rainbow that signifies that vital combination of Sun and rain, which promises fertility.

THE CAULDRON AND THE HORNED GOD

For a time, the Underworld god Bran the Blessed also had possession of this cauldron. In the Bran myth (the Mabinogi story, "Branwen Daughter of Llyr")[5] the cauldron is used to restore slain warriors to life, which makes it a suitable metaphor for the Celtic afterlife in Annwn, where heroes live again. But its provenance given in *Branwen,* which describes the origins of the cauldron before it came into Bran's possession, leaves us in little doubt that it is that same cauldron of Ceridwen. The finding of the pre-Christian Celtic Gundestrup Cauldron in Denmark during the nineteenth century would appear to confirm not only that the Taliesin and Bran myths were around for a very long time before they were written down, but that when they were written down they were accurately transmitted.

The interior of the much decorated Gundestrup Cauldron depicts dead warriors being plunged into the cauldron to be reborn, as was the case with Bran's cauldron. This is also, of course, a motif for initiation, where, for example, Gwion is consumed by Ceridwen to be taken into and then reborn from her cauldron womb. On the exterior of the cauldron is a squatting figure surrounded by animals. This humanoid figure, often taken to be the god Cernunos, is wearing a headdress of antlers, with each antler having seven tines. We are reminded of a poem called *The Song of Amergin,* Taliesin's Irish counterpart, with the line "I am a stag of seven tines."[6] The animals that surround the figure may be taken to represent animal forms into which the initiate and the Goddess have the ability to transform to achieve a mutual instinctive mode in which to meet and interact. They may also represent Cernunos as the traditional horned god and lord of creatures. As we shall see in our next chapter, the two images are in fact complementary, for the initiate in "romancing the Goddess" becomes her consort and master of her creatures, which is the archetypal role of the horned god.

One creature of particular interest shown with the Cernunos image on the cauldron is the ram-headed serpent, which the figure holds in his hand. The serpent represents the inner earth power, the dragon power whose archetypal image is in the stars. This is the power of the inner fire, the same fiery power that Gwion set to the cauldron to initiate his mating with Ceridwen, and the same power that is represented in the Eastern tradition by the serpent of Kundalini. We will see it later in the ancestors of Dionysos. Before the role of priest-kings became divided between priests and kings, or chieftains and bards, this power established the king's ability to mate with the divine. In more mundane terms, this ability translated itself into the phallic power of the horned god (which ensured the fertility of the Underworld goddess) to the benefit of the king's people. This phallicism, later signified by the monarch's scepter and the rods of various biblical characters like Joseph, was, as we have seen, emblematic of the *axis mundi,* the alignment of the earth to the pole star at the center of the archetypal heavens. As the Asherah pole, it signified the arousing power of the Goddess, which in turn was used to romance her and bring fertility, prosperity, and, not least, a new priest-king or a new child of the stars into incarnation.

While the Cernunos figure holds a ram-headed serpent in his left hand, his right hand grasps a *torc*. Torcs were worn by the Celts as neck and wrist ornaments, and appear to have had spiritual rather than armorial or decorative significance. They also appear to be a development of the similarly styled crescent, or broken circle, of earlier *lunula* found in Bronze Age burials. The torc suggests a womb and a cauldron, and also the stellar constellation of the Corona Borealis. The Corona Borealis is the *Caer Arianrhod* in Welsh, and is thus associated with the Goddess who is the starry equivalent of Ceridwen and a frequent antagonist of Taliesin in his later esoteric adventures. The torc shape also relates, as we shall see, to the stone-circle burial complexes in the "womb and tomb" rites of sacred kings.

The Celts saw the heavens stemming from the goddess Arianrhod, whose name means "silver wheel," and it seems likely that in the original myth, Arianrhod masturbated her brother and lover, Gwydion, to ejaculate the Milky Way (called the *Caer Gwydion*) so that she could then weave the mucus threads of his sperm into the order of the archetypal stars. In this, the original cauldron was Arianrhod herself, and the spilling of that cauldron was initiated by Gwydion's desire for her. For the heavens are a leaking cauldron, the same cauldron that was cleaved open in both the Taliesin story and in the Bran myth. When our ancestors looked to the night sky they saw the blackened base of the cauldron heavens that had been bathed in the fire of the daytime Sun. The result of this perpetual heating was that the cauldron began to leak and the essence of light within it, the Awen, shone through the holes as the evocative archetypal patterns of the stellar constellations. The patterns of the stars were the glimpses that heaven gave them. Yet to truly know the light the cauldron had to be cleaved open.

This cleaving of the cauldron is not unlike the biblical rending of the veil, which symbolizes the mating of heaven and earth. It is the rending of the Goddess's virginity, it is the bursting of the dam of desire so that "being" may ensue. Qabalah had a tradition that heaven burst open to spill the light that it contained, and thus spill out the archetypal stellar patterns, the Tsdeq, that flowed down in the pattern of the Tree of Life, or indeed flowed down through the mediation of the Asherah pole. The speckles upon that pole, the same speckles that are to be found upon the body of the Hathor cow, are to all purposes the speckles of Awen upon Gwion's finger. They are the stars that are also the Sephiroth, the spheres of the Tree of Life. They are also the seven lights of the Menorah, or the seven-fold stag's horns worn by Cernunos. Thus we see the female inter-mediary, the conduit of the cauldron as a star-goddess who becomes an Underworld goddess mediating through seven levels of being to apportion the liquor of light and enlightenment, the liquor of what shall come to pass in earth from the womb of her own being. Yet in this apportionment she motivates, as a mother motivates a child to her breast, and is then herself stimulated to release the precious liquor, the Awen. In the initiation of Gwion that stimulation leads to the cleaving of the cauldron with a great orgasmic cry.

The Welsh myths are somewhat more earthy than their Hebrew counterparts in their conceptualization of this, but the principle re-mains the same. Heaven, as the Jewish conspirators of Jesus's time knew, and as the bards of Taliesin's time also knew, needed to be ro-manced and coaxed a little. This was the job of the priest-king as horned god, horned as was Moses, horned as was the Knights Tem-plar's *Baphomet,* horned like the figure upon the Gundestrup Caul-dron. The Taliesin poem *Preiddeu Annwn* says: "and before the cold place the horns of light shall be burning."[7] Again we are reminded of the horns of Hathor, Hathor in the cold, unstimulated under-world cave, for Hathor in this aspect is the Egyptian equivalent of Ceridwen, and the cave is both her cauldron and her womb. The figure on the Gundestrup cauldron is therefore the initiate as Cer-nunos, wearing the horns to achieve that same animal transforma-tion to align to the Goddess, and as proxy for the horned god to become her consort. Yet in this he will be the rutting stag, the horned one, and she shall be the young speckled doe with whom he must mate to bring the patterns of the stars, the right flow of the Awen, to fruition in earth.

As to the later assumption of Taliesin into the womb of the Goddess, this was the lot of all sacred kings, so that they might know rebirth in the stars. Bronze Age and Neolithic tombs were intentionally womblike structures, and even now we may see these forlorn mounds swollen up like the pregnant belly of mother earth or as an upturned cauldron so that its Awen may flow out onto the land. They were also built with ditches around them so that when filled with water the mounds appeared as islands, not least the island upon which Taliesin met Ceridwen. Interestingly, sets of antlers have been found in a number of such tombs, and as we shall see, these tombs held a particular fascination for the Taliesin bards, as can be seen in their writing some two thousand years after the tombs' construction.

THE CULT OF THE SACRED KING

The Welsh mythological archetype for the sacred king was Bran the Blessed. The myth of the Welsh Bran tells how he gave his sister Branwen in marriage to the Irish king, Matholwch. But having moved to Ireland with her new husband and borne him a son, Branwen receives ill treatment from Matholwch and his court, and virtually becomes a prisoner. When Bran hears of the shame heaped upon his sister he invades Ireland, easily wading the Irish Sea because of his giant stature and towing his lilliputian fleet behind him. Although he manages to defeat the Irish and liberate his sister, the magical cauldron is shattered, and shortly after this Bran is mortally wounded. He asks his companions to cut off his head and take it back to Wales, for we must remember that the taking of heads in war was Celtic custom, and the head contained the soul. This they do in order that Bran's head does not fall into Irish hands, and the head, the focus of his immortal soul, remains animated and continues to speak and sing to the seven companions who accompany it. These seven are comparable to the seven *Heru Shemsu* of Egyptian myth who accompanied the body of Osiris. We shall meet them in chapter 10.

Eventually the seven take the head to an island (probably Lundy in the Bristol channel) and are told by the head that it will continue to remain in this animated, communicative state unless one of them opens a window facing southwest. This is probably a later addition to the myth, and means "opening up to" Tintagel, where Arthur was conceived, for the Arthur cult replaced the Bran cult. Inevitably the window does get opened and the head dies and begins to putrefy. The seven companions then take it and bury it in London under the white mound where the tower of London now stands, and where it is said to preserve Britain from invasion.

This is only an outline sketch of the myth, but in it we see a king who fights and suffers for his sister-mate Branwen, and undergoes voluntary death and decapitation, then lives on until replaced by another hero-god. The parallels between this and the story of Jesus would not have been lost on the bards. Branwen encapsulated the sovereignty of Britain; she was as much "the bride" as biblical Israel was. Bran goes to war and gets himself mortally wounded so that she shall be free, even though she dies of remorse shortly afterward. But the Bran mythology is very much older than Christianity, and in it we see the ultimate polarity of the sacred king volunteering to mate with the "great taker," the Goddess who is death, so that the tribe may prosper. Bran, in effect, subsequently becomes, like the sacrificed and mutilated Osiris, king of the Underworld and of death. By implication he becomes the consort of Ceridwen, who is the queen of the Underworld of Annwn.

The image of mating with the Goddess in death was a partial allegory for the Taliesin bards. Certainly something in them had to die so that they could be reborn, but that death was psychological.

Like the soldier Merlin they may, for example, have to suffer a complete breakdown before illumination sets in. In the bucolic existence of the Bronze Age and Celtic peoples, the image would have been of the Corn King, of the stubble of the old crop being burned away before a new crop could sprout up. This image of psychological death followed by rebirth to illumination is the perennial twice-born image of initiation. The Goddess, or her representative, breaks to make. In the Taliesin myth Gwion is forced not only through a series of transformations but, in the process, a series of terrors and potential deaths.

But in the pre-Celtic Bronze Age, "the old days," the time of Bran the Blessed, death was not psychological but actual, and the "break to make" process involved actual dismemberment.

In *Awen: the Quest of the Celtic Mysteries,* Mike Harris discusses the sacred king cult and the Bran, and other mythology attached to it in what Robert Graves called The Hercules Cult:

> Graves identifies the practice of the sacrifice of surrogate sacred kings with the widespread classical cult of the sacrificed Hercules and indeed Hercules does appear as "Ercwlf" in a Taliesin poem "Marwnad Ercwlf" which Graves cites to indicate that [the] Taliesin [cult] was familiar with the Hercules mythology. It appears however that the myth of Hercules [originally the Greek Heracles] grew from, rather than originated, Bronze age cult practice which extended from the Mediterranean and through Northern Europe and Britain. The chalk figure of the sexually potent Cerne Abbas giant in Wiltshire is an obvious example of a later British devotion to Hercules, and his ability to initiate fertility. The Cerne Abbas monument does however seem to be of comparatively late date, probably in the Romano Celtic era, by which time the ancient Bronze Age practices had been affirmed in the Romanised Hercules myth.
>
> The Hercules cults, it is said, made their victims drunk (or, I suspect, administered adder venom to them or had them bitten by adders, viz the serpent being held by the figure on

the Gundetrup cauldron), then tied them to an Oak tree at the centre of a ceremonial circle. The victim, Graves claims, was fastened in the five fold bond inverted on a lightning blasted oak tree with the five extremities of neck, arms and legs secured in an inverted pentagram/star posture. He was then put through the five fold death of scourging, blinding, castration, impalement and, finally, dismemberment with his successor in sacred kingship cutting off his head as an act to symbolic continuity. This ceremony would take place at the time of the Summer Solstice, when the sun is at its zenith, because as a representative of the sun God the victim would be assumed to be at the height of his Herculean powers and therefore able to fertilise the land most potently. His vital blood would be caught in an urn to be sprinkled on the tribe and, after disjointing, parts of his flesh may have been roasted and eaten by a selected group of warriors who would thus share in his strength. The stone circle at Moel Ty Uchaf in Gwynedd was shown by Professor Thom to be laid out in perfect pentagrammatical geometry, with its open burial cist at the centre of the pentagram.

As De Santillana and von Dechend note in *Hamlet's Mill*,[8] the attributes and adventures including betrayal by women, of Llew, Hercules and the biblical Samson (in the book of Judges) are pretty much identical. The "betrayal by woman" which this composite Hercules suffers, may well reflect the temporary affection given to the sacrificial victim prior to his death.

The evidence seems to indicate that late Neolithic and Bronze Age sacrificial practices were remembered and/or adopted and perpetuated in Celtic mystery practice, but came to describe the mythical death and rebirth of the initiate bard, the Taliesin, rather than the actual slaughter of a priest-king. That these practices had originally been preserved in Greek, and later Roman, mythology, affirmed them as the practices of an Erclf/Hercules cult to the Celts, who later came under Roman occupation and influence.

Moel Ty Uchaf is a Bronze Age site of particular significance in that while being comparatively small, it is probably one of the best preserved and least tampered with prehistoric sites in Britain. As we have already said, Professor Alexander Thom found that this circle was constructed on exact pentagonal geometry, a task undertaken some thousand years before the Greeks were credited with devising the geometry of dividing a circle into five. It consists of a horseshoe or corona of stones in a torc shape imitating the shape of the Cor Borealis, Taliesin's prison of Arianrhod in the stars.[9]

As noted in the foregoing, all the heroes associated with this sacred king cultus are "betrayed" by women. In the illustration of the stone circle at Moel Ty Uchaf, which Harris shows and notates with the ritual sacrifice of a sacred king, the stone circle is, of course, the Goddess. It is shaped like a cauldron womb and like the starry Caer of Arianrhod, which draws the initiate in. In this, Arianrhod, with her "silver wheel," may be related to Arachne the spider, in which the circle becomes her web. But this drawing-in is not treachery or betrayal, for the sacred king goes to her willingly. In this it is no more a "betrayal" than that of Adam by Eve. It is the female power drawing the initiate close to whisper "what if?" in his ear and motivate him to see somewhat beyond himself, as Ceridwen did with young Gwion. Subsequent terror and sacrifice are not, therefore, vindictive, but the "breaking to make" process of transformation enabling the Goddess to give rebirth to an illuminated initiate.

The Goddess calls to the initiate and he answers and fertilizes her, and dies in the process. Yet he dies to a higher life, for he has fertilized her with the seed of himself, that she may give rebirth to him. The process is mutually fulfilling, and this reborn son is born to serve her purpose, which is one of mediation in anticipation of the marriage of heaven and earth. For she holds within her being the star patterns, the archetypal forms, which are her dowry to all who would mate with her.

THE FAERY PARTNER

The Goddess may summon her initiate, her Gwion, her sacred king, in three ways. The first way is through the "Goddess within," the Jungian anima within the male psyche, the archetype of the desired one that is set into the psyche of all mortal men. The second way is through an inner being, a faery woman, a Ceridwen who is the summation and oversoul of all such faery women and "white ladies" from Annwn. The third and most complete way is through another mortal woman, a priestess. In the latter case, which, rightly understood, is the highest level of polarity in mystery work, the priestess must herself go through the necessary trials and terrors, the deaths and rebirths, to be able to be "as the faery woman." In this she must become "great giver, true taker," and she must know how to transform her priest with love and compassion. He, in his turn, will transform her.

As a prelude to this, however, both priest and priestess may know inner instruction from a being from Annwn, a faery partner. While the emphasis differs in the training of men and women, such training is initiated by desire, the most potent initiator of all polarity. This also, in terms of magical technology, generates enough of an electro-magnetic charge to bring about an initial interaction. While it may appear that the initiate is drawing out or evoking the beautiful faery being, the reverse is inevitably the case. Like Thomas the Rhymer and the queen of fair Elfland,[10] the initiate is being drawn of his or her own free will into a state of proto-creation, where the necessary adjustments may be made. These adjustments may prove painful, but they are necessary. They show illusion for what it is, and in doing so have given rise to endless instances in folklore of faery being deceitful and callous, but this is not the case.

After spending the seven years in Faery, Thomas the Rhymer returns to the world, yet cannot speak of the things he has seen. Like the warriors reborn from the cauldron, the ability to speak of their initiation, their rebirth, is embargoed even as the ceremony of initiation into an outer world Mystery Order is bounded by oaths of secrecy. What can be said is that the experience of such a Faery initiation is sensual in the extreme, but that the sensuality is a means to an end and becomes superseded by a deep sense of kinship.

In that the association works initially through the senses, it essentially works through a tangible sense of place, and is very much set within the land and the mythical parameters of one's own culture. It is one of those esoteric principles that is given rather than sought for, but such a gift becomes more likely after meditation upon the appropriate mythology. In this we can do little better than return to the story of Taliesin and Ceridwen, and undergo the trials and tests of Gwion through regular meditation and ritual. The following meditation or pathworking may be used to do this.

CERIDWEN'S ISLAND

You are standing at the edge of a great lake swathed in the mists of autumn. Feel the gravel of the shore beneath your sandaled feet and hear the solitary cry of the lapwing in the reeds. Here is a place of anticipation and mystery and becoming. Little can be seen in the mist rising from the still water like vapors rising from some great cauldron, and the solitary bird call echoes over the flat dark lake, and it seems as if you are standing not only on the edge of the lake but upon the rim of time itself.

Peer into the mists, and let shapes swirl in the mind's eye, strange otherworldly shapes beckoning us, inviting us into their world. Now, as the sound of the lapwing dies, we hear another sound behind the gentle lapping of the water in the reeds. There is the regular splash of a paddle coming toward us, the swish of a light craft surging through the reeds, and then through the swirling mist we see a figure.

He is hunched over the single paddle of the craft, wrapped in a dark cloak held at the shoulder by a great silver clasp that glints in the dim light. His beard is black, yet his head is bald. He has dark, piercing eyes and a hooked nose. He looks keenly at each of us in turn, then brings the craft to rest. Now see that he is accompanied by a young man and woman. The young woman is fair and beautiful, but the young man is hunched, dark, and ugly.

The man standing says: "I am Tegid Foel, the king of the lake, and these are my children. The fair one, the maid, is called Creirwy, which means 'dear one' in my tongue, and the boy is called 'Agfaddu,' which means 'darkest.' If you would enter my kingdom and know the riddles of my spouse, the witch, you may only come by this way with the three of us. Will you come?"

Now you are being given a choice: you may agree to submit to the perils of this adventure, or turn aside now and return to the world you know. Such are the choices of initiation: to choose to sup from the cup or cauldron or to refuse the opportunity of enlightenment and go on your way. So you must decide to enter into this adventure or to treat it as mere childish fantasy. If you do so choose, you step into the coracle.

With several strong sweeps of the paddle, Tegid Foel propels the coracle out onto the mist-shrouded lake. There is an eerie stillness about the lake, and indeed about him and his children, none of whom speak or look at you as the boat slides across the dark water. You peer into the mist and wonder where this strange trio is taking you. Then suddenly in the mist there is bulk, something dark and solid looms up before you, and you realize that you have come to an island out in the lake. The coracle grounds on a small pebble beach that is littered with driftwood and animal bones. You step out and start to walk up the beach, then turn back for a moment to ask Tegid and his children which way to go, but they and the coracle are gone in the mist, and you seem to be alone. You walk up the beach and get the impression of a figure ahead of you, standing on the edge of the bushes . . . it is so difficult to see in this mist.

The figure, as you come to it, is not a figure, at least not now. It is a head, a human head impaled on a pole. It is a marker, and despite its grotesque significance to our modern thinking, it is a sign of spiritual enlightenment. To the Celts the head was the seat of the soul, it was what contained the spiritual essence. This sign, therefore, tells you that if you would seek the lessons of the Celtic initiation, if you would seek to touch your own soul essence, you are on the right track. So you pass this grim marker and glance up as you do so. In some way the head is familiar to you, and the eyes are open, following as you pass by and looking into your very soul. To all who assay the path of initiation, it asks the questions:

"What seek ye?" And you should answer: "I seek to know."

"Why so?" asks the head. "So that I may serve," you reply.

So you examine your motives, look into yourself, then pass on into the undergrowth of this mist laden island on some lake at the edge of time.

Now on the path ahead you glimpse something white, an animal, half hidden by the bushes. You go forward and find a white sow waiting for you. The animal waits, and then with a grunt she turns and heads along the path with you following.

Following the white sow, you pass through small plantations of stunted oak and hazel, and then suddenly you find yourself squeezing through a thicket of hawthorn. The sow squeals ahead of you as if she has been pricked by the hawthorn, and then there is silence. You push forward and come through the thicket into a clearing. There is now no sign of the sow, but in the center of the clearing stands a mature woman in a rough spun white cloak.

She stands beside a great dark cauldron that is hung over a fire. Strange smells waft across the clearing in the fumes from the bubbling brew, which seem to have some kind of narcotic effect on you. There are half-seen things in the smoke and mist. The woman looks up and asks:

"Will you tend this hearth?" You answer that you will.

"By what name would such a one be known?" she asks.

"By the name Gwion Fach."

"Then whoever would tend the fire in the name of Gwion Fach, know this: the fire is for the tending, but the cauldron is not for the tasting."

So Ceridwen leaves you as Gwion to tend the fire that the cauldron may be kept brewing. And you lay twigs to the fire, and the cauldron bubbles and spits, and a drop of the brew spits out and lands on your finger.

It burns, so you put your finger in your mouth. Now, tasting this forbidden brew, you seem to plunge into a swirling vortex, and see many things forbidden to mortals, things that are the province of the Goddess, things of the Underworld that is called Annwn. And above the rush of the blood in your ears you hear the cauldron crack and a great scream, and suddenly you know that Ceridwen is obliged to kill you. So you flee.

Yet now being skilled in the magic of the transforming cauldron, you change yourself to a hare, that you might flee more quickly. But Ceridwen, knowing this, becomes a greyhound.

Then you become a fish, that you might swim from the island to evade Ceridwen.

But she becomes an otter and swims after you.

So you rise from the water and, calling again on the magic of the transforming cauldron, become a sparrow.

But Ceridwen, seeing this, becomes a hawk and sweeps down upon you.

It seems now that your fate is sealed and that you must die, but seeing a farmstead below, you tumble to the threshing floor as a grain of corn.

Then Ceridwen again changes her shape from red hawk to red hen, and she settles upon the threshing floor and pecks among the grain, and she swallows the grain that is Gwion, the seed of yourself.

Now she changes from her hen shape back to human form, and despite her years she finds herself to be with child, for the seed grain that is Gwion grows within her.

Be aware now that the seasons have turned and that she has given birth to you. See her fashion a bag and feel the dark as she places you in it. Then you feel the constant sway as she walks with the bag to the sea, then salt iciness as she throws the bag into the sea.

There is a kind of numb timelessness, and then suddenly there is gentle light. The bag is opened, and you feel the radiance about you and a deep contentment, like the contentment and sense of fulfillment that follows sexual intercourse.

You close your eyes and sink into a kind of reverie, when you open them again you find yourself in the coracle and a tall shining figure propels the boat. For now our boatman is tall and upright, dressed in white robes with flowing white hair and beard, and about his face there is a kind of light. He or she propels the craft across the water, and the mist is lifting and the Sun is coming through.

You glimpse the shoreline ahead of you, the shore of the world that you know, and overhead is a rainbow joining the world of Annwn to the world that you know. Then the craft grounds upon the shore of your own time. You step out, bid the one who propels the boat farewell, and the mist returns and falls like a curtain. Return through this curtain to normal waking consciousness.

CHAPTER SEVEN

OWAIN AND THE LADY
OF THE FOUNTAIN

In the story of "The Lady of the Fountain,"[1] we are taken to the very heart of the Celtic mysteries, and in doing so we start upon our own journey back to the source. When the bard Taliesin claims in the "Hanes Taliesin" that he has conveyed Awen to the deeps of Hebron, it is from the Fountain of the Lady, the wellspring of creative inspiration who is none other than the White Goddess herself, that he has had resource. We therefore discover from this that Taliesin, who clearly has knowledge and understanding of the inner processes of the fountain of Awen, is revealed as one of its Guardians. Moreover, as one who is capable of moving or manipulating the fountain's energy he can also be regarded as an initiate of the Temple of the Sea and the Stars, for he is working upon the higher levels of creation in which the formative patterns of the prephysical world are empowered by the deeper currents of the stellar worlds.

As we have seen, this patterning, this forming of the etheric templates that takes place beyond our physical boundaries of time and space, takes no regard of the apparent disparity in time, space, and culture between pre-Celtic Britain and pre-Christian Israel. The visionary Celtic imagination and bardic eloquence ensouled it with their poetry to form a record of the making of these patterns. Their sensitive and intuitive response to the essentially feminine nature of these mysteries makes them accessible to us in ways that the scribes of the Old Testament do not. And yet the Celtic faery—the Sidhe or the Shining Ones—are very close relations of the Beni Elohim or the Annunaki. The more things change the more they stay the same. The bards of Celtic legend, unlike their Hebrew counterparts, did not fight shy of earthly reality, and they offer us many evocative and powerful descriptions of how the mythology's priests and priestesses—the equivalents of its Miriams and Marys, its Moses and David—relate to their worlds of above and below, each in polarity to the other.

Of special relevance to the substance of our study is that the Celtic myth is unsurpassed in world mythology for its recognition of the nature of faery. The Irish folk soul in particular is permeated with the spirit of the Faery Kingdom, which still lies very close to the surface of that land and its people. And so when we come to those ways in which, having passed the nadir, we may start to take the long journey back to the one source of all living creatures, we must, along that way, pass back through the faery world, and in doing so reintegrate its spirit with our own.

At the heart of this is found the greatest mystery, because the Lady of the Fountain is both the substance of the fountain and *that which causes it to flow.* She is the embodiment of the land from which the fountain of wisdom flows, yet we see how she also directs its power to serve a particular end, which in this instance is to inspire and to call to her the one she has chosen to serve her within her Temple. Let us then regard the upwelling Fountain of the Lady as the central altar of that inner Temple of the Sea and the Stars, to which many Sun priests and priestesses are drawn in order that their work may thus be empowered from this source. One such priest, less well known than his contemporary King Arthur, is Owain, son of Morgan le Fee and Urien, King of Gorre. The story of how Owain becomes the Sun priest or guardian of the fountain is the story of an initiatory journey of service that encompasses the human, faery, and animal worlds. In many ways it mirrors the bet-ter-known story of Taliesin's progress from child to one who is of

"Radiant Brow," but while the main axis of Owain's relationship is between himself and the inner world goddess of inspiration, we can at the same time very usefully explore the nature and purpose of those he encounters along the way.

The story of Owain's progress appears in the collection of Celtic and pre-Celtic stories called the *Mabinogion,* and also in Chretien de Troyes' story "Yvain, the Knight with the Lion," in the collection of stories called *Arthurian Romances.*[2] Further material occurs in another *Mabinogion* story entitled "The Dream of Rhonabwy." The nature of the relationship between the Lady of the Fountain and those with whom she works is concerned with the soul's undertaking of that unreserved dedication of service to the land and to the sovereignty of the land that calls men and women to any manner of task even unto death. It is of especial interest to us, however, because within the evocative language of the Celtic storytellers are revealed the stages through which each potential priest or priestess must pass if they look to serve within the Temple of the Sun or the Temple of the Sea and Stars. Such is the power behind the story that it functions even now as an initiatory journey that can be undertaken by anyone who seeks to walk in these ways. We must be in no doubt that the powers that inspire these stories are every bit as real and as potent in the twenty-first century as they were two thousand (or more) years ago. The path that they lay before the reader, with its symbols, challenges, and encounters with the guardians of many thresholds, is a path that has been walked by those who have now passed on into the stuff of legend.

Owain is the hero of the story. By way of his ancestry, he is half human and half faery, so by nature of his birth (a conception clearly brought about by the direct influence of the Lady), he already has a foot in both worlds. Eventually, near the end of the story, he becomes the "husband" of the Lady, and by the time he has achieved this status he has learned to work at all levels. But there are others in polarity with the Lady of the Fountain, and by examining them we also learn more about her, for in their spheres of action we can see reflected the Lady herself and the demands she makes on those who would serve her. The strange archetypal figures of the Black Knight, the Wild Herdsman, and the Yellow-Haired Man work in her service—though all in their various ways. Briefly, for we shall look at these in more detail, the Black Knight, abrupt in his appearance and his dismissal from the scene, represents the human race. The Yellow-Haired Man, a curious figure who presides over a dreamlike, otherworldly castle, seems to represent the memory of a previous race, while the Wild Herdsman or keeper of the animals is essentially a contact who totemistically bridges the connection between the animal kingdom and the stellar constellations.

The stages in Owain's story, from his conception to final apotheosis as guardian of the land, are stages through which all who seek to serve the land must pass. His parentage and the place and nature of his conception have been chosen by the Lady, and it is evident that considerable care has been made to ensure that the mating takes place only between the two chosen parents and none other. We find Merlin acting in a similar manner when he arranges the mating between the Atlantean priestess Ygraine and Uther Pendragon. The result of this manipulation was not entirely successful in its outcome, to say the least, and Arthur, the child of this union, was likewise unable to successfully "marry" the faery and human worlds within his Kingdom.

As with the other remarkable conceptions that we have noted so far, the manner of Owain's conception is strange indeed. It takes place in the twilight of the no man's land that lies between this world and the next, a place normally only encountered between sleep and waking, when the boundaries of consciousness are loosened, or entered in vision by those who deliberately seek to walk between the worlds. A Qabalist would describe this place as the interface between Briah and Yetzirah, but the Celtic bards visualized a place of inner earth lying between the cold stars and the deep black waters. To this place representatives of two different races have been summoned: Morgan, queen of Avalon, and Urien, king of the land, variously described as Rheged or Gorre. Rheged is a known country, although Gorre has more of an otherworldy feel to it.

Owain's mother, Morgan, is a richly composite character who, typically of Celtic mythology, contains three distinct aspects within herself, having evolved from three separate sources. Her earliest appearance is as the great queen of Irish legend, the Morrighan, who hovers as a black bird of death over the battlefields, or who is seen as the Washer at the Ford who oversees the rites of passage between the worlds. In Welsh legend she is the daughter of the king of the Underworld, and in Breton legend she is primarily a healer. We see these three strands coming together when Morgan (and two other queens who are really aspects of herself) takes charge of the dying King Arthur and ferries him across the waters into the safe harbor of Avalon, from where, when healed of his wounds, he will return. Later storytellers misunderstood her true function, of course. She is found throughout the Arthurian mythos in brief and sometimes disruptive appearances. It is certainly the case that later chroniclers and interpreters of the myth have not viewed her in a kindly light, and a certain amount of collective shadow has attached to her. But she is faery, not human, and may not easily be judged by the rules of good and bad that were learned by humans in the Garden of Eden. Her true archetype is that of the destroyer, the one who embodies the functions of death and destruction in order that the cycle of rebirth and renewal may continue, and this is not one that is happily accepted, particularly by the Western mind. In a manner that is only too familiar she has gradually been demoted to the role of interfering sorceress, but her true identity is as the queen of the Underworld. If we see her correctly she is far more closely allied to the other great dark queens of myth and history, and in this category we would also place Mary Magdalene. Like the Washer at the Ford, Mary Magdalene recognized the imminent death of her lover,

Christ, and made due preparation for those rites. The ancient rhyme puts it beautifully:

> Qui bien beurra
> Dieu voira.
> Qui beurra tout d'une baleine
> Voira Dieu et la Madeleine.

William Sharp (writing as Fiona Macleod) also perfectly understood this, as he describes in his short story called "The Washer at the Ford":

> It is Mary Magdalene my name is, and I loved Christ.
> And Christ is the Son of God,
> And Mary the Mother of Heaven.
> And this river is the river of death, and the shadows
> Are the fleeing souls that are lost if they be not shriven. . .
> The Washer of the Ford stooped once more. Low and sweet,
> As of yore and for ever, over the drowning souls
> She sang her immemorial song.[3]

At all events, the meeting between Morgan, in her aspect as the Washer at the Ford between the worlds, and King Urien is not a sweet and gentle affair. Other mortals and faeries alike are kept away from this place by howling dogs that drive them away in fear. Even the great queen herself does not appear to have played an entirely willing part in the process, as she tells Urien when he arrives. She has been fated to wait there until she has conceived a son by a Christian. She doesn't tell him how long the wait has been!

Urien, on the other hand, is a well-documented historical figure. He was a sixth-century clan chief of the Novantae tribe who occupied the land known as Rheged, which stretched from the southwestern peninsula of Scotland down through the Borders and into Cumberland and Northumberland. Many of the tribes of that time were at least nominally Christian, and we have no reason to believe that Urien was not. His Chief Bard was one Taliesin who describes him as "Lord of the cultivated plain."

Whatever Urien's religious persuasion, the crucial point is that he was not of the same world as Morgan, but had equally responded to a call from the inner worlds and had arrived at the Ford that was not of this world. Morgan came from the world of faery; she was not subject to the normal human cycle of life and death and the normal human measures of morality, of right and wrong. Urien is of this world, a recognized historical figure who had embraced Christianity.

It is also interesting that Morgan does not appear in her "normal" form as the queen of Avalon, nor does she use any of the shifts of shape that would have been at her disposal, but appeared to Urien in a guise that must have lacked a certain allure. Moreover, Urien is not a warrior about to die, but lives to return a year later to find that Morgan has given birth to two children, Owain and Morfudd. But then the experience of making love with the queen of the Underworld is likely to be transformative, to say the least, and his "death" comes in the consummation of their mating in the cold dark waters of the river between the worlds. In fact, the whole episode is starkly powerful in a way that cuts through any illusion we may have as to the glamour of such an encounter. One can only wonder at the depth of character of Urien given that he was summoned to such a mating, and at the requirements of the inner worlds that it should be deemed necessary. Both he and Morgan appear to be curiously uninvolved in what takes place, even though what is required of them is achieved: the birth of a future guardian of the fountain whose parentage is part human and part faery. The demands of the Goddess are not easy, even for those of nonhuman origin. But by virtue of this harsh initiation, Urien momentarily experiences the paradisal state of unknowing that existed before the fruit of the Tree of Knowledge of Good and Evil was tasted. The function of Morgan as the Washer at the Ford, therefore, is as one who washes away the stains of the world, who *undoes* what happened when Eve asked "what if." It is she who initiates into the world of faery and, as those who have experienced this initiation will tell you, it is not an easy thing.

Owain is, therefore, initiated by virtue of his parentage into the dynamics of the inner earth. His mother, for all her dealings with the human world, remains entirely in allegiance with the world of faery and to its laws. Not unusually, the chroniclers tell us nothing of the history of Morfudd, Owain's sister who shared the same parentage.

The story of Owain's life and continuing adventures show how he came to fulfill his destiny as intended champion of the Lady and eventual guardian of the fountain. He was initially taught his skills by someone who was the equal of sovereignty in a wisdom that only comes from the very highest level, someone who was rooted in the folk soul of these islands and who understood its power and purpose. "The Dream of Rhonabwy"[4] describes how Owain was taken under the aegis of Bran the Blessed, otherwise known as Bran the Raven, and thereafter became known as the Knight of the Raven. The magical significance of this has many layers: the raven was once the sacred bird of Apollo the Sun God, and at that time was not black, but silver. This raven is said to hold many powers, all of which were of use to Owain: the powers of memory, vision, and prophecy, and the ability to find hidden treasure. In other words, the knowledge of the sequence of the past and future, and the ability to perceive what is hidden under the illusion of the mundane world, all very useful skills for one who is destined to work upon the inner levels.

That Owain should have come under Bran's tutelage is no surprise, as we already have this association in the raven totem of Morgan in her aspect as the Morrighan, the scavenging raven of the battlefield. Much may be said about Bran, one of the oldest of the guardians of Britain, but briefly, the well being of these islands was said to have rested upon the safekeeping of his head under the White Tower of London—the same head that was dug up again by Arthur in a moment of hubris. Moreover, Bran was associated with the royal game of Gwyddbwyll, also called "Bran Ddu." The game was played upon a black and silver checkered board, which represented the inner dynamics of the land. Its pieces represented the archetypal powers, and the movements of the pieces about the board symbolized the inner destiny and evolution of the land and its people. "The Dream of Rhonabwy" tells of a curious incident in which Owain appears to be standing in direct opposition to King Arthur, although the nature of the conflict being worked out through their game would appear to be one that comes from a very deep level indeed. The story tells of how Owain's ravens are fighting King Arthur's soldiers in a battle that is clearly not an outer world battle but is taking place at an inner level. To this end, Arthur is seated upon the mantle of invisibility, *Gwenn*, a device that appears necessary to enable him to work at an inner level, although Owain seems not to need such a prop. ". . . they were deep into the game when from a white red-topped pavilion with the image of a pureblack serpent—bright-red poisonous eyes in its head and a flamered tongue—came a young man. . . . The lad said to Owain, 'Lord, is it with your permission that the emperor's (that is, Arthur's) young lads and servants are harassing and molesting your ravens?' 'Your move,' said Arthur." Several more games follow, during which Owain's ravens gain the advantage over Arthur's men, such that "from now on it will not be easy to defend this island." But matters are brought to a head when Arthur "squeezed the gold men on the board until they were nothing but dust; then Owein ordered Gwres son of Rheged to lower the banner, and when this was done there was peace on both sides."

This extraordinary passage poses many questions concerning the real nature of the threat to the land that is symbolized by the image of the poisonous-eyed, flame-tongued serpent. Although the storyteller does not make direct allusion, but prefers to use very evocative imagery, we cannot escape the reference to the Edenic serpent and the conflict that ensued. Similarly, the story leaves us questioning who the land's true guardian was, and who was on the side of right.

However, the story's interest to us at the moment lies in the fact that by this time Owain was clearly a master of the Gwyddbwyll board, and had been entrusted with the inner guardianship of the land at the highest level. It is this ability Taliesin describes when he talks of his own manipulation of inner powers: "I conveyed Awen to the deeps of Hebron."

But while Owain learns skills of this order from Bran, the Lady of the Fountain sends her own tutor to instruct him in other ways of service. She sends her daughter Luned to him. Luned is outspoken and blunt, more than happy to tell Owain or anyone else exactly what they ought to be doing. Evidently nothing is to be left to chance or the vagaries of Owain's psychic perception. The manner in which Luned speaks her mind is often quite humorous, but the point is that she is absolutely clear and unswerving in her perception of, and dedication to, what the Lady wants to achieve. The pairing of Luned and Owain throughout the story is a perfect example of how a man and woman working in polarity in service of sovereignty may together achieve the highest results. When he falters in his course she guides him. When she goes too far and steps beyond her abilities, he rescues her—and vice versa.

Having achieved the birth of her potential future champion, the Lady of the Fountain must keep him on his course by setting tests on his path. And so we read in "The Lady of the Fountain" that Owain, having become a knight in the court of King Arthur, learns how another knight named Cynon has encountered the guardian of a fountain under a tree in a great valley—a Black Knight who knocked him off his horse and then rode away on it. Owain asks why he doesn't go back to have another try. Cynon responds with words to the effect that Owain should put his money where his mouth is, and it is this taunt rather than any response to the promptings of his higher nature that first sets Owain on his path.

He spends some time in the stage of the seeker who, turning away from the comfortable habits of the mundane world, journeys into the discomfort of the unknown. Owain rides "to the bounds of the world and the desolate mountains." His first encounter is not with the Black Knight, but is a surreal, dreamlike sequence of events. On reaching a valley he comes across the two youths, each with a gold circlet about their yellow hair, each dressed entirely in gold and carrying bows and arrows of ivory and gold. Bizarrely, they are shooting the arrows at their knives, which are also made of gold. They are watched from a distance by the Yellow-Haired Man, similarly dressed. The man takes Owain to his castle, which is uninhabited except for twenty-four girls who, without speaking, attended to his—and his horse's—every need. Owain tells the man the whole of his quest, and that "seeking the knight who guards the fountain would I wish to be." The whole sequence has the otherworldly feeling of a dream about it, but there are several significant facts in this sequence. First, the owner of the castle is kind and courteous, and keeps watch over an orderly, bright, sunlit family. There are no shadows or darkness in this castle, and its solar qualities are emphasized by the number of maidens, twice twelve, who attend to his every need and produce every good thing. It is a place of blessing and abundance.

Owain continues and meets the same Black Man that Cynon had previously encountered—the one-eyed, one-footed wild herdsman who sits upon a mound in a clearing in a great forest, surrounded by a thousand animals. This encounter does not present a challenge so much as a stage through which Owain has to pass. The impression we get of the meeting is that Owain has passed the test already by virtue of who he is. He gives Owain the directions he needs, and our hero journeys until he reaches the fountain.

The fountain and the various symbols and artifacts that surround it each have a particular meaning. Descriptions of the fountain are found both in "The Lady of the Fountain" and "Yvain, the Knight with the Lion." Each offers a slightly different description of the fountain, and it is worth considering them both. Owain finds the fountain beneath a tree. This fountain is a bubbling spring that arises from the deep earth. In "Yvain, the Knight with the Lion" we are told that the tree is a pine tree and that the water of the fountain or spring is bubbling as if it were boiling, so we might well imagine that there is some considerable force behind it, and that it produces a cloud of mist or vapor. Beside the spring lies a marble slab, or a great stone, or a great emerald stone. Attached to the marble slab is a silver chain, and attached to the silver chain is a golden bowl. The stone is hollowed out "like a cask," and there are four rubies beneath it.

To take each in turn: the tree is both the human backbone and the glyph of the world axis on which is hung the totality of experience from the lowest worlds to the highest. It is the Tree of Knowledge of Good and Evil that grew in the Garden of Eden, but also, in potential, the tree of everlasting life.

The bubbling fountain is the Awen, the unceasing flow of inspiration from the inner world that can manifest in the outer world as the life-bringing waters of the earth. For example, the yearly inundation of the Nile was seen as the life-renewing energy that brought renewed fertility to the dependent land, and also brought down the blessing of the great goddess Isis and the renewal of spiritual energy from the star Sirius. It is the joyful surge felt within the body when filled with life and creativity, carried along on a wave of expression of inner truth. It is also the medium by which the impulses from the deep earth are transmitted about the planet.

The golden bowl is the essential body of the seeker, the precious temple of the indwelling spirit. The physical body mirrors all things and is an expression of all things; the golden bowl is the sacrum, the seat of the soul, the vessel formed by the pelvic girdle and the protective ring about the hara, the center of the life force. Just as pure gold is "incorruptible," so is the pelvis in the human body the last bone to decay.

The silver chain that connects the bowl to the stone is the umbilical cord by which the soul is connected to all lives and all levels.

It is the silver cord that can be seen with inner sight when traveling upon the astral planes that connects the etheric body on the astral with the physical body.

In the marble slab we see the physical body of the seeker and of the earth. It also represents the ashlar, the finished block of stone, the summit of achievement and work. It is the complete and whole person, the Adam Kadmon, the perfected man. But the additional detail given by Chretien de Troyes takes the symbolism further, because the emerald slab brings in the deeper connection with the legend of the emerald that fell to earth from the crown of Lucifer, the Archangelic light-bringer. Inherent to the cosmology of the angelic and faery worlds is the story of how the greatest angel of them all "fell" not immediately to earth, but initially to Venus, which in planetary terms represents the higher self of the planet earth, and which is also said to be the place of origin of the high priest Melchizadek. From Venus the Archangel plunged to earth, the emerald in his crown becoming embedded in the planet's heart as he did so, but becoming the light of the world of faery, who recognize him as humankind do not. Other legends describe the emerald as the green stone of the Grail. It is described here as "hollowed out like a cask," which suggests that it has become a receptive vessel.

Beneath the emerald slab shine four rubies, the inner dragonfire of the earth, the kundalini serpent energy that lies coiled at the base of the spine. But here we also find a connection with faery, because these four lights also represent the lights of the four cities of the faery Kingdoms of Falias, Gorias, Finias, and Murias, or as the four corner towers of an inner castle, at the center of which lies the emerald green stone of the inner earth.

So we see that these vivid images that speak directly to the imagination represent different worlds and different levels of reality that have been brought together at the foot of the World Tree. They represent the physical earth and the "higher self" of the perfected, sacred earth; the physical, etheric, and spiritual bodies of the seeker, and the two worlds of human and faery. (The initiation of the animal world has already been taken to a certain extent by the safe passage past the keeper of the animals, although more of this is still to come.) And so those who come to this place are presented with a set of highly significant and charged emblems that, it can be said, encapsulate all that evolved from that first moment under the World Tree when Eve set it all in motion by asking "What if?" It is the seeker's task to find a way to return to that moment: to literally "get it together." In other words, the seeker must recognize and then align the inner with the outer, the higher with the lower, this world with the other world, and to express them within him- or herself in true balance and alignment. By this means will harmony and balance be reachieved. The Celts may not have voiced the words "Tsedek" or "Maat," but they knew their meaning.

Needless to say, the task of getting it all together is no easy matter. Like other seekers who had come that way before him, Owain takes the bowl, dips it into the spring, and throws the water onto the slab. This small ritual action is deceptively simple! Owain is literally taking his life in his hands by picking up the bowl; he offers it in dedication to the Lady of the Fountain, and to demonstrate the strength of his dedication he fills the bowl—his body—with the Awen of the fountain. Having received this empowerment, he then pours the water onto the hollowed emerald. By doing so he is making a symbolic sacrifice of his own lower self, which has been filled with the power of the inspiration of the fountain and is *returning in dedicated service* to the powers of the inner earth, to sovereignty. This is a ritual enactment of the occult dictum "I desire to know in order to serve." It is not sufficient merely to receive the gift of Awen; it must be used in dedicated service.

The result of this action is what, in psychological terms, would be described as extreme mental, emotional, and spiritual disturbance. In the story it is described as a violent storm of nature in which loud thunder precedes a hailstorm so fierce that every leaf is stripped from the tree. This is the often apparently brutal stripping away of the clothing of illusion, which can overwhelm the rational senses and leave only the bare skeleton of truth. The process is one that sooner or later is almost inevitably experienced by those who are sincere seekers, and may indeed be experienced several times. It is akin to what has been called the "dark night of the soul," or a psychotic episode, or a spiritual crisis, according to the system of thought that is followed.

But Owain is not deterred, and having ridden the storm the clear light of heaven dawns, the tree is filled with birds and the air filled with their song.

Having survived this far, Owain is now ready for the next challenge, and the black rider appears. In occult teaching the image of the rider on a horse is often used as a meditative exercise designed to reveal to students the nature of the relationship they have with their lower self or personality, and can quickly reveal exactly who is in control. The previous knight to encounter the black rider was Cynon, who was unsuccessful in his challenge; the black rider knocked him to the ground and rode off with his horse. In psychological terms the black knight also represents the shadow: those parts of the whole self that are repressed and denied. In the deeper mythological language of the story, the black rider is the guardian of the threshold, and stands before the seeker and the fountain, the one chosen by the Lady who will ensure that none but the bravest and truest knight can reach her. It is not a selfish whim on her part, nor an idle or meaningless test, but is for the most part a means by which the seeker is protected from that with which he or she cannot yet cope. There is no point in attempting to gaze upon the higher realities unless one is prepared, body and soul, for the experience.

As for the black rider, Owain, unlike Cynon, "received him and encountered him with spirit." We must assume he was successful in this, because the black rider, although wounded, leads him on to "a great shining city," which we learn is the home of the Lady of the

Fountain. He rides across the drawbridge—the Abyss in Qabalist terms—and into this innermost castle, but the portcullis drops down and cuts his horse in two, leaving Owain "in a quandary." He and the front part of the horse are safe but stuck between the gates, while the back half of his horse has been shut outside. This represents the dropping away of the lower self, which has no place in this deep inner place, although Owain is still not able to pass through the final gate into the courtyard of the castle by himself. A final guide, Luned, the "daughter" of the Lady of the Fountain, appears and rescues him by opening the last gate. It transpires that the black rider, who is now revealed to be the husband of the Lady, has died of the wounds caused by Owain. In case Owain falls prey to the fatal error of pride and believes that he has somehow deserved spiritual riches, or at least the Lady's hand in marriage through overcoming these challenges, Luned soon puts him right when he confesses to her of his love for the Lady. "God knows," she said, "She loves not thee, neither a little nor at all." One is reminded of the final revelation made to the initiates in the Greek Mysteries at Eleusis, who, expecting perhaps to receive the glorious gift of enlightenment, are told only that "there is no God."

The remainder of the story tells how Owain eventually becomes the consort and champion of the Lady of the Fountain. He thus "guards" the fountain for three years, although this overused term actually describes a position of high priesthood. He returns after three years to the court of King Arthur, but still has lessons to learn concerning the proper relationship between the inner and outer worlds, staying too long in the outer world and finding the Lady again only with some difficulty and consequent further challenges. This is the way of the initiate: to find a way in which to balance and integrate the inspiration of the inner worlds within the outer; to find a way in which to take the fruits and results of such inspiration right down into the mundane world. The story of Owain and the Lady of the Fountain, although couched in very readable and enjoyable allegory, nevertheless represents an indication of the path of service that can take the seeker into the very heart of the mysteries that this book explores. Anyone who seeks understanding of and initiation into the inner powers of nature will find that the story of Owain sets out that path very clearly, and that the inner powers work through the symbols that are encountered with a presence that is very real indeed.

The following ritual can be used as a means of initiation into that inner world. This ritual is not so much a "one off" as one that will take shape over a period of time. The preparation is as much a part of the magic as the ritual itself.

You must first collect the symbols that you will encounter at the fountain, and then consecrate them. It is possible to buy them, but the magical and talismanic effect will, of course, be much stronger if you have made them yourself and thereby made them your own. You will need a "golden" bowl. Be aware that it represents the temple of your physical body, and make it yours by whatever means you are inspired to use. If in doubt, ask! The inspiration of the Lady of the Fountain is there for all.

You will also need a length of "silver" chain to represent the etheric cord that attaches your physical body to your astral body. Again, find a way to make it, and be aware of what it represents as you do so.

You will also need a large stone to represent the marble or emerald. Use your imagination. It is possible to buy polished granite or marble offcuts from a stonemason, or you could make a pilgrimage to a place that has especial or sacred meaning for you, and take a stone from the ground. Ensure that this does not in any way damage the site. Again, ensure that the stone represents the sacredness of the good earth. Attach the silver cord to both the stone and the bowl.

Set the fountain next to the stone. You may like to attempt this ritual outdoors, in which case you can use a stream or pool, but working outside presents its own hazards. You will need a chalice or cup that contains water. Obviously, it is best if the water has come from a sacred spring, and you may like to find a local holy well for this purpose.

The stone is surrounded by four "rubies," one at each corner, to represent the four kingdoms of the inner earth. Red candles are the obvious answer here, but this part of the ritual brings the faery world into the magic, and this in itself is almost another ritual. If you do not yet feel confident in this area, you may wish for the moment to confine yourself to thinking of the four quarters as the four elements. If you wish to explore the Faery Kingdoms further than this book can take you, then the work of Bob Stewart is highly recommended.

This preparatory work should be done with care and attention. A talismanic power will begin to build around these symbols, which will bring your work to life and make it real. When you are ready, familiarize yourself with the following pathworking by reading it through several times. Once you are familiar with the sequence of events, you will find that in meditation the images will arise and develop in your mind of their own accord, and that you no longer need to follow their exact sequence.

THE LADY OF THE FOUNTAIN:
AN INITIATION INTO THE WESTERN MYSTERIES

When you are ready, assemble your symbols in the center of your place of working.

Light a single white candle and place it at the center, stating out loud that it represents the one true light. Say your name and state your intent to dedicate yourself to the service of sovereignty, the Lady of the Fountain. Light the four red candles, one at each corner of the stone. You may wish to make an invocation, as you light each candle, of the four elemental kingdoms, and/or of the Faery Kingdom. Seat yourself in meditation, and then visualize the following pathworking. Take it slowly, and allow time for each image to build in your imagination.

You are walking across an empty plain underneath a night sky filled with stars. It is winter. You have left behind the warmth and comfort of your home and companions many days ago and are journeying to the distant horizon and beyond. There have been no signposts on this journey, only your conviction that you will find what you are driven to seek. You walk onward with determination; the only sound is of your feet striking the ground beneath you with regular step. As you proceed, even the stars seem to fade into the black sky.

You come to a dark river that flows silent and deep; the river between the world of humankind and the otherworld of faery. Beyond the river, on the other side, is a white mist. A faint howl of dogs floats to you, an eerie sound that comes from all directions and none. Upon the other side, at the water's edge, kneels an old woman who is dipping a white, blood-stained garment into the river as if its dark waters will take the stains from it and carry them to oblivion. She lifts her head as you approach, and stands. Her face swims in and out of focus as you look at her. Her eyes are deep and bright, not those of an old woman. As you gaze at her you see different patterns within her, different figures superimposed upon each other. You see a tall dark queen upon whose head shines a heavy crown that bears a single ruby. You see a cloak of black feathers enfolding her like wings, and the hooded head of a raven whose eye gleams keenly. She is Morgan, queen of Avalon. You realize that she is waiting until you ask the right question. In your own words, you tell her that your desire is to serve the Lady of the Fountain who is the sovereignty of the land.

She steps into the river and walks toward you. Without hesitation you also wade into the water. Curiously, it does not strike you as either cold or wet, but is more of a deep enveloping darkness that has a strange but comforting familiarity about it. You experience the sensation that your garments are floating away from your body and that you are standing naked within the water. The water, like an invisible current, surges about you and you feel cleansed, almost as if the water penetrated your very bones. You feel the touch of her hands upon you, and her arms are about you. She is neither cold nor wet, but holds you with a warmth and strength that is immensely reassuring. You are aware of her energy and you experience fleeting visions of her own land and people, the faery folk of the Underworld, but before you have time to understand them she withdraws her touch and vanishes. You find yourself bursting upward through the water, your lungs gasping for air, your legs pushing upward toward the light. You break through to the surface, the water (simultaneously) falls away from you, and you are standing on dry land with the warmth of the Sun's rays shining upon your face. You have arrived in a place of great light and goodness. Take time to look around you, and do not be afraid.

You become aware of a figure who stands near you. He is Owain, one who has taken this journey before you. He is kind and wise. He is cloaked in the brown robes of earth, and carries a staff. He holds out another cloak, which you take and wrap yourself in. He takes your hand. You have the consciousness of the earth—you are one with the land and she is one with you. You feel her movement through space, turning about the Sun through light and through dark.

You walk with Owain through grass green as emerald, and arrive at the edge of a forest. You step inside into the cool green shade. You reach a clearing at the heart of the forest. At the center of the clearing stands a green mound, and upon the mound, cross-legged, sits a giant of a man with one eye in the middle of his forehead. At the sight of you he stands and roars with a voice that reaches to the very edges of the forest and beyond. You realize that the forest is full of wild creatures: birds and animals of every shape and kind that live here in peace and contentment. You may find that one wishes to make itself known to you and to accompany you on your journey.

You walk deeper into the forest, and as you do so a half-seen presence builds about you—the faery folk—inquisitive creatures who come to the edge of your vision, and tall, shining, spear-carrying warriors fade in and out of the green light. You reach another clearing and here, at the center, is a pine tree that reaches straight and tall to the sky. Its roots are entwined around a huge stone that gleams like an emerald and appears to be rooted deep within the earth. Upon the stone are four rubies, one at each corner, that burn with an inner flame as if from the fires of the Underworld Kingdoms. By the side of the stone, attached to it with a silver chain, is the golden bowl that you recognize as your own. It stands by the edge of a spring of water that bubbles up from the ground with a ringing sound of tiny silver bells.

Prompted by Owain, you kneel in devotion to the sacred presence of this place. You search you heart for truth and purity of intent, and ask for the blessing of a vision of the Lady of the Fountain. Wait in silence until this is granted, and make contact with the Lady in the way that seems most fitting to you.

When you are ready, in your imagination, stand, take the golden bowl, dip it into the spring, and throw the water onto the stone. Pause for several minutes in your meditation, and take note of anything that now occurs.

When you have completed this stage of the meditation, give thanks and a gesture of farewell to the Lady and to Owain for guiding you, and to the animal or bird that accompanied you. Slowly let your focus return to the outer world, where the golden bowl and silver chain you have prepared are placed before you. Carrying with you the knowledge and awareness of the events of your meditation, and with ritual intent, pick up the bowl, dip it into the water, and splash a little water onto the stone. Repeat out loud your statement of intent and dedication. Return to your seat and again pause until you feel that your work has been accomplished.

When you are ready, extinguish the candles, make a statement or sign, or say farewell and thanks to those you have invoked. You may wish to pour the water from the bowl and chalice onto the earth. Keep a record of resulting dreams and changes. You may wish to return to this ritual from time to time.

CHAPTER EIGHT

THE INNER FIRE

FORCE AND FIRE

Both physics and metaphysics agree that creation is permeated by some invisible yet almost tangible force. A universal energy pervades all things. In the Taoist traditions it is called *Chi;* in the Shinto, *Ki;* in Hebrew it is *Ruach;* in Sanskrit, *Prana;* and in the Brythonic Celtic tradition it is called *Awen.* This force is what Dylan Thomas described as "the force that through the green fuse drives the flower,"[1] and in traditions that retain some appreciation of a mother earth it is seen to be essentially feminine and dynamic.

In the Brythonic Celtic tradition the Awen proceeds from the cauldron of a triple goddess. The cauldron is receptive and yet the Awen is dynamic. In the Tibetan tradition the potential of the Prana lies dormant in the earth under the presidency of the goddess Kundalini, yet in its movement it is under the dynamic direction of four goddesses, each of whom is assigned to one of the elements. Physics also sees the universal force that emanated from the primal Big Bang as being fourfold. In mythological terms these may be thought of as the four rivers that flow out of Eden. The intangible progression of that fourfold force (strong nuclear, weak nuclear, electromagnetic, and gravitational) may be seen in the fledgling laws of quantum mechanics, particularly as they apply to the sub-atomic realm. This is the area that Western occultism calls the *etheric.* Fourfold consciousness may also be seen as part and parcel of this quadruple emanation. Science, at least in quantum mechanics, is coming to the conclusion that mind and matter are inextricably joined, rather like the waves and particles of its quanta.

The object of raising the inner fire is to identify with the universal force as a means of achieving changes in consciousness. In this process we are (in a sense) affirming the relationship of mind and matter, at least matter at the subatomic or electromagnetic/etheric level. The objective of such changes in consciousness is to furnish the adept with the three traditional attributes required for his or her work: personal transformation, inner power, and mystical devotion. The mechanics of raising the fire itself are mostly operative on the etheric level, where physiology and consciousness overlap. However, the changes themselves have the potential to build bridges to other modes of being and consciousness that lie far beyond the etheric.

The raising of the fire is not the raising of the universal force itself. That universal force is already within us, albeit in a dormant state, for human nature is part of all nature. The inner fire awakens the universal force. Hence, Tibetan mysticism makes the distinction between a universal Prana and the individual Tapas, the fire in the blood that in Welsh is called *Hwyl,* which must be activated to let Prana do its work. In Celtic mythological terms we are required to light the fire under the cauldron to activate and realize the Awen. The Tibetan yogin awakens the goddess Kundalini; we, like Gwion, awaken the goddess Ceridwen, mistress of the cauldron of transformation, in which the Awen is contained.

The objectives of initiates of the Western Mystery Tradition are not those of the Tibetan yogin. The word "yoga" may be broadly translated as "union," but the union that magicians primarily seek is an identification of their own human nature with the powers of all nature that the Goddess exemplifies. The initial motive in white magic is to enable effective stewardship in creation. Personal spiritual development and mystical devotion cannot and should not be entirely separated from this, as we shall later discuss, but in this first instance we are raising the inner fire to facilitate the practical magic that enables stewardship.

In terms of practical magic, as distinct from mystical endeavor, this is very much a "local affair." As we have stated, the process operates at an etheric level, and etheric conditions are very much related to a land and its people. Eastern tantric and kundalini yoga techniques are underpinned by a philosophy that is geared to etheric and cultural conditions in the East, and are therefore not ideally suited to the Western European folk soul, although both techniques are similar. This is because what Tibetan yoga calls Tapas, the fire that connects the yogin to universal energy, comes from the land, and its application and results are colored by both native environment and native mythology.

THE ETHERIC AND THE AURA

Metaphysics and material physics are agreed that both the earth and human (and other) life forms that inhabit it have an inherent electromagnetic field. Russian researchers interested in this in terms of human physiology discovered what they came to call a "Biological Plasma Body." What they call "plasma" seems to come close to what we would describe as the inner fire, but the word "plasma" has a number of meanings. In terms of physics, as opposed to biology, plasma is an ionized, electrically neutral gas that can contain an electromagnetic field. The ionization of such a gas occurs at phenomenal temperatures akin to those that occur in nuclear fission, so the idea of an inner fire seems entirely appropriate. The electromagnetic field contained, and indeed maintained, by this fire is what metaphysics and magic call the "aura."

The aura is seen to provide the underlying etheric/subatomic framework for the flesh and blood body, but as Heisenberg showed, human consciousness is capable of altering the wave and particle behavior of this subatomic world. Occultists have always maintained this, if in other terms, and medicine has long been aware that consciousness can cause psychosomatic effects and biological changes.

PHYSIOLOGY AND CONSCIOUSNESS

This realization has been put to positive use by enlisting the patient's consciousness as a therapeutic device. Visualization techniques have, for example, been used to help combat the progression of carcinogenic cells, and meditation techniques are taught to regulate blood pressure. Neuro-Linguistic Programming attempts, as its name implies, to access and reprogram areas of consciousness that govern neurological mechanisms both for therapeutic purposes and general attitudinal adjustment, although both are inevitably two sides of the same coin.[2]

Alternative and complementary therapies presently enjoy a very positive renaissance. Some of these, like acupuncture, use direct mechanical intervention to regulate the body's electromagnetic field, while others use media that stimulate appropriate biochemical mechanisms. Still others, like hypnotherapy, work on a psychotherapeutic level. In practice, most therapies employ a combination of physical and psychological media. Even so, perhaps more of the healing process depends upon empathy or *polarity* between the consciousness of the patient and the consciousness of the healer, or the facility in the healer's consciousness to mediate "the fire." What is clear, however, is that all such therapies seek to deal with *causes* at the etheric level, rather than just with *symptoms* at the physiological level. This necessitates the stimulation of what our Russian friends called the Bioplasmic Function to effect modifications in the body's etheric/electromagnetic substructure. This is also the starting point for our magical endeavors in stimulating the Bioplasmic Function of raising the fire, even if technique and motive are somewhat different.

CRYSTALS

One form of intermediary substance used in both alternative therapy and magic deserves some mention here. Quartz crystal has enjoyed increasing popularity in recent years as both a magical and therapeutic adjunct. Crystal healers place quartz crystals on the body, mostly on the chakra points. A number of acupuncturists also use crystals rather than steel needles, primarily because crystals are noninvasive and painless. Personal experience indicates that the crystal, if placed at the correct meridian point, will still make the necessary modifications in the body's electromagnetic field for healing to take place.

There now seems to be reasonable evidence that our ancestors were also aware of the mediatory effect of crystals upon electromagnetic fields. Tom Graves and others suggested more than twenty years ago that the Neolithic and Bronze Age people who built the stone circles, alignments, and burial chambers did so, among other reasons, to perform a certain type of acupuncture upon mother earth herself to modify her electromagnetic field. More recently, the finding of the ice-preserved body of a Neolithic hunter in an Italian Alpine glacier showed that our distant ancestors were not only aware of what we may describe as acupuncture principles upon the body of the land, but were aware of these principles upon themselves as well. Thanks to the keen observation of one of the doctors attending the postmortem of the ice-preserved body, a number of tattoos were seen to align to known acupuncture points. These points were realized to be the same ones that the doctor, who was also an acupuncturist, would have used to treat the diseases that the postmortem indicated that the man had suffered from. How these points were addressed in a premetal culture remains a mystery, but it may well have been through the application of crystals to effect, then as now, therapeutic changes in the body's electromagnetic field. This certainly seems to endorse the theories of Graves and others that our Neolithic ancestors were aware of acupuncture principles, whether upon the land or themselves.

The majority of stone circles in northern Europe are constructed from granite with a high quartz crystal content, and cists covered with milky quartz are frequently found at such sites, especially in Wales. A number of stone circles surveyed for geological anomalies have also revealed radioactive hotspots. These seem to lend some credence to ideas of inner fire and the heat at which a plasma is generated. Similar isolated flares are revealed in Kirlian photography of the human aura.

None of this should surprise us in terms of quartz crystal being able to modify electromagnetic fields. Crystals do, after all, have pieso-electrical properties, and under pressure produce electrical charge. In terms of the physics of the electromagnetic spectrum, glass is the prismatic material for the wavelength of visible light, as any child knows when he or she sees the wonderful rainbow effect of a glass prism. Because the less tangible ultraviolet wavelength carries higher electromagnetic energy than visible light, prisms must be made from quartz crystal. Magical experience has shown that quartz crystal used in magical implements and magical cere-monies does in fact produce electromagnetic and, consequently, often physical, effects. The quartz seems to act as a particle acceler-ator that naturally causes heat. In that magic is the "making of changes in consciousness," and given that consciousness has effects upon electromagnetic media, this is not surprising. We should re-member of course that the machinery that facilitates the use of consciousness is electrical. Brain enables mind through electro-chemical transmission.

We know of one magical ceremony in which crystals were used as a meditation focus, which caused the crystals that were used to "charge up." Some twenty minutes after the ceremony, having been removed from the room and taken to various locations, they were suddenly extremely hot to the touch. Healers often experience this same intense heat when placing their hands upon a patient. In such cases, even though the heat generated is not of the order of that generated in nuclear fission, which would effectively produce a plasma, we may still assume the operation of some sort of "fire." In all these procedures something that registers to the senses as intense heat is being generated. Furthermore, this generation of heat is, in most cases, being initiated by deliberate operations of consciousness, activating and changing the electromagnetic/etheric substance of the "Biological Plasma Body" that consciousness contains.

We are seeking transformation of consciousness so that we may, in terms of magical as opposed to mystical or therapeutic application, act effectively as intermediaries between the archetypal and material worlds. To do this we have to be able to tune human consciousness to the seven wavelengths or states of that intermediary area in nature that the Celts called Annwn and the Egyptians called the Duat. To do so we take up that Ariadne's thread of inner fire at the etheric boundary where our own physical world touches the inner world of Annwn. This is the point at which we set the process of raising the fire into motion, the point where our feet touch the crust of the good earth, the boundary where physical appearance and sensation touch upon instinct, feeling, and, not least, memory. Because this region is the etheric, we use etheric technique.

THE CHAKRAS

The inner fire is a device that connects. It is the medium through which synchronizations are made in personal consciousness with other areas of consciousness. Human consciousness tends to perceive both its inner and outer environment in a sevenfold way. Sacred space and the Qabalistic "Cube of Space," as well as the Caers of Annwn, are intermediary sevenfold constructs through which we seek to synchronize personal consciousness to inner, wider consciousness. This is best thought of in terms of tuning personal consciousness to the various wavelengths of consciousness and being within creation. Such wavelengths exist in terms of the energy levels shown on the electromagnetic spectrum. In the electromagnetic aura of the human constitution we find seven major, corresponding points, although there are many others. These are, of course, the chakras. While these function through the etheric mechanism of the human constitution they may be seen as junction boxes within the human electromagnetic body. The inner fire is therefore visualized as coming from the deep earth, from Annwn, and activating each of these centers or junctions to make the synchronization. When that synchronization is complete, it is possible to access and synchronize each of the modes of consciousness and being of all nature.

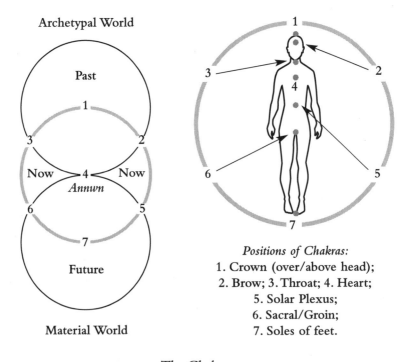

Positions of Chakras:
1. Crown (over/above head);
2. Brow; 3. Throat; 4. Heart;
5. Solar Plexus;
6. Sacral/Groin;
7. Soles of feet.

The Chakras

The word chakra means "wheel." This implies that each center within the human aura may be visualized as a wheel or, more exactly, as a spinning vortex of fire.

This idea of "wheels" also implies that in the concept of our ancestors performing a type of acupuncture upon the land herself, we may, in such constructs as stone circles, see representations of terrestrial chakras. This is not as outlandish as may be supposed, and may help to explain how human chakras also function. We have established that these circles are made of stones that have a high quartz crystal content, and that radiation hotspots often occur in the vicinity of such circles. We have also seen that crystals appear to be able to promote subatomic particle acceleration. Modern particle physics uses large "circles," cyclotrons (like the CERN one at Geneva) to accelerate particles by electromagnetic pulse. In this, subatomic particles and antiparticles are accelerated to almost the speed of light in attempts to replicate, among other things, the conditions of the Big Bang. In doing so scientists hope to recreate the primordial energy from which arose the four forces that hold the universe together. The heat generated under such conditions is tremendous. Among the particles created in this way are bosons, described by physicists as "salamanders" because their being is in and of fire. In addition to these fiery primordial force effects, particle acceleration also, because of the immense speeds involved, plays games with time. We may imagine that while stone circles acted rather like cyclotrons, stone rows fulfilled much the same function as linear accelerators.

A magic circle, with the participants in a ritual spaced around its periphery, works in much the same way. The trained consciousness of its operators provides the electromagnetic pulse of consciousness, which more or less invokes the primordial forces of the universe, and not infrequently plays games with time. Like a chakra in the individual human system, a magic circle creates a vortex that can synchronize the consciousness of those involved with other modes of consciousness and being that exist within the various energy matrices of the universal force.

It is further stated that each chakra is of a threefold nature. In pagan Celtic terms we may think of this as a synchronization with the inner powers of nature, the powers of the triple goddess. This means that at each of the points of synchronization she may offer us a mode of conscious synchronization that pertains to each of her three aspects of form: archetypal/stellar, Underworld/transformative, and material/created powers.

There are also considerations here of space/time, in that contact with the embryonic prenatural world of Annwn connects us with the three states of past, present, and future. Time is better perceived as progressing in a vortex or spiral, like a chakra, rather than in the linear terms we are generally used to. As we have seen, one of the aspects of the acceleration of particle energies is that they play games with space/time. Contact with Underworld states and other beings in Annwn is typified by contact with inner world beings through time, often called the "ancestors." R. J. Stewart's *The Underworld Initiation* states that the raising of the inner fire is a prerequisite to contacting the ancestors. We should be aware however that these may not only be ancestors from the past, but also from parallel time and future time. The inner fire can access the facility of prophetic vision that has itself been called "remembering the future."[3] We should also be aware that in physically contemplating archetypal or stellar patterns, we are, in terms of conventional physics, contacting the stellar past, due to the time that starlight takes to reach earth.

Annwn, while being between the archetypal and material worlds, is seen as being beneath or within the earth. This is the symbolism used in the *Preiddu Annwn,* where the Underworld of Annwn is shown to have seven modes, or Caers, approached through subterranean burial chambers. Thus the bard makes the journey and raises the fire through these seven Caers by synchronizing one of the seven modes of personal consciousness to each Caer. The poem is quite specific about this interaction of human consciousness and the levels of consciousness in Annwn, telling us that the journey is through seven Caers from which "only seven return."[4] This inner bardic journey is the course of the inner fire, the Ariadne's thread that connects our perception to the seven major levels of consciousness and being that have been spawned by the universal force that is personified essentially by the Goddess.

The following diagram, "Wavelengths of Being," indicates the chakras in the human constitution and the levels of conscious experience they may represent. It is generally agreed that these major chakras align to the spine as a kind of axis through which the inner fire is conducted. The diagram compares this with traditional graduations of colors of visible light on the electromagnetic spectrum, and the wavelengths of sound represented by musical intervals. These are outer devices that, by mantric and visualization technique, can be used to "accelerate" the waves and particles of our inner "Biological Plasma Body." The wavelengths of the electromagnetic spectrum are also shown, as are the Caers of Annwn. However, none of these corresponded exactly, and the correspondence of these various wavelengths and levels should be taken as analogy rather than actuality. This is not to say that such analogies may not be profitably worked with.

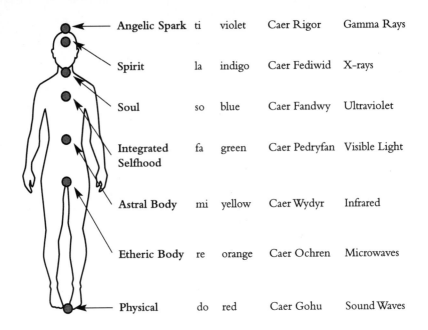

Angelic Spark	ti	violet	Caer Rigor	Gamma Rays
Spirit	la	indigo	Caer Fediwid	X-rays
Soul	so	blue	Caer Fandwy	Ultraviolet
Integrated Selfhood	fa	green	Caer Pedryfan	Visible Light
Astral Body	mi	yellow	Caer Wydyr	Infrared
Etheric Body	re	orange	Caer Ochren	Microwaves
Physical	do	red	Caer Gohu	Sound Waves

Wavelengths of Being

Similar graduations and systems to raise the fire also occur in traditional Western Qabalah, and the Tree of Life glyph could have been used to depict much of the foregoing. Anybody who chooses to apply these methods in a Qabalistic setting by building the Tree in the aura should read Israel Regardie's *The Middle Pillar.*[5] A Christian interpretation may be gleaned from chapters entitled "The Fiery Spear" and "The Serpent Flame," which appear in Gareth Knight's *Experience of the Inner Worlds.*[6] (The exercises given by Knight are taken from Anthony Duncan's *The Lord of the Dance.*)[7]

THE FIRE

When we come to consider the fire, the power itself, we come back to that much misunderstood word "polarity." In as much as this inner fire, the medium of interaction and synchronization of wavelengths, is part and parcel of the fundamental power within nature, it enables what Taoist philosophy calls Yin and Yang, and what Western magic calls positive and negative, or, more properly, dynamic and receptive. In this, it appears to have a masculine or dynamic side and a feminine or receptive side. These stereotypical labels are by no means fixed, but the fundamental powers within the universe have an ebb and flow, a give and take, a velocity and gravity. In other words, particles have both negative and positive charge, and nature operates on interaction and balance. Qabalah recognizes this in that the Tree of Life has one negative and one positive pillar, and a central pillar of equilibrium between the two. Such are representations of the workings of polarity in nature and human nature. In the raising of the fire the magician becomes the middle pillar.

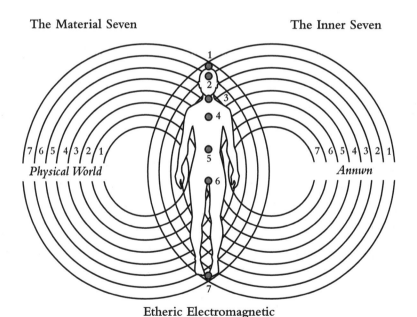

Material Seven/Inner Seven

DRAGON FIRE

In Celtic terms, this fundamental power and its polarity may be represented in two ways. The first way, in common with many ancient mythologies, is by the sexual magnetism between gods and goddesses as a kind of cosmic libido. Frequently these relationships are shown to be between brother and sister. This seemingly incestuous state of affairs indicates that the male and female components of the relationship stem from one "parental" source.

The second and not unrelated way in which the power of the universe is shown is by the fiery power of the dragon. This derives from the constellation of Draco, the dragon, which held the ancient pole star to which the phallically evocative axis of the earth was once aligned. (It is now in Ursa Minor). The phallicism of this concept went well with the realization that the axial tilt of the earth enabled the seasons, the ebb and flow of nature, and thus fertility, and of course gave credence to the god and goddess concept of the fire as a representation of stellar or cosmic libido and consequent birth and growth.

These ideas are not as quaint as they may first appear. The worlds did, as any astrophysicist will explain, come into being from the gas clouds of interstellar hydrogen ("dragon's breath"?) that were emitted by the orgasmic explosion of the evocatively named "Big Bang"! That the power was seen to come from "within the earth" yet had stellar associations need not be seen as a contradiction. The ancients believed that the stars were also present within the darkness of the earth and meditation upon this will reveal that this was something more than quaint analogy. There is of course "fire" at the core of the earth, Dante's mystical speculations on hell and ice notwithstanding!

The association of "dragon's breath" with this fire of Annwn and the triple goddess may also be seen in *Prieddu Annwn,* when Taliesin describes the cauldron of Annwn, the cauldron of being, as "warmed by the breath of nine maidens."[8] In addition to this being both an acknowledgment of the triple goddess (3 x 3 = 9) and the gestative (3 x 3 = nine months) powers of the cauldron, this also suggests that at one mode of operation the fire is mediated by the planetary powers. The fact that these are represented as being ninefold rather than sevenfold is because the ancients assumed the seven planets to include the two dragon nodes.

THE RED AND THE WHITE

The most famous of all dragons to appear in Celtic myth are those perceived by the boy Merlin, beneath the rock upon which Vortigern was trying to build his tower at Dinas Emrys. The tower kept collapsing due to earthquakes. Deep within the rock Merlin found a red dragon and a white dragon twisted in "conflict," but we may take this conflict to represent a state of dynamic tension, of polarity. This power within the earth, the power to initiate an earthquake, becomes translated to the wider context of being able to order events in the stewardship of the land. In the myth, Merlin is taken to Vortigern's stronghold to be a blood sacrifice to establish the axial tower of Vortigern's sovereignty, but escapes his fate by issuing his first prophecy. Instead of experiencing the spilling of his blood, Merlin therefore experiences fire in the blood: the red and white dragon fire. We may wonder if the ancients knew that blood is composed of red and white corpuscles.

The sacrificial rites of sacred kings who mate with the Goddess in death and align the tribe to the benevolence of the earth has been dealt with at length elsewhere. By Merlin's time the tendency to use surrogate sacrifices had, it would seem, gained ground! However, we should note in passing that originally "the red and white," the blood and semen of the king, were offered to the Goddess in sacrifice so that she may both empower and be fruitful from these essences of sovereignty. On a more profound level, the king's red blood represented the outer world of humanity, and the white essence represented the stuff of the Goddess, or her faery representative in Annwn.

In the red and the white we see the conjunction of inner and outer, of positive and negative, male and female, a conjunction implicit in the polarity within the inner fire itself; therefore, to know that polarity in whatever way and at whatever level is implicit in the ability to raise the fire and effect changes in consciousness.

The same symbolism occurs elsewhere in Celtic myth, in *Peredur,* for example, where a tree is encountered at the bounds of Annwn and the material world. The tree has one half of its leaves green, but the other half is aflame. This is a variation of the idea of red and white, of the polarity between inner and outer, of force and form. Trees are in any case evocative of the power within nature, the inner fire, the rising of sap from deep earth in phallic and fruitful manifestation. It is believed that sacred kings were sacrificed upon lightning-struck trees in the rites of Hercules. One may be tempted to speculate here upon an ancient understanding of the electromagnetism manifest in lightning and the relationship between lightning and the earth's magnetic field! This natural magnetism of the earth may itself be equated with a mythologically "sexual" magnetism that the earth exerts upon her consort, be he the horned god, the sky god, or an ancient, sacrificed, sacred king in the rites of Hercules.

In addition to Merlin and his red and white dragons beneath Dinas Emrys, we may notice the same inner fire symbolism cropping up to facilitate concourse between the worlds at other similar locations. This is particularly so in the legends attached to Glastonbury. In these the red and white symbolism encompasses several layers of myth and meaning. First there is the Tor, said to be the realm of Gwynn ap Nudd, one of the lords of Annwn, around which the seven-leveled "maze" winds like a dragon or dragon fire through the seven chakras of the land. Even today, two streams flow from the deeps of the Tor, one of clear white water emerging at the White Spring, the other red because of its chalybeate content, emerging at Chalice Well. Again, the flow of streams as electromagnetic adjuncts should not be ignored. Many an ancient sacred site is set over a subterranean water course. In addition to offering magnetic anomalies, such inner waters are seen in the Celtic tradition as access points of human perception to the inner levels of faery or Annwn.

The spectral hounds of Gwynn ap Nudd, which move between Annwn and underneath Glastonbury Tor and the outer world to collect the souls of the dead and unite them with the ancestors in the Underworld, are said to be white with red ears. In an uncanny parallel with Merlin's Dinas Emrys in Wales, there was actually an earthquake in medieval times that demolished a church to St. Michael on top of the Tor, of which only the tower now remains.

Other evidence of this power of the inner fire being placed in a Celtic Christian (but feminine) setting in acknowledgment of the Goddess occur in other British and Irish legend at Glastonbury. St. Margaret was one of the trio of female saints appointed to the patronage of Glastonbury Abbey. The selection of a saint associated with far off Antioch seems at first to strain credibility. St. Margaret appears to have been selected, however, because a dragon was central to her legend, thus her association with the red and white dragon symbolism of the place. St. Brigid too, in her Christianized version, became associated with Glastonbury, having gone there from her abbey at Kildare in Ireland.

The association of Brigid again brings in the symbolism of the "white and the red." In her pagan incarnation she was said to be the daughter of the Dagda, and thus mistress of the cauldron at the center of what the British Celts came to call Annwn. She was also patron of the fiery activity of smith craft. When she made the quantum leap into Christian sainthood, her feast day was set at the old Isis festival of Imbolc. She was a saint of (red) fire, and a perpetual fire was kept at Kildare for many hundreds of years after her death. Her "whiteness" came from both her patronage of milkmaids and her role as the wet nurse of Christ.

All this serves to show that Celtic magical practice held its own understanding of how and why to raise the inner fire, its goddess associations and, in the red and the white, its inherent polarity that could act as a bridge between the inner and outer worlds. It is time that we examined that polarity.

POLARITY

We have come a long way from talking about the activation of the human aura through seven chakras to facilitate a synchronization in consciousness with the sevenfold powers of being, the powers of the Goddess. We touched briefly upon the sacrificial rites of sacral kingship in a "mating" or "synchronization" with the Goddess who represented this power, this inner fire within the Underworld deep beneath the landscape. We have described how this dragon power or inner libido is cited in primal myth as the mating of gods and goddesses.

We may picture this in terrestrial terms as the land representing the body of the Goddess and the ley lines within the etheric of the land being rather like acupuncture meridians comprising her electromagnetic aura. In the East these are actually seen as "dragon lines" within the land and provide the *raison d'etre* for feng shui! For a sacred king to synchronize his own aura with that of his lady the land, in imitation of that original cosmic libido, we must assume the synchronization and surrender of the king's own etheric essence in sacrifice.

The associations between sexual climax and the surrender and expiration at death are complex and profound. The aura signifies the human etheric body and the etheric body, which supports physical life systems and experiences powerful stimulus when subject to sexual magnetism. In sexual arousal the fire in the blood associated with raising the inner fire is apparent in chemical changes in blood and brain and in the way that blood behaves, not least in its stimulation of both male and female genitalia. The process of raising the fire is, in other words, an etheric or bio-electrical process, and the most efficient way of initiating such a process is through the polarity of sexual magnetism or the acquisition and direction of magnetism through sacrifice.

Not all polarity is "sexual," of course, and the raising of the fire and the synchronization of the human aura with other levels of being certainly also facilitates polarity outside of any sexual context. The process itself, however, is most efficiently initiated by the polarity of human sexual magnetism.

There is an inherent gender polarity within every human being, and there is the internal polarity known to Jungian psychology that manifests in dreams as the "contra sexual image." The incubi and succubi demonized in medieval religious belief typify such phenomena, which may at some stage result in external projection. In more positive terms it is possible to develop such internal polarity with archetypes of the unconscious as a starting point to reach for a more profound contact with one's own selfhood. This is what many schools of yoga seek to do, endeavoring to establish union with an internalized higher self.

MYSTICAL UNION

Such internal "vertical" polarity may in time break the bounds of magic and progress to mysticism. In Judeo-Christian mysticism this means that the internal polarity between self and soul has been overridden by an external relationship between the soul and God. As the Christian mystic Anthony Duncan puts it, "A man would seek himself, let him beware, he is in mortal peril of beholding God."[9] In this, the raising of the fire or the will to raise one's nature to union has been elevated to establish a relationship, a synchronization that is beyond either one's own nature or indeed all of nature. A higher will, the will in which all nature lies, has answered that call for union. Such an answering is called "grace" in Christian mystical tradition. Yet even in this we see the red and the white of the wine, and the host as the symbols of the mystical marriage that the Christian Eucharist represents.

Although Christian tradition would balk at the association, this really becomes a mystical expansion of those ancient rites of sacred kingship. As we have seen, the Bronze Age sacred kings were sacrificed voluntarily so that the king, the father of the tribe, could mate with the Goddess, the tribal mother, who was represented by the land. Frequently the body of the sacrificed one would be eaten by members of the tribe while his blood and semen would be spread upon the good earth, and his bones set within a womb-like burial chamber to indicate a mating with the Goddess. In the Christian Eucharist, the body and blood of the "sacred king" are symbolically consumed by the worshippers in a mystical union. In the Bronze Age context, that union enabled changes in nature, fertilizing the mother goddess to make healthy children, fine animals, and abundant crops by changing the underlying "fire," "the green fuse," the will of all nature. In the Christian context the idea is that the mystical union changes human nature to align with divine will.

In this we meet a curious legend that attests to what may be called a cross between pagan magical practice and Christian mystical theology. This typifies the tragedy of one of many broken threads by which Christianity, in its divorce from a pagan past, lost its anchor to the good earth.

There is a legend that a cry was heard at the crucifixion of Christ: "Great Pan is dead." Gareth Knight, in his book *The Rose Cross and the Goddess,*[10] takes this to mean "Great Pan is *changed.*" But first we have to establish just who or what Pan represents.

PAN

Within the polarity that is integral to the inner fire with its complementary aspects of negative and positive, external and internal, masculine and feminine, and red and white, we discover the Goddess and her consort. Her consort is the personification of the power that arouses and fertilizes her to form the growing earth. The pagan religions of northern Europe knew this consort as the potent horned god whom their sacred kings represented, and the classical pagan mysteries knew him as Pan. The Goddess may represent the star-white pattern or the cauldron womb of creation, but the horned god represents the fire-red arousal and the will by which it is fertilized. Pan's power is the Welsh Celtic Hwyl, the instinctual passion that set every sacred king to seek his union with the Goddess. At the coming of the One whom Christianity might call the "once and future sacred king," Pan does not become obsolete. As Knight points out, if he did, the planet would die! But like the instinctual half-man, half-beast of human nature, he might become "changed."

Occult philosophy is inconsistent in its treatment of Pan and his function in the scheme of things. Pan is readily identifiable with the less classical horned god, or *Cernunos,* the horned one of northwestern European tradition, but opinion varies as to his relationship with other inner beings and thus his true function. The native British tradition tends to view the horned god as the consort of the Goddess and the keeper of her creatures. The creatures referred to are generally assumed to be the animal kingdom, but other opinions place his presidency over the flora as well as the fauna of our world. The horned one is also seen as a guardian of the inner levels: those very levels that the "raising of the fire" seeks to access. But what most commentators agree upon is that Pan or the horned god is absolutely identified with the virility of the living earth. In this he becomes a convenient consort for the Planetary Being, although his relationship with the Goddess is something more complex than a straightforward "Lord and Lady" relationship.

Pan is very much the guardian and the guide to the Goddess, or at least to certain aspects and functions of the Goddess. The Goddess as the Great Cosmic Mother is an aspect of Godhead, who thus existed before all being. The Planetary Being is certainly not "the

Goddess" in this sense. When we come across Pan as her consort and keeper of her creatures, therefore, we are examining a relationship with the Planetary Being, the Goddess-inspired impulse of form in nature.

The Greeks identified the Egyptian god *Min* with Pan, probably because he was represented with an erect phallus and because Min was worshipped originally as a god of vegetation and protector of crops. Greek statuary associates Pan with the Horae goddesses, who were responsible for the seasons and the encouragement of the growth of vegetation. The fertility motif is further emphasized by Pan's love for Selene, the Moon. Pan is also depicted as a shepherd of flocks, half animal, half human, hoary, hairy, and past his best, unlike the svelte company of heavenly Mount Olympus. His name is said to mean "all," in the sense of one power of virility in all that has life in earth.

Pan's Celtic counterpart Cernunos has the same horned and creature symbolism. On the Gundestrup cauldron he is shown in a provocatively "yogic" posture holding a serpent, and his horns are each of seven tines. He is surrounded by animals, showing him as keeper of the creatures of the Goddess. These creatures are totem beasts that signify, like the seven tines, various modes of consciousness, or indeed the overall "animal" instinctual level at which human nature may initially touch all nature. This instinctual level is the same common ground upon which Taliesin first meets his goddess Ceridwen in a series of complementary animal transformations. The serpent that Cernunos is shown to hold on the Gundestrup cauldron may be thought of in terms of the serpent fire of Eastern kundalini yoga, or as dragons in the later Celtic tradition.

Tying Pan or Cernunos to theology is a difficult task. The horned god, more than almost any other pagan concept, came to be vilified and misrepresented by the medieval church. In other words, the concept of the inner fire within the good earth and its personification was intentionally demonized by a Christianity that decided that the power of Christ and the archangelic Michael had to all intents and purposes killed Pan. However, great Pan was by no means dead, but "changed," as Christian perception witnessed a changed inner fire moving through creation. Unfortunately, that change was to an unpolarized, patriarchal force that lacked the female balancing dynamic.

In pagan mythology Pan is the force that fertilizes the form of the Planetary Being. He represents the purposeful directed power (symbolized by a thunderbolt or phallus) from within the land, the force that the Planetary Being must weave into form. He is therefore very much associated with the sexuality and fertility impulse that typifies its initial reception in the human psyche. Yet the horned god is in effect his own censor. He is the key to and guardian of the power by which the Planetary Being may be aroused, and he guards his consort the Goddess from the vulgar and profane. Without the aspect of the fire that Pan represents we are unable to activate the inner processes of nature, not least our own nature, even our genetic nature. The initial raising of the fire and calling of the ancestors through the genetics of our blood is very much tied into a relationship with, and acceptance by, the guardian or horned god, Pan.

When we begin to raise the inner fire we are therefore concerned with the instinctual arousal that Pan represents. But this is only one half of the equation, the dynamic force, for as the fire is raised it must have the capacity to *form* and consolidate itself at the various levels of consciousness represented by the chakras. The two parts of the fire, the yin and yang, the dynamic and the receptive, must complement each other just as their subatomic and cellular counterparts or the red and white corpuscles in blood do. This dual aspect of energy may eventually be wedded to the archetypal thoughtforms to which the Planetary Being and her human children aspire. As we begin to raise the fire toward those archetypal patterns in order to awaken the Planetary Being in a balanced way, we also consolidate the correct balance for the physical, etheric, and astral mechanisms of our human constitution to operate safely and effectively.

UNION

We have seen that raising the inner fire is about desire, relationship, and union. We may now look again at the threefold options of union that each chakra represents. These may be thought of as:

1. Mystical union: the soul's relationship with the Creator.

2. Magical union: the relationship of human nature to all nature to facilitate magical or inner stewardship of creation.

3. The union that represents integration and transformation of individual human nature in the complete and realized self.

All of these are initiated in the raising of the inner fire, and all of them are described in varying degrees throughout the magical and mystical treatises of human metaphysics, from the much misunderstood Knowledge and Conversation of the Holy Guardian Angel to the journey of Taliesin into Annwn. None of these experiences induced by the raising of the fire takes a single exclusive track. Achieving inner union of self, of one's own nature, induces a unity with all nature. Such a unity with creation may further induce a feeling of unity with the Creator, whether that Creator appears at the door of one's heart in the guise of a male or female deity. Furthermore, it may manifest in the unity of one individual soul with another. The fire of desire must in all these instances eventually bring about that union we call love, not least the often misunderstood love of self.

PRACTICE

Some Considerations

The fire is, as we have seen, of a dual nature, and we could do worse than to express this duality in terms of gender. Tibetan Tantra does this, but can be misinterpreted as an excuse for sexual high jinks. This is not to say that sexual magnetism may not be used to great effect in magical work, but it's a question of emphasis and intention. This presumes that we have to express this in terms of polarity, and that such polarity has to be realized in some sort of masculine/feminine relationship. Such may find magical, as distinct from mystical, expression in three ways:

1. An internal relationship with the opposite gender within oneself: a polarity between one's own outer masculine and inner feminine, or vice versa.

2. A relationship with a being from Annwn, a faery Lord or Lady in polarity with the incarnate magician.

3. A magical relationship with an incarnate magician of the opposite sex, working on a priest/priestess basis.

None of these ways of working are completely separate from each other, but in all of them the contra-sexual images within each individual psyche are stimulated. The analogy in all cases is to simulate union with the God or Goddess, and thus synchronize one's own chakras to those of a being who embodies the complementary and empowering side of the universal force, the all-nature.

PRIESTS AND PRIESTESSES

In magical terms, rather than in terms of mystical union with Godhead, the most effective and profound exercise of raising the fire is between a human priest and priestess. The power of projection may be used to great effect in this, provided that both are clear that it *is* projection! This projection of stereotypical and archetypal images may be made in the journey up through the chakric levels to the extent that priest and priestess initially represent the faery Lord and Lady, the empowering beings of Annwn, to each other. They then raise the power to archetypal levels, and not only symbolize *but realize* the God or Goddess to each other, an Arianrhod and Gwydion, or an Isis and Osiris. The effects and realizations of this are profound. This was probably the way in which the archetypal Adam and Eve were intended to conduct their equal sovereignty and stewardship of the good earth, but for us fallen mortals there are pitfalls.

That which empowers magical polarity between men and women works from the etheric or instinctual level, so that sexual magnetism is being used to initiate the raising of the fire. The man and the woman are there together, physically, not only as powerful projections and almost tangible evocations of the magic, but also as flesh and blood sexually active human beings who are for a short while pretending to be gods and goddesses.

To raise the fire and elevate consciousness beyond the lower chakras under such circumstances requires practice and discipline. If the pair manage to elevate consciousness and complete this mutual raising of the fire and opening of consciousness, then the operation may be earthed in flesh and blood sexual union. Indeed, to consciously raise the fire together is to know the complete dynamics of sexual union, beside which mere physical intercourse is a pale shadow of the real exercise of human sexuality! But to anticipate this is a distraction, and even to complete the operation and earth it in physical union may, unless the priest and priestess are partners in outer life, cause problems. Even without physical consummation, the spiritual and emotional union thus forged will unite them to an extent that begs such unity in outer as well as inner life.

The saving grace of the physical consummation of the relationship, especially in the longer term, is that it obviates the risk of either or both parties becoming fixed in the superhuman projections they magically employ. Men and women who sleep and wake up together realize themselves to be fallible flesh and blood humans. If they can do this and nonetheless know that each fulfills and represents the God or Goddess, the other empowering part, one to the other, then they are truly what men and women should be to each other. If on the other hand they become locked in some unrealistic otherworldly state of single or mutual projection and, say, the priest consolidates his priestess in the projection of an Isis incarnate who can do no wrong, then not only is the relationship unhealthy, but its very un-worldliness will mean that the magic can never fully function.

THE FAERY CONSORT

This is the danger inherent in working with a discarnate faery part-ner, the danger of glamour cited by all those old-fashioned occult textbooks. Even so, this was the way, in ancient times, that it was worked in order to achieve the synchronization of levels to secure right sovereignty. The king, or later the bard, was assumed to mate with a faery being who could empower him and set the correct ar-chetypal patterns in his aura and thus, by extension, into the aura of the tribe. But this relationship must be consummated in terms of the material world, which is perhaps why Arthur and his kingdom eventually fail. Working with a faery partner is a step on the way, not the final step.

What generally happens in reality is that an inner faery relation-ship is operated by a magician who "earths" the relationship with his or her outer partner (who generally isn't a magician), and this tends in many instances to bring the magic full circle. However, if the outer relationship is not fulfilling, then unearthed backwash of inner power will tend to drive the magical partner to seek fulfill-ment elsewhere.

Mutual regard and trust is as important in working with an inner partner as it is in a flesh and blood priest/priestess relationship. This can take a good deal of time to build, but when it is built the faery partner may become all but tangible on the border of the ultra-violet wavelength on the edge of visible light, and almost tangible to the other physical senses of smell and touch. Sometimes crystals may be used to establish the synchronization in wavelengths to bring this about.

Such relationships do not normally come easily, but tend to come as the natural progression from working with the inner fire, and through that of operating in the faery realm. In other words, by the time a faery partner becomes apparent the magician is usually well-schooled in making the journey into Annwn/faery and of operating the techniques that the faery consort will empower.

WORKING ALONE

Nobody really works "alone," at least not for long. The very fact that one is raising the fire and opening up other centers of consciousness that synchronize with those of Annwn will soon mean that inner relationships are made. Intention has a lot to do with how these subsequently become elaborated. Sometimes they may not develop along lines of quasi-sexual partnership, but may nonetheless embody all the warmth and trust that such a partnership should encapsulate.

To the mystic, such alliances may be fleeting and incidental, for he or she is induced to make union with his or her angelic spark, and thus with the mind of God. This is what the "Knowledge and Conversation of the Holy Guardian Angel" is really all about. It is a "conversation" that is given rather than sought. To the Christian mystic the union will be immediate and personal, and while not overtly sexual will nonetheless have a sense of both passion and fulfillment. It is not for nothing that nuns refer to themselves in their Christian calling as brides of Christ. The same fire is in play here, the same components of the journey to union, except that the soul experiences and translates them in other terms.

Many magicians will to some extent be mystics, although few mystics are magicians. But it is impossible to raise the fire through one's chakras and know the inner side of creation without forming a relationship with the Creator. At its most profound the magical relationship between a priest and priestess may well resonate the mystical relationship of the soul with divinity: seeing the God or the Goddess in one's partner. Such an experience tends to make profound sense of the Christian Mass: "this is my body which is given for you," and, "this is my blood which is shed for you."[11] The Eucharist, rightly understood, celebrates not a memorial but a marriage.

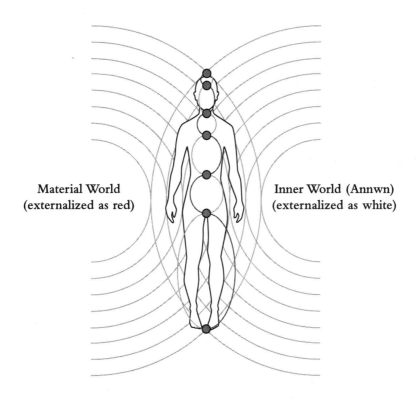

Material World
(externalized as red)

Inner World (Annwn)
(externalized as white)

The Red and the White

METHODS

Raising the Fire Alone

Stand or sit in an upright chair. It is essential that the spine is straight. As a prerequisite to the raising of the fire, it is no bad thing to:

1. Put yourself into your sacred place—a temple if you have one—and invoke the power of that place, such as the Master of your inner temple.

2. Draw a sphere or circle of light about you, and, if you wish, open the quarters in the names of appropriate inner plane beings. This depends largely upon any set purpose that you may have for raising the fire.

3. Having opened, sit quietly for a few moments contemplating what you are about to do. While you are doing this, breathe in the fourfold manner and visualize the breath moving through your body as you do so. Now see your breath winding in vaporlike swirls at the points where your chakras occur.

4. Hold out your arms sideways, bent at the elbows, so that your upturned palms are level with your chest. Be aware of a point of light, like a small silver ball, in the palm of each hand. There are practical advantages to actually holding a quartz crystal in each hand to symbolize this small ball of light. Now visualize a line of silver light extending from each palm so that the two lines of light meet at an infinite point above you. Keeping your arms and hands held out, see this triangle of light form over a pyramid over you, whose base is at chest level. When this has taken on some solidity, be aware of another pyramid, inverted and thus "base to base," with the upper pyramid going down below you, sharing its base at your heart level, with its lines extending inward and downward to meet at an apex that touches the center of the earth.

Now be aware of both pyramids around you as one construction of silver light, with its upper apex in high heaven,
its lower apex at the center of the earth, and its four shared
base points at your heart level. Then at your heart center see
the seventh point. This is the construction of sacred space, or
the cube of space, which also signifies your aura.

5. With your arms still out and palms upward, visualize a spark of
   fire high in the heavens at the upper apex of this pyramid, the
   "above" of your sacred space. See that fire ray outward and downward, running along the lines and angles of the pyramid and
   down to the earth's core. As the fire touches the earth's core, be
   aware of an "answering" in your heart center, and see and
   feel for a moment a green glow at the center of your heart.

   The concept of the descending fire as a prerequisite to raising the inner fire will be familiar to some. Whatever your
   belief system, it establishes awareness of the source from which
   both you and creation are empowered and sustained. This
   variation of using a sevenfold Cube of Space to accommodate
   the "fire from heaven" brings in some additional ideas. It
   establishes the idea of a sevenfold construct in creation and
   applies it to the portion of creation, which is you. In theological terms, it acknowledges the divine raising of the inner fire,
   which is directed inward into creation, as in the Qabalist doctrine of *Tsim Tsum* and of divinity internalizing creation
   within itself. In more practical terms, the pyramid construct is
   a powerful intermediary device for linking between inner and
   outer levels. It can represent in its seven angles the intermediary Caers of Annwn, and relate these to the personal Sacred
   Space of the aura.

6. You are now ready to raise the fire. This will differ between
   men and women because male energy tends to work outward-
   inward and female energy tends to work inward-outward. In any

case, be aware of two dragonlike convolutions of fire coming up beneath you from the earth's core. One of these will be red fire, and the other, white fire. Be aware of your breathing working in unison with the upward progress of these two dragons until they fuse at a point where your feet touch the earth. Now see them conjoin and turn in a great whorl of red fire at your feet. If you wish, you may intone a suitable note as the conjoining fires in this chakra substantiate themselves.

Now, concentrating upon this chakra, see the two streams of fire emerge from it as the two dragons separate and rise up through your feet. For women, the white dragon will rise through the right foot and the red through the left foot. For men, the white dragon will rise through the left foot and the red through the right foot. See the two streams of fire extend up and inward to conjoin at the sacral chakra. In doing this, be aware of the progress of the fire and the progression of the chakras being related to the axis of your spine.

See the sacral chakra substantiate itself in a whorl of orange fire, and, if you wish, sound the appropriate note within the rhythm of your breathing. The polarity of the fire will change in association with the colors, in effect crossing over at each chakra.

The two streams of fire continue to be drawn upward through the chakras in rhythmic breathing. At this stage do not dwell overlong on any particular chakra. Continue to raise the two streams with them conjoining, establishing, and crossing over until the crown chakra above the head is reached in a blaze of violet light. This blaze of light then explodes like a fountain over your head, and from it the colors of the rainbow cascade down and around you.

Be aware now of these colors vibrating around you in an ovoid of sparkling light, and feel each color answering to a chakra. It will take time to be able to do this exercise and reach this stage easily. When you have done so, you will be able to select the color in your externalized aura, relate it to a particular chakra, and move your consciousness into the level that that chakra and its color in your aura signify. This can also be used in a self-healing way to examine the aura, look for discrepencies, and undertake the appropriate form of self-healing. It is very important, however, at the conclusion of any work, to reabsorb your aura and draw the fire back down into the earth, then to deconstruct the pyramid and return everything progressively back to the starting point of normal consciousness.

RAISING THE FIRE WITH A PARTNER

When working alone, the polarity is internal—between the masculine and feminine within. In working with an outer or inner partner the principles are exactly the same, but the technique is adjusted to accommodate the two sets of individual consciousness involved in the operation.

The preparation of place and breathing is commenced with the partners, actual or inner, facing each other. The sexual magnetism is allowed to build. Both partners, if not already standing, come to their feet and hold out their arms as before. Each now visualizes a triangle of white light with the apex above themselves. Having established this, they hold the image and move toward each other until they are almost touching. They extend their arms forward and past each other so that the man's upturned palms are at chest level on ether side of the woman's body and her arms are likewise extended to reach to either side of his chest. As this movement is made, the apexes of the two individual triangles are seen to fuse above them and the upper pyramid is made. The lower pyramid proceeds down from this, extending to the center of the earth. When this has been completed in visualization, the fire from above is seen to activate the lines and angles of the pyramid to form one area of sacred space about the two people. This technique can also be used for mediation to the deep earth.

The fire is raised by drawing it up as before, except that now the woman draws up the white fire and the man, the red. Each, however, projects the fire that they are drawing up through the chakras of the other, again achieving the crossover at each chakra. Color and sound is used as appropriate for each chakra. The vibration of the notes helps to synchronize the "arrival" of the fire at each chakra so both partners know where they are! It is also a very powerful adjunct to the blending of the two streams of energy. When the crown chakra is reached the rainbow light is seen to cascade down around both in one aura.

The object of the exercise is *energy exchange*. As in the old sacred king formulae, the king supplies the outer contact and it is through him, emblematic of the father of his tribe, that the bounty of the Goddess manifested. She or her faery surrogate supplies the inner energy, but her own energy is supplemented by the king's dedication and desire, which was the focus of tribal belief. We must always remember that the relationship, the polarity between inner and outer, is always a two-way street. "For the inside to have meaning there must be an outside."[12]

Finally, it must be repeated that no technique for raising the inner fire is risk free. This is especially so when working with an inner or outer partner. These are the methods and rationale of dedicated practical magic, and practical magic, despite New Age optimism, is not all sweetness and light. These techniques require a great deal of meditation and contemplation of motive. Sexual or autoerotic adventure is not a legitimate motive! We have indicated the theory, practice, and pitfalls, but do not make any recommendation. Self-knowledge and discrimination are among the essential lessons of magic.

CHAPTER NINE

MERLIN AND GWENDDYDD

THE POTENCY OF POLARITY

One of the fundamental principles of all magical work is the occult law of alternating polarity, which is to say that whatever is potent, or "positive" on the outer plane will be receptive or "negative" on the inner planes. Conversely, that which is "negative" or receptive on the outer plane will be potent or "positive" on the inner planes. Common parlance recognizes this principle at work whenever there is perceived to be a "power behind the throne." The practice of alternating polarity can be found at the basis of Western Magic in the partnership of Merlin and his sister-priestess, Gwenddydd.

It comes as something of a surprise to think of Merlin as anything but a solitary magician—apart from his brief and misunderstood encounter in later life with the Nimue, the ambitious young faery who only wanted him for his magic. The image of the archmage of Britain working side by side with a priestess sits almost as uncomfortably in the imagination as does the image of Jesus and Mary Magdalene exchanging a kiss. The same censorship we have encountered many times before has been applied to the magical relationship that should properly underpin the Western Magical Tradition. Whereas Merlin is a universally known figure, his "sister" Gwenddydd (she is called Ganieda in Geoffrey of Monmouth's account of the life of Merlin)[1] is almost unknown. Yet the brief accounts available to us of their partnership are sufficient to show that their relationship was in every way equal and that the creative spark of their priesthood can still be found at the heart of the Western magic if one cares to look.

This was put very clearly, and by none other than Merlin himself, in a communication given to Colonel "Kim" Seymour and Christine Hartley (referred to as CCT), two members of Dion Fortune's Fraternity of the Inner Light in the 1930s. It is recorded in one of the excerpts from their magical diaries found in Alan Richardson's *Dancers to the Gods,* in which they had both traveled in vision to the cliffs of Tintagel to be met by Merlin, who appeared to them from out of the mists in a sudden burst of hot sunshine.

> I think Merlin used hypnotic suggestion. He gave us a clear picture of Lyonesse, before it was drowned, and said we had been brought from Atlantis to teach, and that life after life for thousands of years we should work together as priest and priestess, trained to work as a functioning pair before Atlantis was destroyed. We should rebel and fight and hate each other at times but in the end fulfill our destiny as priest and priestess—a functioning pair. He gave us a shadowy glimpse of many lives as servers of the ancient Wisdom which then lay before us. Then he told us to look back. And we saw an immense line of ancient Adepts—high priests and priestesses stretching back into the dim ages, and we now work for them as they worked in the past. . . . Merlin placed his right hand on my nape of the neck and on CCT's and drove an immense current of force through me and through her. It shook me like a leaf in the wind.[2]

From other comments in these diaries it would seem that CCT identified her part of this contact as Morgan le Fey rather than as Gwenddydd, but we should not worry about the apparent identity of any inner plane communicator; what matters is the substance of what is communicated rather than the name of the contact. The communicator here would certainly appear to be Merlin, and he makes several interesting points. In addition to the obvious reference to Atlantis, he makes the further suggestion that the islands of Lyonesse, lying between the Southwest tip of Cornwall and the Isles of Scilly, are a manifestation of that aspect of Atlantis that fed specifically into the early mysteries of the British Isles. Part of this kingdom was called Cameliard, whose king, Leodogrance, was Gwenevere's father. But what particularly draws our attention is that the line of teachers that emerges from Atlantis in the vision conjured up by Merlin is of high priests *and* priestesses, a line that is typified by Seymour and Hartley, "trained to work as a functioning pair."

POTENT IN THE OUTER

Long before he became active as a magician, the Merlin of the early Celtic bardic writings and of Geoffrey of Monmouth's account was a soldier and a statesman. He was physically active in the service of the land. His task was deeply and intimately connected with the future of Logres: with the concept of kingship and succession, of battles fought in the name of the land and its sovereign, the guardianship of the land, and of the elemental forces that play upon it. The brutality and hurt of such service was also his; he was driven mad by witnessing battles in which many of his friends were killed, and it would seem that he was responsible for the death of his sister Gwenddydd's son.

Merlins' service to the land, no less than the other priests we have seen in these pages, was inspired by and dedicated to the queenly sovereignty of the land herself as manifested in her representatives: the flower maidens of sensual beauty, the priestesses of magical power, and the earth-mothers of wisdom. The archetype of the threefold goddess is represented within the life of Merlin no less than any other avatar: his earthly mother, his wife Guendolena, and his priestess Gwenddydd. There is a fourth—the faery-woman Nimue, who appears just before his death—although, of course, the "gwen" element in their names quickly identifies Guendolena and Gwenddydd as women of the Otherworld.

So let us start with Merlin's mother, another surprise. We some-how assume that Merlin just arrived without the hindrance of the normal paraphernalia of birth—as if real magicians should be free of an earthiness that is not part of the real magic. But tradition is clear that Merlin was born of a mortal woman even though his father was not of this world, and this places him firmly in the tradition of avatars whose conception and birth are brought about by the union of a discarnate male and an incarnate female—"the sons of God and the daughters of men." The Anglo-Saxon writer Layamon describes what took place: ". . . there dwell in the sky many kind of beings, that there shall remain until domesday arrive; some they are good, and some they work evil. Therein is a race that cometh among men . . . and many a fair woman through their craft childeth anon."[3]

And what of the unnamed woman whose actions brought into birth the greatest magician in the history of the Western world? Layamon tells us that she was the daughter of the Conaan, king of Wales. When she was fifteen she dreamed often while asleep of a fair full knight arrayed in gold. She murmured softly to him in her dreams:

There is a youth comes wooing me:
O King of Kings, may he succeed!
Would be were stretched upon my breast
With his body against my skin.

Her desire brought her wish to reality, and thus was Merlin born. Unlike Hatshepsut, who made sure that the whole of Egypt knew of the union of her mother and the god Amun that resulted in her own birth, it would seem that no one, least of all Merlin, cared to acknowledge this unnamed woman. For the rest of her story there is only silence, and the quiet of the ages has smothered the cries of his birth. We wonder if she told of what she knew, watching her son grow into a golden child, a troubled youth, and a wise man, or kept her secret with bewilderment or shame as she sank into the darkness of the age. After the birth of her son she re-

tired to a nunnery, and we can only speculate on the probable reaction of those about her that made this necessary. Later writers,
reflecting contemporary opinion, confused the Otherworld "daemon" responsible for this conception with the later word "demon,"
and thus neatly inferred that the activity of devilish powers was at
the bottom of it all rather than the knowing undertaking of a
union between the worlds.

To the current generation, on easy terms with the culture of
extraterrestrials, aliens, abductions, and walk-ins, but sometimes
naive of the deeper implications, this is pretty run-of-the-mill
stuff. Much as we may celebrate or deplore the vast shift in public
consciousness that has made it commonplace, it is within this
process that the very heart and mystery of the workings of polarity
are found; an incarnate female working with a discarnate male.
The energy is so finely modified, so carefully tuned, that the product of this union of opposites initiates the process of fertilization
and brings a new life form into manifestation. Many questions are
raised. What precisely is achieved by "virgin birth"? Is the genetic
makeup, the DNA of the resulting individual, different from that
of "normal" humans? May we assume a greater knowledge of the
individual's higher purpose or destiny, enhanced abilities and powers, less of the normal restrictions imposed by physicality, and a resulting increase in ability to shapeshift? It is strange how this
process, once a closely guarded secret of ancient and former civilizations, should now be subject matter for popular entertainment.
It may be worth musing on how we appear to have lost control of
it from our end of things. What was once in Atlantean times a
carefully monitored and disciplined technique of high magic
(whatever our opinion as to its morality) is now a matter in which
we appear to play little part beyond the passive role of victims of
"alien abduction."

But the association of Merlin with genetic engineering is part of
the esoteric tradition that recalls how he brought about the union

between Ygraine and Uther Pendragon. Ygraine's name, which is derived from the Gaelic "Greine," meaning "the Sun," reveals her identity as a priestess of the Sun Temple of Atlantis, and her presence in Cornwall at this time as the wife of the Duke of Gorlois is testimony to that continuing tradition working through into the mundane world. The magical diaries of CCT and Seymour also record that they remembered their own earlier landing in a previous incarnation on Cornish shores after the destruction of Atlantis and their infiltration into the civilization they found there at the time. They came with the realization that they should rely on the fact that for a while they would not be recognized for who they really were. By use of magical art Merlin brought about a mating between the bloodline of the priesthood of Atlantis, which was represented by Ygraine, and the line of the kings of Albion in Uther Pendragon. There is every reason to believe that this was a further initiative stemming from the Temple of the Sea and the Stars to establish a new Sun Temple in Britain, although one questions how successful this attempt proved to be.

MERLIN'S WIFE

Of Merlin's wife Guendolena we know even less, although the idea of him participating in scenes of domestic bliss can seem a little incongruous. But we do him a profound disfavor by denying him—and ourselves—the worldly end of the axis of polarity. His magic worked within the world, not in spite of it. Just as the image of Merlin the magician has tended in popular imagination to degenerate into the irascible wand-waving figure that is the stuff of cartoons—flowing robes, pointy hat, and solitary—so the demise through the centuries of the woman of magic now goes almost without comment. We see it still at work in the characterization of that other great magician, Gandalf, in J. R. R. Tolkien's *The Hobbit* and *The Lord of the Rings*. Gandalf also appears to act entirely on his own, and without in any way denying the profound achievement of these wonderful tales, it has to be said that this is unfortunate. The result again is the denial of one half of the vital element of polarity. The real achievement of the magician, the avatar, the miraculous child of the virgin birth, is the bringing down of power, inspiration, and vision *into physicality*. And an essential part of this process must be the full integration of the magician (of either sex) into the physical world into which this power and inspiration is to be embedded.

Guendolena's name means "almost white" or perhaps "white ring" (*gwen* means "white"; *dolen* means "ring"), and this is the only clue as to her nature, the all-revealing "wen" that persists like an indelible dye to reveal her origin in the world of faery. Some legends accord Merlin the responsibility of building in the outer world the "white ring" of stones we call Stonehenge, but if in the end it was his priestess Gwenddydd who brought him to a full awareness of the real power of the white ring, it was his wife Guendolena who initiated him into its more sensual joys. We may liken her to Blodeuedd, the flower-bride whose marriage bed is an initiation into the pleasures and pains of earth. When Merlin went into hiding in the woods, driven mad by the violence of the battles he had fought and unable to bear the brutality of the real world any longer, it was Guendolena who sent a musician to find him and bring him back to sanity through the healing powers of music. However, the marriage does not seem to have lasted, nor did it produce issue, and Guendolena soon disappears.

Merlin tells of these things himself. In *Affalannau (Apple Trees)*, he speaks aloud of his distress to an apple tree that has witnessed his previous happiness as a young man:

> Before this madness came upon me
> I would lie beneath its boughs
> With a pale maiden, slender, willing . . .

But things are now very different:

> At daybreak the tale was told me.
> They came at dawn. They told me
> That I had angered the king,
> Three times I had angered him.
> Christ! I should have died myself
> Before the blood of my own sister's son
> Was red upon my hands![4]

MERLIN'S PRIESTESS

This brings us to the main relationship in Merlin's life: the relationship with his sister Gwenddydd, a priestess in her own right. Here we find the essence of magical work, and one that, when worked with in meditation and inner vision, proves to be of abiding inspiration, guidance, and empowerment. Here is a perfectly functioning priest and priestess partnership that exists in reality and for all time upon the inner planes, ready and waiting for those who approach in sincere enquiry. Merlin as a lover, as brother to a sister whom he dearly loves, as a priest and prophet, and as guardian of the folk-soul of Britain; and Gwenddydd, his partner in love and magic, source of inspiration, and apparently the possessor of an ancient knowledge that she brings to Merlin in the form of a ritual of initiation. Here also in the poetry are images that cut through the glamour of the magic and are not only very moving in themselves but, because they speak in the common language of humanity, convince us more than anything else that these two are "for real."

It is through the extremes of suffering and isolation that the breakdown of Merlin's personality occurs. When the moment is right, Gwenddydd returns to him and the real magic begins. Initially she enables him to move toward the fulfillment of his gift of prophecy. In the poem entitled *A Dialogue between Myrddyn and His Sister Gwenddydd*, we are shown exactly how this is done. It opens with a brief hint by Gwenddydd of her true origins, to which we shall return later.

> I have come to you from out of the North;
> I rule those lands; I bring their beauty with me.

Merlin's reply to this is poignant, and he reveals a vulnerability and sad acceptance of his state of mind:

> There have been many battles at Arfderydd and Erydon
> Gwenddydd, my sister, I am hurt
> And my senses are numb—

She makes no attempt to soothe him with soft words, to heal his madness, or to suggest that he should do anything that might bring peace of mind or ease his suffering. Neither does she comment upon the death of her son at his hands. The interaction between them here is entirely that of priest and priestess, and all worldly considerations, agonizing though these may be, are put aside. Gwenddydd comes to Merlin deliberately to act as the catalyst that will break open the "numbness" that has overcome him; to free his prophetic soul and to push him relentlessly into his true magical vocation. And so in her questioning of Merlin she is persistent to the point of relentless, refusing to be satisfied with his answers but drawing from him the fullness of his prophetic utterances. She alternately praises him:

> You are known throughout the world, my brother,
> And have fought with courage.
> You have been my partner through many Ages
> And your voice speaks the truth.

She plays upon his distress as if this were a necessary technique to keep him in the required state of mind to continue to prophesy, and driving him to continue when it appears that he is on the point of giving up before the job is finished:

> I see the tears fall upon your face,
> But I must urge you—
> Don't leave me now
> Don't return to your silence.

All the while questioning:

> I must ask you, my brother
> My fearless fighter who is known throughout the world
> Tell me of the future
> Tell me of the bold heroes—
> Tell me who, and why, and when?

Knowing that it must be so, that this is their task, their service to the higher good:

> Not I alone but all people
> Seek guidance from your words.

Until finally Merlin reaches the end:

> I have told you all, Gwenddydd
> Queen to many Lords,
> It will be as I have told you
> And this is now my prophecy!
> The line of Kings must end!

They part with an acknowledgment of the high powers that they serve, and of the resting place that befits them both and to which they will eventually return:

> While I live I will not leave you
> Our hearts and minds are one
> Until we reach the castle of eternity,
> The castle at the roof of the sky,
> May God protect my Gwenddydd!

> My dearest one! We know that we will part.
> When the battles are ended
> And you are laid to rest within the Earth,
> Kings will mourn your passing.
> But for now, awaken from your dreams,
> Turn the pages of the book called Inspiration
> And be free from your sorrows.[5]

We will do well to give the description "sister" or "twin sister" a wider interpretation than the merely familial, and not assume that there had been a double virgin birth. There was, after all, even then no other word to describe a female partner in magic. The identification of them as twins puts them firmly within the age-old magical tradition—that of twin souls, of two facets of a single spark of life, incarnating together down the planes and down the centuries in dedication to the work and of service in partnership. We may look to the first and foremost example of this relationship in Isis and Osiris, brother and sister and lovers: the perfect pattern for a priest and priestess partnership and one that laid down the pattern for all those who follow their path. In this tradition the word sister is simply a convenient peg on which to hang the many facets of a relationship that is functioning fully on all levels: physical, emotional, mental, and spiritual.

GWENDDYDD, MAGICIAN OF BRITAIN

As to where Gwenddydd comes from, we have only her own description to go on:

> I have come to you from out of the North;
> I rule those lands; I know their beauty.

This tells us that she has held a position of authority in the north, and history records this as having been in the court of Rhydderch, to whom she was married. But she also knows of the beauty of all places, and "north" may be interpreted as something more than a region in Britain. In this sense it is more usefully located in the description of the lands of Hyperborea, the land at the back of the north wind. Greek legend records that Apollo visited this land once every nineteen years, and their implied location lies beyond the veil of reality, within another dimension that corresponds to the inner earth. In fact, passing through the veil of Boreas that blows from the cold darkness of the northern skies would appear to provide entrance to the otherworld of faery. Irish legend records something very similar in the stories of the early, perhaps prehuman invasions of Ireland, and it is described how the Nemedians, one of the first groups of settlers, were driven from the land by the next wave of invaders. A few of them returned to Greece, but most of them fled "to the north." Much later this latter group returned to Ireland, where they were now called the Tuatha de Danaan, the faery race of the children of the great goddess Danu.

Further dynamics of the magical relationship between Merlin and Gwenddydd are seen again in a later work, "The Story of Myrddin Wyllt," from the sixteenth-century *Chronicle of Elis Grffudd*. Again we see Merlin at the height of his madness:

> . . . so unstable in mind and senses that he would not live within dwelling houses . . . but in caves in the rocks and in arbours of his own work in the glens and woods on either side of the river Conway. To these parts and places Gwenddydd his sister would come . . .[6]

In this story Gwenddydd has a series of dreams that she brings to Merlin in order that he might interpret them for her. But before this can take place there appears in the narrative a curious sequence in which she brings him food—wheaten bread—and no less than five different drinks, each drink in a different vessel. We could assume that her brother had developed such wayward tastes in the midst of his affliction that she was obliged to toil up the hill to his cave laden with a hamper full of rattling bottles and jugs, but there is more here than meets the eye. In fact, here in a veiled and condensed form is no less than an exposition of the several strands that together form the Western Magical Tradition.

Gwenddydd brings him ". . . various drinks in various vessels, *every drink in its grade* as nature demanded, as wine in silver, and mead in a horn, and the beer in sycamore, and the milk in a white jug, and the water in an earthen jug. All these she placed in order besides the bread and butter . . ."

THE INITIATION OF MERLIN

". . . Gwenddydd revealed herself to her brother, to whom she showed the drinks in order, as she had placed them in order." It was probably on this occasion that Gwenddydd first "revealed" her true appearance or her full powers as a priestess to Merlin. Certainly in this story she is in charge, she is the initiatrix, and she is shown to have knowledge of the many traditions that inform the Western mysteries.

The sequence of events that follows would appear to be none other than a ceremony of initiation for Merlin in which Gwenddydd as priestess presents him with the symbols of the various traditions of magical wisdom. He ritually sips from the different vessels, each of which contains the essence of a magical tradition. The presentation in the heightened atmosphere provided by Merlin's extreme emotional state (and perhaps also by his deliberate fasting) serves as a trigger to release past lives and experiences, past initiations and achievements. This process is part of all magical initiations, although in this instance Gwenddydd is the catalyst for bringing to his waking consciousness the memory of past lives and work. We saw something very similar in the "Hanes Taliesin," where the poet Taliesin recalls in turn each of his previous incarnatory experiences and gathers together into his current lifetime the wisdom gained in each former incarnation.

There are five vessels because five is the number that signifies the tasks and trials of humankind upon the planet earth. Each is made of a different material and, it is emphasized, presented to him in a certain significant order: silver, horn, wood, china, and earthenware. The symbolic vessels of these five "grades" or levels of magic are inclusive of color, material origin, the plant and animal kingdoms, and the planetary or stellar correspondence, and by drinking of their substance or rejecting them, Merlin indicates his own relationship with what they represent.

The following text displays the significance of order of the vessels and their composition and contents. These are only suggestions, and it is through individual meditation that further realizations and connections will be made.

Vessel: silver, horn, sycamore, china, earthenware.

Color: bright/shining, yellow, multicolored, white, brown.

Planetary Correspondence: Moon, Sun, Venus, Stars, Earth.

Liquid: wine, mead, beer, milk, water.

Origin: fruit of the trees, bees, grain, cows, from God.

Properties: wealth/poverty, sickness/health, sense/madness, strength/energy, to benefit humankind.

As in the book *A Dialogue between Myrddyn and His Sister Gwenddydd,* which uses a similar technique of question and answer, the significance of what lies behind each drink and each vessel is brought out in a series of questions and replies between the two magicians, a traditional procedure that is undertaken in order to bring to full consciousness the meaning that lies behind a symbol. In the first three instances—wine, mead, and beer—Merlin reveals that he knows the symbolic meaning of these substances, that he has experienced and understood them. In other words, he has already passed the particular initiation symbolized by the liquid and its containing vessel.

He equates wine in the silver Moon-vessel with spiritual poverty: it makes those who drink it "poor from being rich." He is acknowledging the nature of that which appears attractive, but which seduces and misleads into loss of contact with the earth and resultant impoverishment. The "test" here is the initiation of the Moon, that of discernment between false magic and glamour, as symbolized by the false light of the Moon and the true path of spiritual enrichment that is rooted firmly in the earth. In Qabalist terms, this is Yesod.

He knows that mead, made from the six-sided golden honeycomb, symbol of the Sun, is health-giving only up to a point. The test here is that of the initiation of the Sun, or Tipahareth. In any occult work the Sun is the center of being, the center of the individual's energy at the Solar Plexus, and the central point of our planetary system. Many of the mysteries of the Sun were lost in the fall of the Atlantean Sun Temple and still await rediscovery.

Thirdly, beer is presented to Merlin in a vessel of Sycamore, a tree traditionally associated with the mysteries of the Goddess. Whatever his previous incarnatory experiences, it would seem that much of his current incarnation is concerned with his relationship with the Goddess as mediated by his mother, his wife, and his priestess. The sycamore bowl represents the mysteries of the goddess Hathor, among whose many titles was "Lady of the Southern Sycamore." But this is the initiation of Geburah, and within the sycamore bowl is beer, also the drink of Hathor in her aspect of the destroyer. The reference is to the legend in which Ra, Hathor's father, the god of the Sun, decides to destroy humankind and asks his daughter to do this for him. She carries out his instructions so efficiently that he begins to change his mind, but has to find a way of stopping her without himself incurring her wrath. When the seasonal festival of beer-making is underway, Ra arranges for the beer to be mixed with red ochre so that it resembles blood. Hathor, thirsty for blood, drinks her fill and falls into a drunken stupor. Humankind lives to see another day, and beer is thereafter drunk at all Hathor's rituals and feasts.

There is a change in the nature of the question and answer sequence at this point because, having recognized the inner qualities of the first three vessels, he neither rejects nor takes the fourth drink, but accepts the fifth.

The fourth drink is milk, contained within a white vessel, and is the symbol of the stars, and of stellar magic. While his words describe the exoteric properties of milk: "this is natural to nurture the weak and to help the Feyble and to strengthen the wretched and increase energy for the strong," in esoteric terms this symbolizes the movement from solar magic to stellar magic. We may call to mind the many goddesses who nurture the questing spirit and soul of mankind with the milk of the stars: Isis, Nut, and Hathor in the Egyptian pantheon, and the Celtic Brigid, Mary of the Gael, foster mother of Christ in Avalon. Merlin neither accepts nor rejects this drink, merely acknowledges it as good, so we are told by this that this initiation is open to him, and indeed we see that later in his life this is precisely the path he takes.

The final vessel is made of earthenware and it contains water. This time it is Gwenddydd, not Merlin, who describes the inner nature and significance of the drink. It is one of the four elements and is sent from heaven by God for the benefit of mankind. It is pure, clear, unadulterated with any other substance, and indicative of the purest spiritual power of the highest source. It is also, of course, indicative of the future age of Aquarius (the water carrier) and the next turning of the cycle of the Sun. Merlin drinks his fill of the water and, when he has done so, is enabled to interpret Gwenddydd's five dreams, each of which are concerned with the inner destiny of Britain.

Of all the alternatives offered to Merlin, paradoxically it is water in its earthenware container that would appear to represent the highest level of initiation. Yet whatever Merlin's former incarnations might have been, his present work on earth is intimately connected with the elements of earth and water. It is Merlin's humanity, his struggles with the very human emotions of anger, grief, jealousy, and sexual drive that are his concern, and he is also concerned with how these emotions might be used to empower his wisdom.

When Merlin has moved beyond the expression of physical sexuality, which is symbolized by the death of his wife, Guendoluena, his relationship with his sister-priestess becomes fully developed. He returns to the woods, accompanied by his Gwenddydd, this time in a balanced state of mind.

PRIESTESS OF THE STARS AND STONES

He asks Gwenddydd to build him a house in the woods with ser-vants to care for his needs. He also asks her to build him another building, remote from the first, "with seventy doors and as many windows through which I may watch fire-breathing Phoebus and Venus and the stars gliding from the heavens by night, all of whom shall show me what is going to happen to the people of the king-dom. And let the same number of scribes be at hand, trained to take my dictation."[7]

We should not take this too literally. The idea of Gwenddydd acting as Merlin's benefactor may confirm what we already know of her as the wife of a king and therefore able to put up the money to build him a home, but that she should become the foreman for the construction of an elaborate bricks-and-mortar and plate-glass ob-servatory does not ring true, and also seems a little anachronistic for the sixth century. The specification for this building of seventy doors and windows must be read metaphorically, for its position within a wood does not provide the ideal site for sky watching! In fact, Merlin was not an astrologer but a magician. He was not a cat-aloger of stellar bodies but a mediator of their energies.

The real observatory, the house in which the stars could be ex-plored, was the body and mind of Merlin's priestess, Gwenddydd. She was the form that housed the way of access to the stars. It was she who had drunk of the fourth cup, the milk, the starry seed of the Milky Way, the bridge to infinite space and the wisdom of the stars, and it is the body and mind of the priestess that holds this matrix. She brings down the patterns of the higher realities and holds them upon the astral planes, within reach of the exploring mind of the priest, who then fires them into action and new real-ity. And so we find that Merlin and Gwenddydd are in fact using the very same magical techniques that we describe in the follow-ing chapter, even though the ritual that the next chapter contains uses the godforms and language of Egyptian magic. Gwenddydd and Merlin are well-versed in many magical systems, and when we look more closely at how they work together as priest and priestess we find many similarities to the ideals and methods of Egyptian magic.

THE TEMPLE OF MERLIN AND GWENDDYDD

The descriptions we have in the early poetry and prose are brief, but there is sufficient detail to enable us to rebuild the temple of Merlin and Gwenddydd. It had "Seventy doors and seventy windows." Seven is the number that provides a basis for every aspect and working-through of the destiny of humankind, from the seven stars of The Great Bear to the seven days of the week. Ten is the number of perfection and completion, and so we have here a temple dedicated to the Great Work, the completion of the journey of humankind.

As is the case with any magical temple, it exists for the main part on the astral plane, built largely through the imagination and ritual action of those who work within it. However, it is keyed into the physical plane by use of certain physical structures, and we may look to various sources, including Geoffrey of Monmouth's work, to build up a picture of the temple and of the magical dynamics that empowered it. Rather than the pyramid or the rectangular temple structures of Egypt, the early temples of Britain were circular stone constructions, of which many hundred still exist. Geoffrey of Monmouth makes a clear association between Merlin and Stonehenge, describing how Ambrosius Aurelianus, king of Britain, sent for Merlin when he needed some advice on the construction of a building worthy of the memory of all those who had been killed in battle in the defense of the land. Wace and Layamon[8] describe how Merlin harnessed unseen forces so that the stones that he considered to be suitable for the job were moved without any physical effort to their present location on Salisbury Plain. The stone circle remains one of the most powerful temples of the land, whether in a physical sense or whether reconstructed in the imagination.

Many more were probably constructed from wood. The circle of Woodhenge once existed close to its stone counterpart, and we find a description of the nature of such a structure given in *The Life of Merlin,* where Merlin, in his first bout of madness, ponders how a grove of nineteen apple trees has disappeared in an inexplicable fashion.

> Here once stood nineteen apple trees bearing apples every year; now they are not standing. Who has taken them away from me? Whither have they gone all of a sudden? Now I see them—now I do not! Thus the fates fight against me and for me, since they both permit and forbid me to see.[9]

The curiously intermittent nature of their manifestation, moving between the physical and astral levels according to how well Merlin's inner vision was functioning or according to cycles of the planets, reveals that there is more to this group of apple trees than a small orchard. Nineteen, a number often found in the number of stones in a stone circle, is the number of years that elapse between each coming together of the cycles of the Sun and the Moon, and this brings us back to the land of Hyperborea. Legend tells that Apollo visited a round temple in Hyperborea once every nineteen years.

There are other connections to be found here with the magic of Merlin and Gwenddydd (and, by inference, with all Bronze Age magical practice) and their Egyptian counterparts. The ancient Egyptians of the early pharaonic period used, alongside several other calendrical systems, the comparatively short cycle of nineteen years. This was because the star Sirius, which was so central to their beliefs, coincided once every nineteen years in its heliacal rising with the New Moon. The heliacal rising of Sirius was of paramount importance in the Egyptian calendar, as it marked the beginning of the new year that corresponded with the flooding of the Nile and the resultant fertilization of the Nile valley. It was immediately preceded by the rising of Orion, the risen, stellar body of Osiris.

In fact, the mention of the "seventy" doors and windows can also be said to be more Egyptian than Bronze Age or Celtic. It is not a number that appears in Celtic mythology, but it does appear in other early civilizations, notably that of ancient Egypt. Seventy days is the period in which Sirius disappeared from the night sky. During these seventy days the star was considered to be in the Duat, that region of the sky that approximated to Annwn and the region in which the initiatory experience of death and rebirth took place. It was here that Osiris, having passed as the sacrificial king through the trials of the Duat, rose as Orion to take his place in the stars. Seventy days was the period strictly adhered to throughout Egyptian history for the period in which the mummification of the human body took place in observance of the soul's passage through the trials of the Duat.

The number ten also held significance for the Egyptians. Each of the gods who were particularly associated with the heavenly bodies had a ten day period or "week" ascribed to them. Perhaps more importantly, it was customary during some periods to paint the interior of temples, tombs, and coffin lids with checkerboards that served as star clocks. These were illustrated with the decans, the stars whose risings or transits marked the hours of the night. Each of the decans shifts up and to the left on the checkerboard grid after each ten day interval, thus forming a diagonal line across the squares. The stars that qualified for use as decans were all those which, like Sirius, disappeared from the night sky for seventy days.

So we find that Merlin and Gwenddydd are together working a system of magic that operates, as does all high magic, at every level. The external structure of their temple may be visualized as a ring of granite stones, or perhaps a grove of nineteen trees. We may also visualize a processional way that winds up through a wooded hill to the temple, something like the Bronze Age stone rows on Dartmoor or the serpentine rows that lead to the circles at Avebury. The processional way contains seventy pairs of stones that, as one passes through them, evoke a gradual transformation of consciousness from the everyday world to the place between the worlds. At the far end of the way there lies a circle of nineteen stations. At the center of this circle lies a cistvaen, a covered rectangular grave.

This circle is where Merlin and Gwenddydd meet to perform their magic, alone within the forest, unaccompanied by the grandeur of ceremony or the chanting of liturgy or the wafting of incense. Their magic is the purest magic of polarity and relies on no techniques or ritual panoply save only that of a man and a woman who have come together to work their magic for many lifetimes—"life after life for thousands of years working together as priest and priestess." And so their magic is the naked power of the bright stars embedded in the hard cold granite; where sharp-bladed grass cuts through bare-soled feet and the door to Annwn lies open. The circle is the combination of the orbits of the Sun and the Moon, a pattern of intertwined energies that weave their two lights, silver and gold, into a twisted rope of containment. Within the circle Merlin and Gwenddydd lose their outward clothing of humanity, and their bodies take on the patterns of the stars. Here they raise the fire of heart's desire. The body of the priestess becomes the fivefold star of Venus, on whom seven swirling clusters of light can be seen, seven windows to the stars. Here, Merlin comes to her, his staff plunged deep into the body of the living earth, its tip drawn into the loving enclosure of Venus. Together they mount the spiral steps within the white tower that leads upward to the Milky Way.

THE WHITE TOWER: A RITUAL OF
MERLIN AND GWENDDYDD

The couple performing this ritual should meet together in a suitably prepared place. It is suggested that you sit at opposite sides of a circle, preferably at east and west, and spend a few moments in silence before you begin. It is helpful to the process of making contact with Merlin and Gwenddydd if you each then describe them to each other. For instance, the woman would describe Merlin as if he were standing behind the man, and vice versa. Take your time doing this; allow the images to build up, as they surely will.

The circle of nineteen stones could be marked with chalk, or with crystals. You may also mark the quarters of the circle with a pair of candles to form a "gate." You may wish to collect physical representations of the five cups and five liquids to have them present in the ritual, although it is not necessary for Gwenddydd actually to present them to Merlin to drink from. The preparatory act of collecting them performs a powerful talismanic function and not only helps to focus your mind on what you are doing, but is likely to throw up some interesting signs and events. However, in the ritual itself it is just as effective for this to be done purely in the imagination. The ritual can be performed indoors or outdoors; it is a matter of weighing the very real advantages of a natural setting with the disadvantages of interruptions, gnats, weather, and so on.

The Ritual

Gwenddydd and Merlin: *[Together light a candle at the center of the place of working, saying]:* The one true light of the Universe.

Gwenddydd: I, Gwenddydd, priestess of the stars and the stones, will build you, Merlin my brother, an observatory, a white tower in the heart of the forest, in which your soul can rise upward on the steps of the spiral stair within to touch the very stars.

[Walk clockwise about the magical circle three times, saying]:

Come with me through the deep silence of the forest, rising upward upon the white path at our feet until we reach upon the summit of a hill and a clearing in the trees, which opens to the clear night air under the starlit vault of heaven.

And I shall tread barefoot upon the soft green grass and trace in the cold dew the encircling girdle of the heavens, the ring of cosmic space. And I shall bring down to rest within it the powers of the Moon and the Sun, and form about us a circle of nineteen standing stones of white granite, the circle of the great year.

[Light the candles at the quarters on this third circumambulation.]

And within myself I summon up the star-fire, and shall empower the stones with star-fire and they shall empower me also. And so here is created an earthly temple of Caer Sidi, the city of the stars.

In the north the Mother, midwife to those who pass through the borders of the circle from life to death, from death to life.

In the east, Merlin.

In the south the flower-bride, Guendolena, wife to Merlin.

In the west, Gwenddydd, sister in magic to Merlin.

Merlin: My sister and lover, let us meet within the circle of stones you have created, mindful of the calling of the stars above and of the answer of the stars within the earth beneath our feet, and of the meeting of their fires within us. We see at the center of the circle a cist, a cauldron of stones, entrance to the inner earth. The capstone has been lifted and placed to one side, and as we watch we see a column of white fire that pours upward from deep beneath the open cist. It pushes high into the air, then slowly begins to turn about itself, and as it turns it begins to form a stairway within itself, a double spiral, slowly spinning, moving both upward and downward simultaneously. We walk into the center of the circle and step together into the turning white fire, which engulfs us, streaming through every cell of our bodies. We become aware that we are slowly sinking downward, and emerge to find ourselves standing on the warm red earth of the floor of a chamber that lies deep within the ground below the circle. At the center of the chamber, beneath the entrance to the world above, is a fire. About the fire, inscribed upon the floor, is a pentagram. At each point of the pentagram is a vessel, a cup, each different in shape and color, each containing a different liquid.

Gwenddydd: And we see that others are with us and stand to the north and the south. In the north, a woman of ancient knowledge and wisdom, the Mother. In the south, a young woman crowned with flowers, the bride. And I bring you five choices, five cups from which you may drink, and I ask their help in this.

Merlin my brother, I bring to you a sycamore cup of beer. Feel the rim of the wood touching your lips, warm, releasing a soft fragrance of sap and resin. For this is the drink of the Goddess, the intoxicating liquor of the rites and mysteries of love. The pleasures of the Lady of Venus are here, made yours for the taking, of she who stands before you now and beckons you to drown your sorrows and weariness in the bubbling depths of the rich malted barley, to fall with her in the tumbling, rolling foam of the ocean waves. Drink if you will.

And I bring to you a silver cup of wine. Look down upon the surface of the liquid and discover it to be a dark sea, rich and blood red, with an odor of ripe fermenting grapes and the bursting bruised juices of the purple vine. For here within this cup is both passion and sorrow intermingled, here is the blood-red rose that blooms to fullness in the fierce heat of the Mediterranean Sun, and here is the burning fire of the love of Mary Magdalene for Christ. Drink if you will, but only drink if you will drink deep to the very end.

Merlin: Gwenddydd my sister, I bring to you a cup of horn that contains golden honey mead. And you find that a light shines upwards from within the very heart of the vessel and illumines your face with a blessed warmth and radiance. For within its depths is contained the essence of paradisal beauty and innocence, the golden light of Eden. Enclosed within this vessel is retained the memory of the first light of dawn upon the earth, when men and women, animals, birds, and the people of the first time, which are called the faery race, lived together in unquestioning harmony. Here is bliss, here is the perfection that once was yours. Here you may for a moment taste its sweetness upon your tongue, if you will have it so.

Gwenddydd: Merlin, my beloved twin, I bring you a white jug containing milk. And I stand before you and dip my hand to scoop up its whiteness. Look into my palm and see that within it is contained a white swirling luminescence, neither solid, nor liquid, but pure moving light. Within my hand you are witness to a vision of the birth of stars. Tiny spheres of solid light rise from below and break the surface like pearls, iridescent, pale. If you wish, you may open your lips and receive the three drops of starlight that fall slowly, individually, upon your tongue.

Merlin: Gwenddydd, my priestess of many lives, I bring before you an earthenware pitcher of water, clear, pure flowing, spiritual sustenance of all life. And this also is a symbol of the planet earth, for whom we live and work and have our being.

Gwenddydd: Let us together rise to the stars in service of this land, for this is our sacred task and our delight. Let me become for you a white tower, an observatory to the stars, with seven levels and seven times ten windows within its walls wherein your soul can rise up to the highest spaces of the stars. And as I build the tower I also will rise up and become at one with the white tower, and bring down within it the substance of the stars so that their courses run through my veins, their substance becomes the substance of my bones, their swirling energies come to rest within my body and the stars became my song.

Merlin: And so Merlin came to stand at the gate of the city of the stars and he entered within the white tower that she had formed for him. And he soared upward upon the seven levels of the stair of her making and reached the innermost height. And thus were the heavens freely made open to him and his hair was drenched with the dew of the stars of the night, and the confining bounds of earth dissolved. He became a strider through the stars and followed in the steps of Gwydion and Idris, and stood at the foot of the milk-white bridge and with his desire formed it anew. And he walked across it, and the borders of time and space melted into the bliss that is beyond all knowing, and he saw, and knew, and understood.

Gwenddydd: And Gwenddydd became a hand-maiden of Arian-rhod the weaver, and entered into her castle of the stars, and with the fingers of her mind she took some threads from the bridge of light that he had made and turned them in her hands and spun them out into a web upon the wheel of the year. And she wove them round the spindle of her limbs and saw how the the glorious Sun moved back and forth through the web of starlight, a golden shuttle, the boat of a million years that ordered and blessed this creation. And when it was completed she reached down from the castle in the stars and placed her tapestry of light upon the earth with love, a net of stars within the circle of the stones. And upon each knot, each joining of the threads, she set a pearl of star-dew, perfect miniature of inspiration and delight, a pearl of memory, of evermore.

Merlin: And he reached out and thrust the base of his staff through the center of her web of light and down to the very heart of earth where it was held fast, the axis, the back-bone, the earthly pole that held the planet to her proper motion. The tip of his staff rose upward to the pole star itself and became joined with the fixed point above, around which moved the slow perpetual dance of the imperishable stars. And held between them in perpetual flow and interchange from earth to heaven, heaven to earth, was Awen, inspiration.

Merlin: The power of the serpent to you.

Gwenddydd: The sight of the eagle to you.

Merlin: The strength of the swan to you.

Gwenddydd: Speak with the voice of the raven.

Merlin: Speak with the voice of honey.

Gwenddydd: Speak the words of the stars.

Merlin: May God bless you and those who are with you.

Gwenddydd: May you find the peace of eternal life.

Merlin: May we find the peace of eternal life.

Gwenddydd: Let us remain touched by the inspiration of Awen. And so let us allow these visions to fade, and let us find ourselves again within the circle of stones, the woven web of light about our feet. And now we are aware of our feet upon the ground in this earthly temple. Our work is completed.

[Extinguish candles and exit the room.]

CHAPTER TEN

PRACTICAL POLARITY MAGIC

The Egyptian mythology, like most mythology properly understood, lends itself to polarity magic. In this instance we mean magic that receives its impetus from the sexual dynamics between a priest and priestess. We have already addressed the distinction that the mysteries make between vertical and (bad jokes notwithstanding) horizontal polarity. The truth is that with real understanding the one will reflect the other. The mystical union known in that most ultimate expression of vertical polarity should be reflected in the earthly (and earthy) relationship between a man and a woman, and the horizontal polarity between a man and a woman should ultimately reflect the mystical marriage of heaven and earth.

In this latter context, the priest/priestess relationship may evoke some very obvious problems, not the least of which is the adoption of rituals like the one presented later in this chapter. While we hesitate to adopt an agony aunt role in this, these are matters that need to be raised and addressed.

THE PRIEST/PRIESTESS RELATIONSHIP: SOME SERIOUS CONSIDERATIONS

Responsible magical fraternities have an almost insoluble problem with polarity magic. More often than not they find themselves approached for instruction by married or partnered people, but rarely by couples. The opening up of inner faculties and the intense urge to accelerate and apply that opening up is sadly on a "percentage of population" basis, a very rare thing. It is also a very individual and personal thing, which is generally most strongly felt in one's thirties or forties. By this time the adventures of settling into adult life and finding one's place in the outer world have passed, and most people are partnered and settled in family life. However, any consequent urge to develop an inner life is rarely experienced by both members of a partnership and, rarer still, in the same way or at the same time. An inner life is a very individual matter, even for individuals who are mated to each other. Magic and mysticism can of themselves set secrets and distances within marriages, with the inner life of one partner becoming as threatening as any extra marital liaison to the other.

That threat may become a very real one if a partner is conducting polarity magic with somebody else and undergoing all the sexual and emotional pressures that the magic evokes. This is but one reason why polarity magic is not a magical procedure to be, as the marriage service suggests, taken "lightly or wantonly." But one is faced with a paradox, for neither may it be entered into "cold bloodedly"; without the potency of both passion and tender affection, the psychological and sensual charge that gives the magic its impetus is lost.

There is no way around this, for the priest/priestess relationship demands it, and the working through of mythology demands at some juncture the expression of the god/goddess relationship through a human priest and priestess. In the archetypal situation of "how things should be," that relationship should result in and be expressed through marriage. Unfortunately, we have inherited our cultural and social conditioning and practices from two thousand years of patriarchal and celibate theology, which views libido as a spiritual inadequacy. Whatever the protestations of modern clerics, the biblical faith upon which marriage is still consciously or unconsciously based is simply a reluctant licensing of sexuality to allow for the procreation of children and the socioeconomic cohesion of the herd. Even in unmarried partnerships the force of this conditioning still persists. Such a grudging attitude to love and desire hardly encourages men and women to see their partnership as an anointing and ordination to their natural priesthood, or its consummation as a sacrament.

This cynical treatment of human love and sexuality, of marriage being a "near miss" with temptation and sin, is at absolute odds with the precepts of the mysteries. In these mysteries the divine power of love touches humankind and is expressed through the human power of life. If we choose to erase the sexual polarity content of the mysteries and the mythology that underpins them, we try to make bricks without straw. The archetypal stories of gods and goddesses and their reflection in human heroes and maidens remind us that nature designed men and women to work the magic of love. The working of the magic is as much a part of our creative mandate as the outer procreation of children, for the sexual dynamics employed evoke the same creative principle. That principle applies the power of love to the conception, birth, and externalization of intangible inner potential into tangible outer life. Children may be the result of such a union, but so may be the realization of another sort of parenthood: the priestly parenting of the principles of heaven in earth. In the mechanics of inner creation, emotional energy is a valuable commodity to nature, and its conscious and committed focus serves both her outer and inner purpose. Consequently, desire as a stepping stone to and from true love serves the marriage of heaven and earth more than we can know.

If you choose to embark upon this specialized and much misunderstood area of magical work, you will find that it imposes conditions that are not apparent in either group or individual esoteric work. The first thing that has to be learned is that "two must work as one" in a synchronization of your inner objectives—which is much easier said than done! But this is more than just a magical partnership, it is the partnership of a man and a woman who in a very real sense may become "mated in magic." In addition to the all too real strains of general magical cooperation, this will place considerable emotional strain upon priest and priestess, and on any relationships that they may have with others in outer life. Even with the whisperings of sages about such "pitfalls of polarity magic" hissing in your ears, you may come to realize that such pitfalls are pretty much unavoidable in our present culture if you are committed to this work. The irony of this is that you work in the belief that such work may one day change that culture! In the meantime the magic must start from a basis of mutual attraction, respect, and affection, and inevitably attraction will soon become "wanting." Whether "wanting" should or should not end up as "having" is something that will tax your subsequent deliberations.

Both magic and sex, exercised in appropriate motive and context, can of themselves be wholesome spiritual experiences in earth (and earthiness) without parallel. Exercised together, however, they have ramifications that go beyond the usual considerations. Like the components of gunpowder, each has a potential volatility when separate, but mixed together they are explosive. But it is these greater ramifications, this explosive power that, like esoteric rocket fuel, makes polarity magic such an essential magical and spiritual activity. Those who anticipate problems or who have been burned by that explosive substance naturally shy away in horror. This horror has fuelled the aberration that sex has no place in spirituality. In fact, the opposite is true, even if the risks are very real. But then all spirituality is a risky business!

While the outer hazards of polarity magic are clear enough for partnered people, there are inner hazards that apply to anybody, whether partnered or single. Anybody who thinks that polarity working or "sex magic" holds out a license to simply exercise sexual excitement or gratification through a magical agenda should think again. What should be contemplated is a magical pairing that potentially transcends most marriages, and if like marriage it is approached merely as a sexual or social convenience, it will end in disaster. The forces evoked in a priest/priestess relationship are those at the very core of all spirituality and all nature. Playing with such forces only to serve selfish ends will attract the retribution it deserves. If two magicians therefore only want an excuse to sleep together, this is not the arena in which to find that excuse. They would do better to forget the magic and simply have an affair.

What we are dealing with are two things. The first, the attraction, is one (but by no means the only) ingredient for the work. The second is the *motive* for the work. As in all magic, motive is paramount. The "morality" of a priest/priestess relationship may therefore appear to crash from the ground fire of religious or social codes, but these are nothing compared to the yardstick by which that relationship must judge itself. In the outer world, a circumstantially adulterous relationship may be founded upon true love, while a nominally "faithful" relationship may be woven from selfishness, tyranny, or cruelty. Human legislation, as we have seen, is a cumbersome device with which to address such matters. We do however have those less tangible tools of conscience and motive: that sense of "rightness" that was called Maat in Egypt and Tsdeq in Canaan. This is the yardstick that should be sought and seriously contemplated.

The fact remains, though, that by the time they are ready to do this work, most magicians are mated in the outer world, and rarely to other magicians. Even if they are partnered or married to somebody else who does magic, it may well be that their magical interests do not coincide appropriately for this work. This means that we are immediately faced with what initiation oaths call "the just dues of others" and the true exercise of conscience will find no easy answers for this.

A number of excuses are easily found. The first one is that as long as the magic doesn't involve physical sexual liaison, all is well. The second says that if physical sex takes place it's permissible as long as it is only in a magical context. The third excuse is that as long as nobody gets hurt that's fine too. The fourth excuse says that the great work of magic transcends the trivial laws to which lesser humans are subject. Most excuses are "lies breathed through logic," so let us examine them.

In the first place, the emotional bond forged between a priest and priestess can be so strong that the step over that fabled red line of physical sex is almost incidental. In the second instance, magic can't be clinically separated from real life. If it is, then it isn't real magic. The whole object of magic, especially in the redemption of archetypes, is that it has to be "lived." The third scenario is one of people not getting hurt by not finding out; but sooner or later they are bound to. Of all the laws that govern human existence, two crop up with awful inevitability. The first is that every man ends up with a drawer full of odd socks, and the second is that there is no such thing as a secret affair—at least not for long. The fourth excuse actually does have validity (if not in the way imagined), although to adopt this as an easy credo is to dance on quicksand . . . and invariably on those "just dues of others."

These are the types of considerations that anybody contemplating a priest/priestess relationship will have to face up to if one or both are partnered to others in outer life. If things go wrong, a lot of people can get hurt badly: promises become broken, "lies breathed through silver" become merely lies, marriages collapse, and children suffer—and all these things negate the spiritual premise upon which such operations are founded.

Even so, polarity magic involving such relationships is more common than imagined, even in groups that might officially deny them. In this we are speaking of legitimate white magical groups, not the doubtful lodges who practice promiscuity as "sex magick" without regard for consequences. If we look at groups that in some instances work a priest/priestess system honestly and honorably, we must look to some Wiccan covens.

In that some Wiccan ceremonies involve actual sexual relations ("the Great Rite") between the high priestess of a coven and her priest, it is interesting to hear what Janet Farrar and the late Stewart Farrar, both experienced and eminently sensible witches, have to say in their book *The Witches' Way*. They make a distinction between what they call "gender magic," which utilizes men and women as "opposites" in rites (such as ballroom dancing does, for example), and "sex magic." Sex magic for them is magic that incorporates actual sexual intercourse.

They comment as follows:

> . . . we would say categorically: sex magic as such should only be worked by a couple for whom intercourse is a normal part of their relationship—in other words husband and wife or established lovers and in complete privacy.

They go on to say:

> . . . if they approached it cold bloodedly as a "necessary magical operation" that would be a gross abuse of their sexuality and their supposed respect for each other; if they rushed into it with a sudden and ill considered warmth, it could have effects on unexpected levels for which they are quite unprepared—worst of all it could effect them unequally, leaving one emotionally overwhelmed and the other with a burden of guilt. Sex magic without love is black magic.[1]

While we would agree with most of what is said, the matter is not for us so clear cut. What they call "gender magic," magic that utilizes male and female partners but has no overtly sexual "action," may bind individual couples very closely together. As may be seen from the "Great Rite," Wicca holds the actual act of physical sex in great magical esteem but does not seem to realize that men and women can become emotionally tangled just as easily by practicing certain forms of polarity magic fully clothed! There is an assumption that by its nature, conventional Wiccan ritual may not tap the levels of power known to other branches of the Western tradition. Whether or not this is the case it has to be said that Wicca is a much more straightforward way of approaching magic, and an honest way of approaching sex in magic. Done well, it is very much a case of "what you see is what you get!" This is reflected in the Farrars' no nonsense approach. Their assertion that "sex magic without love is black magic" quite rightly slaps down the potent quasi-sexual games of lodges who look distastefully upon polarity working as "a necessary magical operation." But this still doesn't solve the problem.

What the priest/priestess relationship seeks, or should seek, to represent is what men and women should be to each other *on all levels.* Ritual magic, whether specifically polarity magic or not, draws all these levels together. For example, the officers in a greater mystery ritual represent and mediate archetypal forces. These forces are then brought down through the levels to be manifested through the intellectual, emotional, and sensual processes of the ritual. If the archetypal forces represented are traditional god/goddess forms, then the polarity between the officers mediating them will be worked out not only intellectually but emotionally and physically. This does not necessarily mean that mythological intercourse has to be translated into actual copulation in the ritual (though under certain circumstances and privately this may sometimes be appropriate). What it does mean is that the emotional and sensual aspects of the ritual will both call for and precipitate intense intimacy. This will not simply evaporate at the conclusion of the ritual. You cannot evoke and enter into the magical situation of becoming a cosmic lover and then just go home and forget about it. If you can, then either you or the magic isn't doing what is required!

In terms of the sexual implications of this, it may be that people who are partnered with another in outer life will go home and work out the effects of the ritual through their mundane relationship. In other words, one evokes the magical relationship with one's priest or priestess and then goes home to express that relationship with one's nearest and dearest. The problem with this, however, is that the "carry over" into mundane circumstances is often unsatisfactory because the nonmagical partner, through no fault of his or her own, is completely unaware of the dynamics involved. To put it bluntly, you may not be able to explain to your partner that you have just done the most incredible ritual that explored the intimate relationship of gods and goddesses and then ask your partner to please stop what he or she is doing and come to bed! Magically speaking, your partner is unable to fulfill the projection and it is unfair and unreasonable to expect that they should.

There is no easy solution that we or anyone else can offer to those who are already partnered in outer life. It appears that in the ancient temples the initiates who performed sex magic were to all intents and purposes members of closed orders and were otherwise celibate. This does not necessarily mean that there was no tender affection, no love expressed in their sacred sex. What it more likely means is that they understood the magical implications of sacrifice. Their sacrifice was to know the feelings of, but deny the fulfillment of, a monogamous relationship that gave emotional security through setting up home together and rearing children.

A priest/priestess partnership may start as mere mutual projection. Magic all too easily enables this, and indeed depends quite heavily on the deliberate projection of archetypal or god/goddess forms onto and by respective magical partners. Projection may therefore be a useful magical servant but a bad master, and magical working relationships between a priest and priestess need to be founded on a good deal more than projection. The projection of images of plaster sainthood upon one's opposite number is unreal, unhealthy, and magically unworkable.

Finally, in this long list of caveats, it goes without saying that serious priest/priestess relationships are long term and magically monogamous. In fact, if you are doing your work as it should be done, you won't want to do polarity magic with anybody else. As in outer life, however, commitment over time can become uneven, and one has to be prepared for the fact that one day such a partnership may be discontinued by the other partner. Magic accelerates personal growth, and while such a partnership should mean that men and women grow together and grow closer in the process, this is not always the way that individual souls evolve!

If the partnership involves physical sexual liaison, especially if other "outer world" partners are involved, it goes without saying that matters such as contraception and sexual hygiene must be scrupulously observed. In cases where one of the partners is single in the mundane world, then it is best to observe magical monogamy. People who believe that they may be able to pursue an open, even promiscuous, sexual/emotional lifestyle outside their magic and maintain a priest/priestess relationship within the lodge, whether physically consummated or not, should think again! It just cannot work that way, except on a superficial level.

If a priest/priestess relationship commences with one or both initiates being single, then one subsequently forms a serious relationship outside of this, their magical partner must be informed, however disruptive this might be. It goes without saying that where a priest/priestess partnership within a magical fraternity fails in acrimonious or emotionally distressing circumstances, one or both partners should leave that fraternity for a time.

While all this may sound a bit "mother hen" and obvious to the mature, it has to be said that men and women who feel that special magical magnetism between them frequently fail to respond in a mature way. It is of course hopeless to attempt to "legislate for love," and every case will be different. But these caveats should be noted, considered seriously, meditated upon by the individuals involved, and discussed frankly. If everybody is completely honest with themselves and their prospective partner at the outset, then a great deal of misery for individuals, others to whom they owe "just dues," and the rest of any fraternity that they happen to work with may be avoided.

A POLARITY RITE

The best way to demonstrate polarity magic in action is to present a sample ritual and commentary. The ritual that follows may or may not have been exactly how they did such things in ancient Egypt, but it is true to the spirit and mythology of those times. Certainly it came from an inner source, but the reliability of both inner source and incarnate recipient may be open to question. No human being may claim infallibility in matters of inner communication, however exalted the apparent source. The following rite must therefore stand or fall on its own merits. Magic is very much an experiential business. The proof of its pudding is very much in the eating!

The publication of this ritual therefore seeks to demonstrate how a committed priest and priestess may, with the inspired use of mythology and in true polarity, further the marriage of heaven to earth. Those who have the necessary insight to read between the lines and the stability and maturity to carry it through will work it as it should be worked. Like so many operations of magic, one comes to it if and when one is ready, circumstances permitting. There is no blame in never performing it, and indeed to do such work at the wrong time, at the wrong stage of realization, and in the wrong circumstances is not advisable. We take no responsibility for any emotional, psychological, or other disruption that ill-considered performance of this rite may incur!

Yet those who never actually perform it outwardly may deepen their understanding by knowing it and integrating its images, thus enhancing their work. We will also demonstrate in our next chapter how those who are not magically partnered in the outer world may work polarity magic on an inner/outer basis with either the priest or priestess being partnered from the inner planes. However, many of the same provisos, especially regarding motive, still apply.

THE PATH OF KHEPHRI

We call this ritual "The Path of Khephri." The construct is simple and dispenses with any ritual frills. Ideally it should be performed privately, and sufficient time should be taken for it to allow images to form and actions to be deliberated. Polarity magic performed by a priest and priestess is "Western tantra"; in effect, it is lovemaking expressed symbolically and elevated to spiritual purpose. As in lovemaking, participants should take their time. Mistakes in performance should not be glossed over as they so often are in group ritual. There is no pressure, and it is better to stop a section and start again. Power lost will rebuild if you get it right. The Egyptian priesthood had time, and rehearsal (interspersed with humor to stop the images that may form and to keep the ritual from beginning prematurely) is essential. Meditation is also essential, not only upon the mythology being employed in order to come to an understanding with and of the powers behind the work, but also to consider one's own motives in doing the work. In Egyptian magic especially there is no room for sloppiness in intention or execution! We do not work alone, and the powers behind this tradition who enable such rites demand that it is done with magical precision. It is for those powers, as well as for the universal greater good and our own development to further that good, that we perform such rites. It is frequently forgotten that the "tracks in space" between ourselves and our discarnate inner brethren are very much a two-way street.

This ritual may be performed with a minimum of clothing but a maximum of jewellery. This is a matter of taste: you need to be at ease but at the same time entering into what you honestly consider to be the spirit of the undertaking. Wiccan participants should be aware that this cannot be performed in the same easy frame of mind as their own skyclad rites. The Egyptian tradition requires a wholly different mindset, which, however one may choose to be dressed or undressed, obviates the easygoing atmosphere of most Wiccan ritual. Clothes or no clothes, erotic or not, this ritual comes from four thousand years of magical conservatism.

MYTHOLOGY AND CONCEPTUAL BASIS

The basis of the ritual is a linking of the seven centers in the human body with the sevenfold symbolism in the stars, reflected in the land through the Egyptian Underworld, or Duat, using supporting mythology and godforms. In this it may be considered to be a "rite of sovereignty," as in the Celtic and Bronze Age mythology. These death and initiation rites are associated with goddess empowerment and transformation by providing access to the archetypal patterns, the Maat, of the heavens, and rebirth as a fully realized human being, a "justified one"—as Osiris and Isis, both to each other and within each self.

The Path of Khephri is the path of the dung beetle, which in mythology rolls the ball of the Sun through the sky, even the inner night sky of the Duat in the Sun's incubation. The death and rebirth of the reborn transformed Sun, or the solar hero in so many myths, is implicit in the Khepher godform, whose winged dung beetle *scarab* symbol was placed over the heart of each dead pharaoh. The scarab had outstretched wings symbolizing solar flight, for the dung beetle takes flight when the Sun is at its zenith.

We remind ourselves that the journey of the soul as the Sun through the seven *arrets* of the Duat was considered to be a journey through the Milky Way, and that this was also considered to be a journey of rebirth through the sinuous starry body of the goddess Nuit. The earthly reflection of the Milky Way was the river Nile, and the rising and fertility provided by the Nile was also governed by the star of Isis, Sirius. The mention of the temple of Isis at Philae accords with the island of Philae on the upper Nile being considered the special earthly dwelling of Isis, not least because the inundation of the Nile was seen to commence from this point. It was also considered as the resting place of Osiris, in effect, the place where Isis finally gathered all but one of the parts of her brother and mate's dismembered body to restore him to wholeness at the culmination of her search through Egypt.

FIRE IN THE BLOOD

This journey through the seven arrets of the Duat, represented in the heavens by the starry body of Nuit, and on earth by the Nile, was attended by seven companions, the *Heru Shemsu,* comprising the four sons of Horus and three other companions. In her own journey to reintegrate Osiris, Isis too had seven companions: the seven scorpions also noted in the rite. The journey through the body of Nuit is in a sense a restorative journey through one's own body, and a journey may be made through earthly Egypt via the river Nile, so the journey through the body may be made via the "river" of one's own bloodstream.

While the sevenfold symbolism may therefore be associated with the seven chakras, a more specific association should be noted with organs related to processes within the blood, including certain endocrine glands, the ductless glands that secrete hormones directly into the bloodstream. They are therefore very much "companions" and helpers along the way.

These associations, though varying from one tradition to another, are not peculiar to the Egyptian mysteries. For example, the sexual symbolism of arousal of the inner fire, or "fire in the blood" that depends upon polarity magic for its execution is obliquely indicated in the red and white dragons (the red and white corpuscles in blood) of Merlin's prophetic awakening. We should note in the Egyptian context that the four sons of Heru or Horus, who are four of the seven companions, are associated with portions of the viscera. Hence, the removed viscera of a dead pharaoh was set aside in four canopic jars, each allocated to the guardianship of one of those four sons of Horus. Horus in a sense represents the son, or reincarnation of the "Osiris," whom the dead pharaoh aspired to become.

THE STAGES OF THE RITUAL

The ritual starts with a composition of place. This may be taken to be the subterranean temple of the dark Isis, as described in Dion Fortune's novel *Moon Magic.*[2] Having envisioned themselves in this sacred place, the priest invokes Ra in the east, Anubis in the south, Hathor in the west, and Nepthys in the north. A huge naked statue of the dark Isis is seen to stand in the center-west with an empty sarcophagus before it.

Holding the visualization of this place the priestess stands before the statue of Isis with the priest behind her. The technique that follows is pretty much the one given by Dolores Ashcroft-Nowicki,[3] where the priestess and priest synchronize their breathing and the priestess prepares a place "within her head." When she has made such a place ready, she draws the priest's arms across her chest so that his thumbs touch the pulse points on each side of her neck. The priest then enters in vision through the chakra at the nape of his priestess's neck to meet the starry Isis, whom she accommodates and represents.

Having made this initial accommodation with the starry Isis through his priestess, the priest gently withdraws, lowering his and her arms to signify that withdrawal. His experience will probably have been somewhat along the lines of Horus being suckled by the cosmic Isis.

The priest then, still holding the hand of his priestess, leads her to a prepared central area of cushions, a "bier" representing the sarcophagus, and gently lowers her onto it. She lies on her back and he sets her arms crossed upon her breast.

The priest stands at her feet, as Horus with the starry Isis, his mother behind him, and reads the charge of the seven over her.

Having read the charge with due visualization, the priest reclines on the left side of his priestess and kisses each of her seven chakra points, from head to foot.

He then returns to kneel at her head to give the blessing and acknowledgment of her fertility. This "fertility" is not so much her personal ability to reproduce, as it is her creative, empowering impetus as representative of the Goddess. The image is of her as the land with him running over her like a river so that she is fertilized by his starseed in his role of son and mediator of his mother Nuit. This is therefore called "the Inundation." To affirm this he stretches out and slides along her body in a sinuous riverlike motion, arriving at her feet where he kneels.

At her feet he again addresses her. In all this he is in a sense convincing her that she is the representative of both Nuit and Isis. He confirms the Nuit association in the "solar birth," rolling a crystal ball, representing the Sun, from her lips to her thighs, as the Sun was seen to enter the mouth of Nuit and to travel through her body, the Milky Way to be reborn from the divided stream of those stars, the open "thighs" of Nuit over a nine-month period.

The priest then affirms the rebirth of his priestess in earth by using the image of the ben ben rising up from the primordial flood as a series of pyramids, each representing a direction of the parameters of being. At these pyramids he sets the seven companions of Horus, to affirm the visceral and chakric parameters of the flow of her blood as she returns to life "as the Goddess."

To affirm her return to life, the priest beats the wings of Horus over her and breathes upon her chakras. Then, taking the pyramids from her, he kisses her upon the mouth and turns her head toward him, kneeling at her head. She raises her head and kisses him on the thigh. In this he appears to be the bull of Amenti, for the thigh of the bull was the constellation of Ursa Minor, and the adze that opened the mouth of the deceased to assure return to life was made in its shape. He then raises her up to stand as the Goddess incarnate before him.

The priestess then prepares her priest to enter the body of Nuit. She sets him on the bier and becomes Nuit to his soul, feeding him symbolically upon her milk of the Milky Way.

She raises him up and becomes the Goddess incarnate to his reborn Osirian self.

The mediation exercise that follows involves the priest and priestess combining to form and visualize one double pyramid as indicated in the ritual subtext. This is done for some time, with the visualization of what is mediated mostly being left to spontaneity.

After this the ritual is wound down, a final prayer is made to Isis, and the temple is closed.

The ancient Egyptian language is used here and there in invocation, and the god names are said in the original Egyptian, rather than the usual Greek. Thus, Osiris becomes Asar, Isis Ast, Anubis is Anpu, Horus is Heru, and so on. No guarantees are made for the pronunciation or grammatical accuracy of the Egyptian passages! All scholarly attempts to recreate the pronunciation of the ancient Egyptian language are only approximations at best.

The "pyramids" that are referred to are small crystal pyramids.

THE RITE OF KHEPHRI

Preparation

Then shall the priestess make ready the star chamber within her mind, called the temple of the Arq, which the priest of Ast shall enter with due reverence.

Within this place he shall sup from the milk of the stars, and having done so shall withdraw and rejoin the priestess.

With due ceremony, he shall help the priestess to lay prone, as if in her sarcophagus. Her head shall be to the east, and the priest shall stand at her feet facing over her and shall invoke:

The Charge

Priest: Priestess of Ast, know that the seven Wise Ones attend thee, hovering as hawks upon the winds of space.

The seven scorpions attend thee and show thee the true Maat.

The seven spirits guard thy sleep, even the four children of Heru, son of Ast, and with them Maa-atef-f, Keri beq-f, and Heru khenti Maati.

The Lord of West is risen and attends thee. He rises up from Philae on the wings of Khephri, the wings of the morning. The fourteen stars shine bright in his being, and the holy branch is in his hand. For he is reborn as Heru, as Amun, and as Apis. He is the bull of Amenti and the collar is about his neck, even the collar of the seven stars, and upon his tongue is the beetle of Khephri and of the risen Sun.

And the bull of the gods called forth the power from the beginning, even the power of Nau Shesma, which is the power of the great serpent called the bull of the gods. And he holds the power of the seven—even the seven uraei and the seven bows.

These things are over thee, priestess of Ast, even as the sevenfold stars shine over the still body of the land of Khem. For he is risen, even as the great river rises and makes the land fruitful. He has seen her, splendid among her seven stars, and the river of his desire overflows and his starseed shall be upon the body of the land. He that died has drunk the milk of the stars and is alive. She who was concealed in mourning is come forth and is bathed sevenfold in his dew.

Affirmation of the Charge

[Priest stretches over priestess and kisses her seven chakra points.]

The Blessing

[Priest places hand on the crossed arms of his priestess, saying]:
  Blessed be all daughters of Ast.

The Inundation

Priest: So does the river of his wanting run over thee so that thou shall be dark and fruitful under the stars. But then shall he wane and the tide shall subside leaving thee potent with his starseed.

[Priest moves back down her body and sits at her feet, saying]:
Think on these things O priestess of Ast.

The Solar Birth

Priest: Think on the brightness of the stars and the dark of the land, and think of the star of the Sun that rises over thee. Feel its warmth upon thy body, as the bright and vital orb rolls over thee.

[Priest rolls crystal ball from the lips of the priestess to her root chakra, saying]:

And when the tide had subsided, the Sun rose and moved like the ball of Khephri over the dark and fertile land of Khem. Blessed be the land of Khem, and blessed be this daughter of Ast.

Rebirthing

Priest: The dry land emerged to rise up to the warmth of the Sun, each mound of new earth standing like a sentinel spirit to guard and guide the destiny of the land, even those sentinel spirits appointed by Anpu guarding the land over which the body of Asar was scattered. And the first mound is of the firstborn of Heru.

[Kisses feet of priestess and places pyramid, saying]:
MESTHA, who has the countenance of a man.
And the second mound is of the spirit who is the second child of Heru.

[Kisses root chakra and places pyramid, saying]:
HAPI, who has the countenance of an ape.
And the third is of the third child of Heru.

[Kisses solar plexus and places pyramid, saying]:
TUAMUTEF, who has the countenance of the jackal.
And the fourth mound is called after the fourth child of Heru.

[Kisses heart chakra and places pyramid, saying]:
QEBHSENNUF of the hawklike countenance.
The fifth mound is of MAA ATEF.

[Kisses throat chakra and places pyramid, saying]:
The sixth mound is of KHERI MAATI BEQF.

[Kisses forehead and places pyramid, saying]:
The seventh mound is of HERU KHENTI MAATI.

[Kisses crown chakra and places pyramid above/in contact with it.]
Priest: These are the paths of the stars upon the body of Khem. These are the guarding ones and the guiding ones of the parameters of the sacred land. They are at thy north and south, thy east and thy west, at thy height and depth, and at the very heart of thee and of the land.

And the wind arose and breathed life into that warm land. And it blew the feather of truth, and with it wrote its signs upon her splendid body. This is the truth that is Maat, and its writing is that of her companion, TEHUTI. For Tehuti is leader of the seven wise ones, and the seven wisdoms, held in the seven stars, are upon her, for hers is the body of Khem. And the seven wise ones who attend hover over her and beat their hawk wings and cool her in the heat of the day. *[Breathes upon priestess's seven chakras, touching them with hawk's feather.]*

So the land rises up from the inundation of the starseed of Osiris. So Khem rises from her darkness, for she is a star-crowned and glorious. And as Ast of all brightness and wisdom, she rises as the highest mound of all, joining heaven to earth.

[Priest takes the pyramids from priestess's body and places them in a circle at her feet. He then kneels at her head and kisses her on the mouth, saying]:
Priest: Re hen en Heru, the mouth of the majesty of Horus. Yet know that I am the bull of Amenti, and the seven stars are upon my collar and turn within the circle of my being. Rise up priestess of Ast and know me.

[Priest then turns the head of his priestess toward him and she kisses him on the thigh. He then raises up his priestess to stand before him. Each slowly raise arms, saying]:

Priest: The honey voice of Ast be thy voice.

Priestess: The wisdom of Tehuti be thine.

Priest: The starry body of Nuit be thy body.

Priestess: Be beloved in my perfect dark.

The Body of Nuit

[Both slowly lower arms; priestess takes hands of her priest and sets him to lie prone upon the bier, setting his body in the correct position. She then stretches herself over him, saying]:

Priestess: I am the rainbow arch of heaven, I am Nuit. I am the arch of the night sky, desired by those who would know the true Maat. The starseed is in my breasts, even the starseed of wisdom, the wisdom of the land and stars.

[Priestess briefly assumes position over him of Nuit, before settling beside (or across) him.]

Priestess: Child of Ast, child of the land. I am the pyramid of the heavens that overshadow thee. I am the most ancient mound that rose up in the sea of space. Feed on me of the starry wisdom. *[Priest raises his head and kisses her breasts.]*

[Priestess then rises and takes pyramids from foot of bier and kneels beside priest, kissing each of his chakras and placing pyramids upon them, then says]:

Priestess: Know through my being the marriage of sap and sinew to the imperishable stars, and know the flight of Khephri in the risen Sun.

[Priestess takes pyramids from the body of priest and raises him up to stand against her. For a while both are aware of the starseed in their respective chakras, and may use the interchange of chakric energy technique to raise

the inner fire between them. They then each hold out their arms sideways to waist level, palms up, and are individually aware of rays of white light forming triangles over themselves with the basal angles of those triangles held in their palms. Slowly holding the images of the triangles, they pass their arms around each other, extending the triangles past each other to form a mutual pyramid of white light with one apex above them both. They must remain absolutely still like this, in absolute control for some time, making sure that the pyramid is solidly built between them. There should be an awareness of (a) their respective star centers/chakras harmonizing, and (b) the axial orientation of this "pyramid," to the (present) Pole Star, the center of the circumpolar round.]

[They should then be aware of the descent of the light from the apex of the pyramid, down through the four sides and extending out to the four children of Horus at the cardinal points. Both raise arms "past" each other, visualizing a pyramid above them and another forming below them, and the two fusing the Duat with the earth. They remain as this for some time, then slowly lower their arms, kiss, and stand apart.]

Priest: Blessed be thou, daughter of Ast, for the true Maat is in thee.

Priestess: Blessed be thou son of Ast, Hept tu Maat, the Maat embraceth thee.

Priest: Auset maa er per maati, seyen sen baiu, sen abiau, sen ukiau. Ma pa ukiau em ast uyset. Apten seyen khepher ma ua.

Priestess: Isis come to thy house of truth, embrace two souls, two hearts, two pillars. As the pillars in thy hall. These embrace to be as one.

[Priest gives thanks to and closes the four quarters. Priest and priestess sit. Pause, salute, rise, embrace, and leave.]

CHAPTER ELEVEN

DIONYSOS AND THE BACCHAE

THE INNER MASCULINE

Any discussion of the polarized relationship between an incarnate human and a discarnate or Otherworld being more often than not assumes that the human is male and the inner world being is female. This is a reflection of several unavoidable truths, one being that men have written most of the material about this subject. Whereas it is common, for instance, for male writers to receive inspiration and guidance from their female muse, perhaps one such as the White Goddess so eloquently described by Robert Graves, the archetype of the male muse who inspires a female writer does not spring so readily to mind. And while it was rumored that the priestesses of Amun who danced in front of his statue were able by this or other means to bring the God to climax in a ritual reenactment of the first moment of creation, one suspects that this may have been more gratifying for Amun than it was for the priestess. The special nature of the relationship between an outer world ruler and an inner representative of the Goddess similarly depends upon the working assumption that the polarity that underpins this relationship is that between the inner, female sovereignty and her male regent, who acts for her within the world.

But this leaves the active, creative woman in search of a context in which she can find an inner (not to mention outer!) male partner who will inspire her without taking over, energize but not frighten, encourage but not control. For a rare example of this relationship we turn to the ancient Greek mysteries of Dionysos. These mysteries lie at the root of much that later found its way into the magnificent conglomeration that has come to be called the Western Mystery Tradition. Together, with the related mysteries of Orpheus, they form an important part of the green ray tradition of magic, as opposed to, for example, the orange ray of Hermetic magic. In simple terms, green ray magic is the magic of the heart and body rather than of the mind; the joyful and exuberant celebration of the living presence of the natural world and its inhabitants. While the physical expression of the mysteries through the typical forms of the green ray—music, song, poetry, dance, and laughter—is open to all who feel drawn to expressing their devotion through these means, our present interest in the mysteries of Dionysos is that from their very initiation they appear to have been specifically aimed at the relationship that exists between a male god and his female celebrants. That is to say, an outer world priestess working with a male inner world partner. These celebrants, the priestesses of the mysteries of Dionysos, were known as the Bacchae.

Of course it is no longer the case that the worship of Dionysos remains the exclusive province of women, even if this was ever so, but the nature of the relationship between a woman and a discarnate male remains relatively unknown territory, and the history of Dionysos and the Bacchae remains one of the fullest explorations of this relationship. Remarkably, it has remained free from male censorship or misguided interpretation. The particular relationship that Dionysos espoused was one in which he inspired and encouraged women to reach out far beyond the normal range of their lives and to touch the hidden heart of their wildest imaginings. But this relationship was not "sexual" in any normal sense of the word, which would imply that there was an exchange of energy that led to the physical sexual act. Although Dionysos invoked and released in the

Bacchae a deep and savage power that, Kali-like, could make or break in a moment of supernatural strength, the women were not engaged in a sexual relationship with Dionysos. Dionysos empowered the women, but he was not the object of the expression of the energy that he invoked in them. He aroused them, but remained the catalyst. The object of the arousal was the personal fulfillment of experience that occurs when a human being is able to uncover and tap into his or her deepest potential and, as an extension of this, the greater benefit that may be brought to humankind. In other words, Dionysos inspired Gnosis, not idolatry.

In the relationship between Dionysos and the Bacchae we see one of the very few examples of the reversal of the more common polarity that exists between the inner sovereignty of the land and her earthly regent, the sacred king. As such, the message of Dionysos remains astonishingly modern in its recognition that while women may choose to find fulfillment in the more traditional role of priestess or handmaiden to the inner sovereignty, there are those who choose to find expression in the active, the powerful, the wild, and the "masculine." It is not always appropriate for women to seek inspiration from an inner feminine figure. Unfortunately, there are very few divine or mythological male figures who offer this type of inspiration to women. The situation is not helped by the common reaction of men (and indeed sometimes of other women), which is to assume that a woman's relationship with an inner male archetype must perforce be of a weird sexual nature, or is threatening to men, or is evidence of an unbalanced personality.

As we have seen, Christ was one of those few who offered genuine empowerment to women. As one ponders the relationship between Dionysos and the Bacchae, the similarities between Dionysos and Jesus become increasingly obvious. The image of Jesus in the hills of Judea with what we now realize to be his inner circle of women followers is not so very far removed from the image of Dionysos and the Bacchae on the mountain of Cithaeron. The sad truth is that such a relationship with Jesus as an inner world and "polarized" partner is generally considered to be blasphemous, frightening, and, for whatever reason, out of the question. The very same censorship that marginalized His relationship with Mary Magdalene and belittled her true status and authority to that of a reformed whore works equally for any other woman who looks for a similar relationship with Him. On the other hand, the "myth" of Dionysos has been protected by virtue of its paganism, and continues to inspire in ways in which Jesus is no longer able. We feel able to accept Dionysos as Lord of the Dance, as the liberating Fool, or as a sexual, inner plane partner, whereas these things are still taboo in regard to our relationship with Christ.

The form in which the mysteries of Dionysos were originally expressed is open to conjecture; as is so often the case in mystery religions, very little has come down to us in written form, and we must rely on fragments of verse and intriguing glimpses on painted jars and faded frescoes. But we are fortunate in that they have been preserved in a later version, albeit one that was intended for public performance rather than private religious observance among the priesthood, namely Euripides' play *The Bacchae*,[1] which was written in 407 B.C. during the author's voluntary exile in Macedonia.

THE BACCHAE OF EURIPIDES

The play was probably written about four hundred years after the first appearance of the cult of Dionysos. While the arrival of this strange new god in Greece nearly three thousand years ago heralded a very different approach of humans to their gods, it has survived within the practice of many green ray magical groups, foremost among which are those that are found in modern paganism and witchcraft. The reasons for this are not hard to discover. More than perhaps any other religion, the worship of Dionysos not only allows but positively *encourages* the free expression of the instincts: it encourages rather than represses the arousal of the lower chakras, it encourages dance and song as essential elements of worship, it demands close empathy with plants, animals, and nature spirits, and, above all, it recognizes the particular gifts and abilities of women in leading worship of this nature. In broad terms, it can be categorized as magic of the heart rather than magic of the mind. It can be helpful to think of Dionysos as the priest of Pan, the male representative of the earth, just as we saw Luned as the priestess of the Lady of the Fountain, the inner female representative of the earth.

In brief, the plot of *The Bacchae* is as follows:

The god Dionysos, a young man, arrives in the city of Thebes, where his mother Semele is buried. It is not clear where he has spent his youth, but he appears to have traveled for some time in the countries "to the north." His arrival provokes a confrontation with Pentheus, king of Thebes, who is depicted as the representative of law, order, and conscious control. (Parallels with the appearance of Jesus in Jerusalem spring to mind here.) Dionysos already has a strong following of women who are called the Bacchae. In spite of calls for moderation from his friends and advisors who realize that the new religion brought by Dionysos has something to offer, Pentheus imprisons Dionysos in the palace stables for inciting riots and enticing women into the mountains for a purpose that, it is assumed, is nefarious. Dionysos escapes from his prison after causing a mysterious fire and an earthquake that destroy the entire palace.

A herdsman enters the scene and describes how he has seen the women on the mountain of Cithaeron and watched how they lived in harmony with their surroundings, striking rocks to produce water and wine, touching the earth to produce a stream of milk, finding an abundance of honey to eat among the rocks, and sleeping peacefully, old women and young, with snakes and wolf-cubs. Among the many women who live on the mountain is Pentheus' mother, Agave. The herdsmen plot to capture the Bacchae and bring them back to Pentheus. But the women realize the presence of the men and run riot, tearing the herdsmen's cattle limb from limb, and then ransack the local villages, carrying their spoils back with them to Cithaeron.

Undeterred by this warning, Pentheus decides to spy on the women. Dionysos advises him to take on the disguise of a woman, otherwise he will not stand a chance of survival, and, thus attired, Pentheus ascends the mountain and climbs a tall pine tree. He is spotted by the women, who uproot the tree and bring Pentheus crashing to the ground. They then tear him to pieces, scattering his fragmented limbs about the earth.

Agave carries his head in triumph down into Thebes, not knowing what she has done until the horrified townspeople bring her out of her ecstatic frenzy to the realization that she has not hunted and killed an animal this time, but her own son. Again, we find echoes in the biblical story of the beheading of John the Baptist, which was said to be at the behest of Salome.

At this point Dionysos reveals himself and tells the Theban people that his purpose all along had been to punish them for refusing to recognize him as a Son of God, the child of Zeus. To achieve this end he had driven the women frantic upon the mountain and engineered the cruel death of Pentheus at his mother's hands. Agave, accursed and wretched, leaves the city and goes into exile.

This, then, is the story as it appears in the play, and there is no doubt that as it stands it is as shocking today as it must have been at its first performance. Nonetheless, it has been suggested several times that *The Bacchae* would make a good magical ritual, and indeed the distinction between Greek drama, particularly tragedy, and magical ritual is a fine one. However, there must be a clear understanding of the play's more disturbing aspects. In part, they are due to the very nature of this new religious impulse, with its raw energy that fills and inspires Dionysos and his followers, and the resultant ecstasy of spirit that can occur when the controls and limitations of the mind are temporarily loosened. At the basis of this lies the belief that this state of being can be brought about by *becoming like God*.

The second uncomfortable element of the play is the revelation by Dionysos toward the end that he has cold-bloodedly tricked everyone by inducing hysteria in the women so that they will bring about his objective of revenge on the Thebans, who did not believe in his divinity. Taken at face value this suggests that nothing in Dionysos' message has any validity. Instead of the expected happy ending, where everything turns out for the best, we are told that it was all a trick, and the carpet is neatly snatched from under our feet. But Dionysos is the joker, the Divine Fool who challenges our prejudices and our comfortable assumptions of the nature and workings of divinity. Like the Fool of the tarot pack he invites us to gather the weight of our old habits into a bundle and to step over the cliff of reason into the unknown. "Expect the unexpected," as one of the women remarks.

What did Dionysos bring that was so different, then and now? The Olympian gods had already been solidly established upon their thrones by the time he appeared on the scene, and his message was revolutionary. His worship encouraged the breaking-down of the normal restrictions of "civilization" and of the conscious, controlling mind. This was done by physical exertion of the body in wild and energetic dance, by the simultaneous (actual or symbolic) abandonment of the controlled orderliness of the city for the wildness of the countryside, and specifically by the loosening of the control of the concrete mind through the moderate consumption of wine. Thus, freed from the fetters of everyday control, the spirit could soar in ecstatic union with the god, *who also took part in the ceremony*. We can piece together from the play the essential components of the original mystery, although, as Plato says: "Many bear the wand, but few are the Bacchae."

DIONYSOS AND THE SERPENT

The mystery of Dionysos starts with his forebears, with the manner of his conception and with his ancestry, which shows us "where he was coming from." Dionysos' mother was Semele, and Semele was one of the daughters of Kadmos, that same Kadmos who killed the serpent Ares and sewed its teeth upon the ground. Semele was sister to Agave, who is mother of Pentheus and who becomes one of the Bacchae, just as Jesus' family were included among his closest followers.

This serpent is as wise as her sister, the Edenic serpent. Here again we find that the story of Dionysos bears close resemblance to the Judeo-Christian myth of Adam and Eve, but of course has managed to escape biblical censorship. Kadmos does not actually kill the serpent but becomes the master of it, confronting the challenge of the deep earth energy and accordingly, his own raw Kundalini energy, without being overcome by it. He controls it and aligns it with his own higher purpose, and thus empowered, he is able to sew the fertile white seeds—the white "teeth" that are released by his actions—upon the ground. They spring up as warriors. Kadmos then marries the daughter of the serpent Ares, whose revealing name is Harmonia. She is the spring maiden, the priestess of the earth mother, the first new life that is released when the serpent is "killed." We have here the Greek version of the eternal myth of the virgin and the dragon, in which the virgin, apparently chained to the dragon and awaiting rescue by the shining knight, is actually the pure and focused expression of the otherwise chaotic dragon energy. Kadmos, having fought and taken control of his own serpent nature, is now in a balanced and harmonious state. As with all sacred kings of myth and history, his own fertility is now part and parcel of the earth's fertility and of the forces of nature with which he is now in empathy.

A significant passage near the end of *The Bacchae* indicates how closely Kadmos and Harmonia are identified with the serpent. Apparently as part of the punishment that he brings to the people of Thebes for not believing in his divinity, Dionysos seems to be condemning them to the awful fate of having to relinquish their humanity and become as serpents.

> Become what you were in the beginning.
> The serpent power was always found within.
> Your wife, Harmonia, daughter of Ares
> Will make this transformation with you.

In Genesis, we are reminded of God's words to Adam and Eve after their own encounter with a serpent: ". . . upon thy belly thou shalt go, and dust shalt thou eat all the days of thy life."[2]

This unlikely scenario reveals Dionysos as being the arbiter of the fate of his own grandparents. But the apparent punishment is really an indication of a much deeper truth working through, in that they themselves are now to take on the form of the wisdom of the serpent and thus become the "testers" rather than the tested. This is in the time-honored manner in which those who master the serpent—whether the serpent within or the serpent without—then become identified with it. In this instance it is their grandson, Dionysos, who makes it so and who promises Kadmos and Harmonia immortal life among the gods after some initial difficult times.

There are many parallels here with the biblical story of Adam, Eve, and the serpent. In this instance it is Kadmos and Harmonia who are responsible for the birth of the race of warriors sprung from the serpent's teeth, and who are also the immediate ancestors of Dionysos the Savior God. The story of this remarkable family from Ares to Dionysos is a compressed version of the story of the earliest days of humanity, although it is distinguished by its complete freedom from the guilt and sin that pervade the Christian version of the same story. We have the same beginnings in the chaotic, untapped potential of the serpent energy that is focused and made fertile by the Michael-like actions of Kadmos. A race of warriors is born (humanity at an unenlightened stage), and they respond with their fists.

Things begin to go wrong, and the sorry state of the world is encapsulated in the character of Pentheus.

Pentheus, whose name means "sorrow" (Dionysos comments that his name "points to calamity"), is a representative of the marriage between the offspring of the dragon-brood and the earthborn. But in spite of his semidivine origin, he has forgotten the bliss of the garden of earth that he once knew, which is the source of the serpent energy within his own body. His ill-conceived attempts to alleviate this sorrow of separation and regain what he has lost possesses him to dress up as a woman and climb the pine tree, the World Tree of Knowledge on the holy mountain of Cithaeron. Although he hopes to gaze blasphemously upon the paradise, he is doing the right thing for the wrong reason, and of course only succeeds in making matters worse. Dionysos the Savior God intervenes and initiates the action that begins to turn events around from this nadir. He restores the severed link with the serpent wisdom by ordaining that Kadmus (the biblical Adam) should take on the identity of the serpent.

DIONYSOS AND JESUS

As a solution to the basic problem of humanity that started in the Garden of Eden, this is a master-stroke! Here is a solution offered by Dionysos, the Perfect Fool, that in every way avoids the pit into which the Judeo-Christian version tumbles. Instead of allowing the unfolding events to be smothered by an insoluble burden of blame and guilt, Dionysos turns the whole scenario upon its head and in effect says to Adam/Kadmos: "*You* become the serpent, *you* see what it's like. Don't leave it to Eve to ask "what if," and then blame her for the consequences, try it for yourself." In terms of individual responsibility, this is the ultimate statement. We find a surprising confirmation of this in the very similar name given to this man from whom the whole of humanity has descended in the Qabalist concept of the primordial human being, Adam Kadmon. Moreover, the Dionysos solution, if we may call it that, also avoids the literal deathtrap of the crucifixion. Dionysos, like Jesus, finds that the people of his native country are inclined to disbelieve in his divinity: they do not accept that he is a son of God. But this is not the ignoble death of Christ interpreted in some circular argument of being "a sacrifice" and therefore noble. For Dionysos manages to achieve a turn in the tide of humanity, live to see another day, *and* establish a cult that remains true to his original purpose and intent.

To return to the story: Kadmos' daughter Semele, the mother of Dionysos, is no ordinary girl, but very much a woman of the earth. In fact, her whole family is an interesting group. Her sister Agave, the mother of Pentheus and the "aunt" of Dionysos, married Echion, whose name means "viper" and who would also appear to have the serpent blood running in her veins. Her other sisters were Autonoe, whose name means "mind of her own" and indicates the progression in this microcosmic family to the clear development of self, and Ino ("she who makes sinewy"). In a further parallel with the Christian story it would appear that Semele was eventually raised up out of the underworld and ascended into heaven. The festivals at Delphi, which included the reenactment of this myth, also included sections that were known as The Return and The Uprising.

Dionysos claims that his father was Zeus—chief among the gods— and is thus one of the many sons to appear in this book who were born of an earthly mother and a sky father. We notice that Zeus is not recorded as admitting to this particular union, and appears to have shown only a very cursory interest in his latest offspring. After snatching the newborn Dionysos away from his mother, whom he had just killed by scorching her with a thunderbolt, Zeus took him back to heaven. In other words, Dionysos died to this world immediately after his birth. However, most significantly, he was then *reborn*. At his second birth—and this time he sprang straight from Zeus' "thigh"—he immediately returned to earth, where he was abandoned in a cave to make the best of things amongst the animals—a familiar story!

Legend also mentions that Hera, wife of Zeus, was jealous of her husband's union with Semele, and in order to get her revenge she persuaded Semele to ask Zeus to reveal himself to her in his true form as a god. This was a particularly nasty trick on Hera's part, and one that Zeus was not able to resist. But there were dire consequences, as his action caused Semele's death. Such petty squabbling in the heights of Mount Olympus hides the underlying truth of what happens when you look directly upon the face of God. But in this case, some good came of it. The house of Semele, which was simultaneously her own tomb and the womb-birthplace of her son, was, from that moment, a source of a perpetual flame, and was revered as one of the places where the creative fire of God had touched the earth.

Dionysos, then, was born out of fire, and would appear to have been a master of fire himself. The perpetual flame that burned over the tomb of his mother is an instance of the female guardianship of the sacred flame. We see it also in the guardianship performed by the Vestal Virgins, or in the perpetual flame that was tended by the priestesses in the sacred order of Brigid. Such women are thus all midwives to the birth of the Son of Light. There are references to this in *The Bacchae,* where on his first entrance Dionysos points to the tomb of his mother:

> This was her home: these blackened stones
> Will burn with the perpetual fire of Zeus—

Later, when he has been imprisoned by Pentheus in the Theban palace, Dionsysos makes the flame blaze to a great height and frightens Pentheus into thinking that the palace is burning down. When Pentheus climbed the pine tree on the mountain of Cithaeron in order to spy on the Bacchae, a flash of fire appears:

> Dionysos! It had to be Dionysos!
> A voice rang out from the empty sky,
> And with the voice, a blinding light,
> A flash of fire which arched from heaven to earth.

This brings us to the most widely acknowledged symbol of Dionysos and the Bacchae, the thyrsos, traditionally a fennel-stalk wand topped with a pine cone. This most phallic of symbols was carried by women, not out of envy, but to indicate that they were able to literally "hold" this energy and manifest it within the world. Something similar is remembered in the ceremony that stands at the center of some present-day witchcraft rituals. At the ritual of the consecration of the mooncakes and wine it is the priestess who holds the wand and plunges it into the chalice held by the priest. The wand as the symbol of fire—the raw, vitalizing, creative energy, the initiating spark of life, is central to his mysteries, and part of Pentheus' error was to place himself symbolically at the top of the pine tree, where only God should be. The rites of Dionysos typically took place at night, lit by the burning torches held by the celebrants.

The exact location of the cave that was the place of rebirth of Dionysos is not known. Although it can be rewarding to attempt to make a correlation between the names of legends and actual physical locations, we must bear in mind that although Dionysos came to earth in a way that had sufficient impact upon the physical plane for him to be remembered and celebrated as a human being, he was also a son of God, and the imprint of his birth attached to many locations. Some legends associate him with the bandit hideouts of the mountainous regions of Thrace, which lies to the north of Greece. Other legends put his "rebirthplace" on Mount Nysa, which is sometimes located in Libya, on an island surrounded by the river Triton. These Tritonian waters were also the birthplace of Athene, who, it will be remembered, was born from Zeus' head.

GUARDIANS OF THE SACRED FLAME

We are provided here with a link between this daughter and son of Zeus, Athene and Dionysos, who each sprang directly from part of their heavenly father's person, both possessing the ability to transmit creative fire from heaven to earth. It was actually Prometheus who stole the fire from Zeus, but Athene assisted him by helping to smuggle him into Olympus, where he took fire from the Sun and brought it to earth as a glowing coal hidden within a fennel stalk— the same fennel stalk that we find in the wand of the Bacchae. The symbolism behind this act is of the "ignition" into a physical flame of the spark from the flame of God within each human on earth. It is an act whereby each man and woman may recognize the inter-connectedness of all things spiritual and temporal, and using this gift, act accordingly to make real the creative fire within the world of form. Both Dionysos and Athene are, in their own ways, guides to this process by which each separate spark eventually must return to the one flame of God.

Whatever the origins of Dionysos, we are told nothing else about his youth and upbringing, as is so often the case with sons of God who walk upon the earth, until he arrives back in Greece from the countries "to the north" (Lydia, according to his own description). However, the manner and circumstances of his birth are important because, as a result of the intervention by Zeus, Dionysos was given the title "Dithyramb." The traditional translation of this is "he of the Double Door," or the "twice-born," a name used to describe the state achieved by those who undergo ritual death, rebirth, and initi-ation into the mysteries of the higher order of things. Thus Dionysos is first and foremost a god who shows the way along the path of initiation into the mysteries: the ritual death and rebirth within the span of one earthly lifetime. The Bacchae, who are the true wand-bearers by virtue of their own rebirth through Dionysos, are now able to act as midwife or initiatrix to others in this process of rebirth since they symbolically hold the sacred fire that is the pure light of spirit.

Having deposited him in the cave, Zeus placed the infant Dionysos in the care of various semi-human creatures. Rather an unusual start to life, but significant to us because the central part of Dionysiac rit-ual, the actual initiation into his mysteries, was a recreation of the moment and circumstances of his birth. The essence of this new religion was the belief that men and women could become as a god, and the rituals in his name were aimed at bringing about the state of consciousness in which this could be achieved. He was raised by creatures who were part man and part beast: Satyrs and Silenoi, wild men with shaggy bodies and the ears, tail, and hoofs of horses or goats, and by the Maenads, or "Mad Women," and the Thyiades, or "Rushing Ones." This is an important element in the story of Dionysos because his followers, as described in *The Bacchae,* foster their identification with the god Dionysos by dressing in goat skins and by the practice of *omophagia,* the consumption of the raw flesh of animals, and the mystical communion that was brought about by the eating of the body of the god. The parallels between this ritual act and the Christian ritual of the Eucharist are clear.

THE FLESH AND THE BLOOD

Dionysos is generally accredited with the introduction of the consumption of wine as a magical technique. Whether or not he was actually responsible for introducing wine to the Greek civilization, he has nonetheless become inseparably linked with it, just as Osiris is credited with introducing the cultivation of wheat to the human race. Whereas religious and shamanic practices of other cultures have promoted the controlled use of hallucinogenic herbs and substances in order to loosen the subconscious from the rational mind, Western mythology has tended only to use wine as a means to this end. Moreover, it was never the practice of the Greeks to sink into drunkenness. They took their wine in small cups, and always mixed it with water. Diodorus describes how "they hold that wine drunk unmixed produces forms of madness, but that when it is mixed with the rain of Zeus the joy of it and the delight remain, and the injurious element that causes madness and license is corrected."[3] It is quite a paradox to discover this control at the heart of what is commonly misunderstood to be the religion of uncontrolled orgy, and to compare this with the modern-day use of alcohol, which almost invariably, by these standards, descends into abuse.

CARRYING THE WAND

The Bacchae describe the experience of being a follower of Dionysos:

> Blessed are those
> Who are called by the gods,
> Who are summoned to the Mysteries
> Of ecstatic union.
> Blessed are those who are purified
> And walk alone in the high places,
> Who enter into the sacred rituals
> Of the Great Goddess,
> Crowned with ivy, bearing the wand,
> Invoking the name of Dionysos!
>
> All joy is here, all pleasure.
> The priest, wrapped in the sacred deerskin
> Falls upon the earth in ecstasy,
> But we, the women, run on in delight.
> The priest, alone, takes the sacrificial goat.
> He eats its flesh, he drinks its blood.
>
> Empowered, he speaks in tongues. We follow him.
>
> The priest now runs with us,
> His holy wand burns bright with fire from heaven,
>
> And the sacred flute is sounding,
> With life, with love, with laughter.

We have here most of the elements of the Dionysiac ritual. The first stage is purification, although the means whereby this was achieved are not elaborated upon. Certainly there was a belief in ancient Greece that the skin of a freshly killed sheep or ram would, if you wrapped it about you or stood upon it, bring about purification and protection. If in addition you slept upon it, it would promote revelatory dreams. A clue is afforded by an incomplete wall painting in a house called The Villa of the Mysteries,[4] in Pompeii. Ten scenes show episodes from the Dionysian mysteries, one of which depicts a woman bowing for flagellation. While this may now raise a few eyebrows, the practice of ritual flagellation, properly understood, is not a matter of torment of the flesh or sexual perversion, but is a technique used to assist in the development of inner vision. It is, for instance, a widely adopted practice in some aspects of modern witchcraft and is nicely explained in one of the older passages in the Wiccan Book of Shadows under the heading "To Get the Sight."[5] This describes a safe and controlled way of developing inner vision under the supervision of a tutor, in which flagellation may be used "very lightly" in order to take the blood away from the brain, stimulate the imagination, and eventually obtain the ecstasy of knowledge and communion with the Goddess. A further passage describes how the same technique can be used to assist in the technique of astral projection, or leaving the body. While it is hard to date some of the passages of the Book of Shadows, it is likely that what is being described is from a long-established tradition and that there is a continuing thread of influence of the Dionysiac mysteries in modern witchcraft.

The next part of the ritual as described by the Bacchantes was the entering into a "secret chamber" within the mountain. This is a common element of religious ritual, particularly if, as in the mysteries of Dionysos, an essential part of the ritual is the contacting of the powers of the deep earth, and thus the corresponding root energy within one's self. In this instance the cave is described more exactly as being the "secret chamber the Kouretes knew" and the "holy cavern . . . where Zeus was cradled." This suggests that not only are the inner mysteries to take place within a cave that was the birthplace of Dionysos, or at least the place where Zeus deposited him after his second, divine birth, but that the cave was also the same place where Zeus was born. So the situation is that the Bacchantes go to the cave to be reborn as Dionysos who was reborn as Zeus.

Dionysos' second birth was rather more propitious than his first, and was attended by Kouroi, eternal youths. This word is difficult to translate, especially because there are apparently no modern equivalents. But we must remember that we are considering events that took place at least three thousand years ago, and that the Kouroi were to a certain extent particular to that time and place. The Kouroi appear in initiation ceremonies as guardians, often in the guise of warriors, who accompany and protect the aspirant as he or she passes through the process of symbolic death and rebirth, a time in which the initiate is particularly open and vulnerable.

Essentially, they are both human and divine; they are of both this world and the inner world, hence their particular gifts in assisting in such rites of passage. A Kouros is an eternal youth. He has grown to maturity but remains in full and unblemished vigor and strength. He is an attendant on the gods, a *daimone*. Strabo describes them as "certain young men who perform armed movements accompanied by dancing." It would appear that part of their function is to frighten away any untoward influences at the moment of birth, and certainly the arrival of Zeus into the world was a hazardous affair, as Kronos, his father, had the unfortunate habit of swallowing his young immediately after their birth. His mother, Rhea, enlisted the help of the Kouroi to frighten Kronos away long enough for the Kouroi to take the infant Zeus into a cave and rear him into manhood. With Rhea absent (or at least discarnate) and Semele dead, both Zeus and Dionysos were brought up *in loco parentis* by an assortment of semihuman creatures. But they themselves became Kouroi in turn, as did Apollo, Orpheus, and numerous other "Divine Youths" who are sent to change the course of humanity and to introduce new elements of the divine plan.

The Kouroi were youthful and androgynous in appearance. In fact, the description of Dionysos when he appeared in Thebes is as good a description of them as will be found.

> A playboy, master of illusion
> Has come from Lydia, drunk on wine.
> With perfumed curls and eyes too bright:
> Beware this toy of Aphrodite!

They brought with them a driving force, but this energy was not particularly sexual or even "male." It was the essence of a particular energy that is normally only experienced for brief moments, but that they captured and retained. It was this energy that Dionysos especially embodied, and the Kouroi were his priests, just as he in turn was the priest of the goatfoot god, Pan.

Teiresias, a blind seer in *The Bacchae,* comments that:

> Dionysos makes no rules.
> His women make these choices for themselves.
> What's chastity? The women chose, they take control,
> The Bacchic rites do not compel,
> For purity lies within, and this all women know.

His words are wise, and behind them lies an understanding that the relationship between Dionysos and the Bacchae is one that includes the energy of polarity, yet transforms it and transcends it.

REBIRTH IN DIONYSOS

It is a very real and deeply felt concern of women that if they "let go" they will be violated, and this fear is no less real whether it is in relation to an outer world or inner world male figure. But the polarity between Dionysos and the Bacchae is not the confrontation of male versus female, and it therefore offers a potential freedom of expression and experience that is not fettered by any limiting preconceptions as to how, or at what level, the polarity will be experienced. It is simplistic to say that Dionysos appears to the women as if he were female, or that the women running free upon the mountain are acting as men. They are accessing other levels within themselves by opening up areas of the psyche that express "maleness" and "femaleness." The women have forsaken their traditional roles within the normal civilization of Thebes and are at a physical level behaving in a wild manner normally more acceptable in men. In this way, they can relate to Dionysos in a way that is free from the normal physical boundaries of sexuality, and this provides almost infinite possibilities in which the creative and empowering forces of polarity *within the psyche* of an individual can be discovered. For the women, this has to do with the discovery of the animus, the masculine within. The key to unlocking this does not always lies in the mimicry "traditional" masculinity. For example, a woman will not necessarily discover her true animus by driving a truck or acting laddish, but rather she will find it through those means that speak directly to the creative masculine spark within her. And for his part, Dionysos does not present a conventionally "macho" male image. The men of Thebes find this disconcerting, but like Jesus, he provides an environment that is sufficiently safe to enable the women to discover a freedom they would not normally be able to explore, and above all, to express the masculinity within them in a way that is unthreatened and unthreatening.

To return to the ritual, after the purification came a period of prolonged physical exertion achieved by running, dancing, laughing, and listening to or playing music, all of which encourage one to break through the civilized bounds of restraint and loosen the deeper instincts. Once this change had been brought about, the celebrant or neophyte would then enter a cave—whether actually or in representation—and, having drunk wine moderately and eaten of the body of the God in the form of raw goat's flesh, would enter into ecstatic union with him, joining ". . . soul with soul in mystic unity."

The play describes how the celebration of the mysteries of Dionysos provides a vehicle for the ecstasy that was ours before the pain of separation from the spirit. Teiresias describes the process as "the two powers which are supreme in human affairs." While Demeter, he explains, provides humans with food for the physical body, Dionysos provides a food for the spirit that will enable humankind to remember the joy of existence before the suffering of this "unhappy race" fell upon them. In fact, it is suggested that the very act of remembering through wine-induced sleep of how the world used to be is the only way in which contact with a pre-Fall existence is retained. The memory of this state lies deep within us all, but is covered by the veils of existence and usually only accessed in sleep, dreams and ritual.

> What are the blessings brought by Dionysos?
> They are counterpart to the bread of life . . .
> From the juice of the grape comes the wine of love,
> The sorrows of life are drowned in wine, in sleep.
> The wine is Dionysos
> And Dionysos is a God.
> You drink of God through wine,
> And through Dionysos flows God's love.

We have here a description of Dionysos as one who has come as a redeemer and who offers a way out from the otherwise hopeless condition in which humankind, cut off from its original state of bliss, forgets what it may be. This escape is achieved through the vehicle of the juice of the earth-grown vine, a juice that Dionysos then *embodies*. By this action he not only imbues the drinker with the experience of the ecstasy of this forgotten union, but also acts as a guide or instructor in the process of remembrance. By this act, Dionysos, whose spirit is voluntarily embodied in the wine, takes upon himself the "sins of the earth," which becomes a libation when the wine is poured out, a symbolic offering of humankind that is recognized and taken up by the gods through the mediation of Dionysos.

We should remember that the name "Pentheus" means "sorrow," although it also suggests the fivefold form that symbolizes humankind.

Through his name, Pentheus is a representative of the state of humankind in separation from God. But he serves as an example of how *not* to achieve the way of redemption that is offered by Dionysos, for he makes the all too easy mistake of assuming that the ecstasy of the women is the result of sexual orgy and, rather than participating in the liberation of the wine and the dance, puts himself in the position of critical observer. This only serves to exacerbate his separation from all that is holy.

The gift of Dionysos is remarkable and timeless. His message is that life will cease to be a futile struggle if you can step away from an unquestioning acceptance of apparent reality and see the reality that lies behind. Or in other words, that unhappiness is a point of view, and an entirely self-imposed one at that. The irony is that pride literally leads to the Fall: the misguided belief that, in attempting to be "more" than we are destined to be, we actually become less through the consequent separation of forgetting. The descriptions of the women on Cithaeron, just as the biblical descriptions of the women followers of Jesus in the mountainous countyside of Judea, tell of a pre-Fall state in which humans, animals, and the life within the trees and rocks themselves form an effortless whole. Through their ritual and ecstatic union with Dionysos the women are enabled to perform goddesslike or supernatural feats when threatened by intruders. Having become like the God/Goddess, they are entirely freed from the normal constraints of physicality and are existing literally in a pre-Fall state:

> The rocks bring forth water
> At the touch of a woman's wand.
> The earth gushes wine
> When a woman plunges her thyrsus into its depths,
> The earth flows with milk
> And gives forth its sweet white stream,
> While honey drips from her thyrsus' tip.

But what is made clear in *The Bacchae* is that to return to a pre-Fall state of existence does not necessarily produce a state where "back to nature" is synonymous with "sweetness and light." Eve was disempowered by Adam and by all those who misrepresented her initiatory, "what if." But, as *The Bacchae* is at pains to point out, there is a lot more than a simple innocence or purity involved in the Dionysian return to this state. Agave, one of the Bacchae who is aroused to a frenzy at the sight of Pentheus in the pine tree as he spies on them, is responsible for tearing him limb by limb in a fury that echoes Set's dismemberment of the body of Osiris. She tears his head from his body, only becoming aware of what she has done when she comes down to the normal state of consciousness symbolized by the city of Thebes, and when the citizens reveal to her that she has torn off the head of her own son. Agave has returned to a place where she is no longer capable of making the distinctions that we rely upon for maintenance of normal human society. She has taken on the archetype of the destroyer, the reductive, grinding-down, death-bringing goddess who, although equal and opposite to the creative, life-bringing goddess, tends to be less appreciated for obvious reasons—and almost entirely ignored by Western mythology.

Here we have the elements of the Dionysian mysteries. The polarity inherent in this lies very much within the individual hearts of those who pursue this way of approaching the Divine within themselves. For women in particular they open up the possibility of a creative relationship with an inner masculine energy, whether this takes the form of Dionysos, or the inner daemon, or a male elemental or faery contact. A Dionysian ritual is not simply a personal communication with the God or inner masculine, but one in which the celebrant becomes like the God—*becomes Dionysos*—and who can say what this experience will be, or where it will lead. There is an apparently "easy" attractiveness of "green ray" magical work, with its song and dance and its joyous physical celebration that has an immediate if sometimes superficial appeal. But at its heart lies an initiatory experience that takes the celebrant outside of all human boundaries in a way that can lead to ecstatic union with the divine. The sadness in all this is that when properly understood the Dionysian mythos offers a way of redemption that is every bit as real and "workable" as the redemption offered by the Church. But ironically, while it has escaped the censorship that has overpowered the true Christian message, it has clearly not attained the status of an international religion. We cannot help but wonder if "Christians" were able to find a little of Dionysos in Jesus and "pagans" were able to discover a little of Jesus in Dionysos; then something of the true Christ might be found.

CHAPTER TWELVE

ARTHUR AND GWENEVERE

THE END OF THE LINE

We turn finally to a couple whose names spring most readily to mind in any consideration of the manifestation of polarity: King Arthur and Queen Gwenevere. Because they are more recent than other mythological couples they are well documented; in fact they are almost household names in the British Isles. But although they represent the apogee of the process of polarity magic that has been described in the preceding chapters, rather than representing the culmination of that process, much has by now gone very wrong indeed. The puzzling truth is that this famous couple achieved only a dysfunctional union—to use an inelegant if accurate phrase. There was an extramarital affair, an apparent lack of progeny apart from Arthur's son, the sinister Mordred, and the couple lived only to witness the final disintegration of their court and kingdom. Yet the persistence with which this catalog of disaster and missed opportunity remains perversely at the center of the myth and matter of Britain is evidence of the continuing role they somehow play in the folk-soul of the nation, even though that role may on closer examination prove to be less obvious than is usually thought. It is rather as if, when looking at this particular king and queen, we peer through the darkened glass of the wrong end of a kaleidoscope that affords us only glimpses of how things once were when Isis loved Osiris and all was well in heaven. We wrongly assume that these dimly perceived fragments are the true and whole picture.

However, we who stand upon the earth and gaze upward at the stars are in a unique position to put our hands upon the rim of this kaleidoscope of fragments and slowly turn its barrels back to their true alignment. It is possible in this way to bring about the re-arrangement of these colorful but fractured pieces to a new pattern of perfection and to allow the full clear light of the Divine to shine right down through. The pattern of archetypes such as Arthur and Gwenevere and the court of the Round Table is not fixed. The force or energy of the powers they contain is controlled by the amount of spiritual energy flowing into them from above, but their form is very much created by we who stand on the earth, and it is our habitual thoughts and conceptions over many centuries that have largely been responsible for the building of their shapes into their present form. It therefore follows that these archetypal forms, which may be described as thoughtforms but on a national level, can also be altered, for good or for ill. When they are worked upon in love, light, and wisdom the process is one that is sometimes re-ferred to as the "redemption of the archetypes," and it is that process with which this chapter is particularly concerned. In order to see how it works we must look more closely at each small part of the pattern by going right back to the beginning, for the fragments of the pattern are many and varied.

Let us then focus for a while on what we have in the stories of King Arthur as they have reached us in the twenty-first century. We have traced the continuing, albeit hidden, tradition of polarity magic that lies beneath the Western Mystery Tradition and explored some of the examples of the relationship that exists between pairs of historical, mythological, and archetypal figures such as Merlin and Gwenddydd, or Akhenaten and Nefertiti. The dynamics of these re-lationships work primarily on the inner levels that lie behind the outer figures of the Arthurian legends—the kings and queens and

the Knights and Ladies of the Court. The relationship that exists between these inner and outer levels has well been called the "secret
tradition" in Arthurian legend, and it would be fair to say that the
tradition that informs the Arthurian mythology contains the essence
of all that we have discussed.

Just as the stories of the Children of Israel are a tantalizing and
ever-changing mixture of historical fact, spiritual reality, and idealis-
tic wish-fulfillment, so do Arthur and the Knights and Ladies of the
Round Table provide an unusually rich and fertile ground in their
fullness of action, their hundreds of named characters, and their
well-documented and eventful plots. Recent research has emphasized the documented historical reality of many of the characters,
and to view them in this way can be a refreshing surprise as well as
help to ground the mythology in physical locations. Up to a point it
doesn't matter whether a character's origin was a small town in
southern France or the astral plane. What matters is whether the
magic continues to work. But this uncertainty may be a reflection
of the deeper confusion that has gradually pervaded the Arthuriad.
This confusion centers upon the nature of the higher spiritual archetypes and the process by which they are brought down through
the characters. While the polarity between the various couples such
as Arthur and Gwenevere or Gwenevere and Lancelot is a matter of
perennial interest, the greater polarity that should provide access to
the highest truths and principles is conspicuous by its absence. The
stories have become secularized and the mighty archetypal figures
that once inspired their actions within the world have long disappeared. There are no gods and goddesses in the Arthurian legends.
Indeed, the mythology of the British Isles as a whole is bottom
heavy. While we have a profusion—and a confusion—of semi-his-
torical characters, the stories are sadly lacking in the deity depart-
ment. One has only to bring to mind the pantheon of Egyptian,
Greek, Nordic, or, as we have seen, early Hebrew divinities to realize that these islands have the doubtful distinction of being arguably

the only Western culture whose mythology has no recognized goddess, no native god. If we wish to look for god/goddess forms we have to turn elsewhere. The earliest written stories, those of the mythological cycle of Irish legend, speak of the Tuatha de Danaan, or the children of Dana, but she has remained a dimly perceived figure outside her native land and the Gaelic Celtic tradition, though possessing richness of story and depth of spirituality has for the most part not passed down into the mainstream of British mythology. This is one of the unfortunate results of the tradition of the priests of the Celtic races, the Druids, whose undisputed wisdom and holiness did not include the foresight to make some record of the nature of their religion to pass on to their inheritors.

The importance of Arthur, Lancelot, and Gwenevere is that they exist in the hearts and minds of the people of the British Isles as guides and representatives of inner truths—whether consciously perceived or not—but the absence of the higher archetypes and divinities only serves to emphasize our tendency to elevate them to a semidivine status that they do not possess. The Arthurian legends can be understood at every level and appreciated alike by children and hardened esotericists; they form one of the most all-encompassing and readily accessible mystery systems available to the modern Western world. It is therefore all the more important that we look closely at what they say, what their basic premise is, and how fully, and in how balanced and true a manner, they represent the nature of inner truths and realities to those who are affected by them. As they provide much of the root material of the folk soul, we are affected by them whether we know it or not.

As we have described in the preceding pages, the roots of the Western Mystery Tradition draw from many nations and many cultures—Atlantis and beyond, Sumer and Eden, Egypt, Greece and Israel, Celts and Saxons, the stars and the deep earth. All these traditions surface in various forms within the Arthurian mythology, not least because it developed so much later than the others. Compared with the high and distant magic of Sumer or the eternal truths of Isis and Osiris, the Arthurian legends in their present form are very recent. And so they act as a whirlpool or vortex that simultaneously draws in and throws out like the cauldron of regeneration that lies at their heart, a symbol of the catalytic process that is performed in the life-blood of the soul of the nation. The legends have stayed firmly rooted within the public consciousness: the stream of books published every year that retell them with both esoteric interpretations and those that appeal to the general reader, continues in ever greater volume. But with this proliferation has come a sort of deadening, a familiarity that has bred, if not contempt, then at least an unquestioning assumption that whatever their origin they still serve the same way they served us a thousand years ago, and that the archetypes that they currently present still function adequately as vehicles for spiritual truth. The truth is that they do not.

So let us look first at the fundamental relationship between the archetypal king and queen of these islands, for theirs is the primary pivot around which the mythology turns. Their relationship presents us with a golden opportunity, as it is continually reinterpreted according to the moral and social climate of the time. But this process is only a projection of our human failures and shortcomings onto the archetypes. Most people would agree that their relationship falls something short of perfect—but then it might be said that, after all, "they're only human," and we are only human, and so by endlessly analyzing the reasons that lie behind this regally failing marriage we may find enlightenment or even encouragement in our own failures and difficulties. The triangle between Arthur, Lancelot, and Gwenevere is reinterpreted by every generation according to its own lights—and darknesses. The Victorian attitude (which still persists) was of righteous outrage at Gwenevere's adulterous behavior with Lancelot, which, it was suggested, was the reason why Arthur's kingdom fell. It was the scene in the Garden of Eden all over again. The solution was to blame the woman and to invent the story of Gwenevere's penitence and lonely death in a nunnery.

Later generations brought a more tolerant understanding, reflecting the social and political changes of the twentieth century. Psychological analysis prompted another look at the stories in the light of Freud and Jung. Gwenevere's affair was perhaps not entirely her fault. Maybe Arthur was just as much to blame as his wife. Perhaps he was too busy fighting and didn't talk to her enough. Perhaps he had problems in bed. But the problem with the reductionist approach is its tendency to sink the entire mythology into the morass of the human condition while preventing any light from the higher levels of the spirit to permeate the gloom.

Another approach to the central pivot of the relationship between Arthur and Gwenevere has been to recognize the inner source of the problem by recognizing Arthur as the Wounded King. This aligns Arthur to the archetype of an avatar, a savior of humankind who bears the pain of an injury that symbolizes the suffering of the human condition and therefore, by extension, of the earth. The Waste Land, all too obvious in our world, is therefore seen to be the result of the wound to the king, who is the representative of the earth. Heal the king and you heal the world. Indeed, he is often now called the Wounded Healer—one who bears an injury or makes a sacrifice that eventually brings knowledge or enlightenment to himself and therefore to humankind. An example of this is the suffering of Odin, who hung upon the World Tree but received through this sacrifice of his lower self the gift of the knowledge of the runes; or Christ, who hung upon the cross of the elements of the world. In truth, it is a process that every soul that comes to earth is engaged in, whether consciously or unconsciously. It is only the sacrifice, the giving up of centered focus upon mundane things, that brings progress to the light above.

But the problem with this approach is that Arthur stays wounded. He does not receive enlightenment; he does not save. He neither changes nor progresses. He fights his dozen battles that appear to have little effect either on the outer kingdom of Britain or the inner kingdom of Logres, or even on the lesser kingdom of his own self. When the time comes for him to bring his future wife home he passively allows another man, Lancelot, to do the job for him. He becomes estranged from Gwenevere and spends the rest of his life as a shadowy seated figure who even, as we are told in *The Mabinogion,* falls asleep when his Knights tell each other of their latest adventures, and wakes up only when his dinner is ready.

All this results in a figure who does not in any way function properly as a king, either as the leader of a nation or as king of his own self. It is as if when the spurious "polarity" of fighting the enemy has vanished, then Arthur progresses no further: when his outer battles finish he loses his *raison d'etre,* the plot of his own life. As Merlin says, riding up on "a great black horse" in the early pages of Arthur's life, described by Malory in *Le Morte d'Arthur:*

> Thou hast never done, hast thou not done enough? Of three score thousand this day has thou left alive but fifteen thousand, and it is time to say "Ho!" For God is wroth with thee, that thou wilt never have done . . .[1]

There is a sad truth in Merlin's summary of Arthur's behavior that rings down to us through the ages, and because he still retains a very powerful influence on the soul of a nation through his continuing function as an archetype, this is something that should concern us very much. It means that when we invoke Arthur, either by deliberate magical act, or by any other means such as reading about him, throwing tarot cards, or watching films about him, we are reinforcing the inadequate form of the archetype, and making it all the more solid and real. Arthur the king represents national pride and the bulldog spirit. He *should*—but doesn't—represent the full power of the central axis that reaches between heaven and earth, providing and supporting the mediation of Divine love to his people and the earthly practice of that love in his relationship with his queen. He *should*—but doesn't—represent the balanced power of the Sun Temple at the center of his kingdom while retaining full contact with the inner wisdom of the Temple of the Sea and Stars, as represented by the many voices of the Lady of the Lake.

In fact, Arthur himself makes no attempt to search for the symbol of spiritual power and grace that is available to him (the Grail) and it is his knights who for better or worse make the attempt to find it. While this lack of initiative on Arthur's part is sometimes explained as his need to stay at home and look after the kingdom, the pragmatic approach ignores the deeper truth that Arthur's kingdom of Britain, or Logres, is best looked after if its king proves to be not only a leader in battle but also a leader in peace, who, having restored physical wholeness to the kingdom, then inspires a spiritual wholeness by initiating the search for higher truth. His knights should not be responsible for this task because they do not stand at the center of the kingdom—Tiphareth, in Qabalist terms—and are not in a proper position to pass down the results of their quest. It is Arthur who should stand centrally upon his kingdom with his heart in Tiphareth and his gaze turned ever upward to the Divine worlds. What brings about the ultimate failure of his kingdom is not the behavior of his queen, nor the threats of the marauding Saxons, but the fact that in the kingdom of his own self there is no love. In addition, he does not give any expression to the polarity that is a reflection of the creative process of Divine love. And so at the heart of his story is his own lack of heart and a staleness, a lack of true purpose, which is by no means the same thing as the sacrificial wound carried by a sacred king.

The symbol that has made his court famous as a place of justice and equality is the Round Table, and this is also, paradoxically, a symbol of the failure that lies at its heart. As a symbol it can work well through many layers: the fellowship of the knights, the circle of the seasons and the year, the greater round of the Sun through the twelve portions of the zodiac. But this symbol is incomplete without a center such as a central Sun or a central symbol of divinity. Arthur should function as a solar hero or as a solar deity, but he does not. There are hints of this Herculean task echoed in the stories of his twelve battles, but in the perverseness of failure that besets these legends, his last battle that should have symbolized the final triumph over the trials of each of the twelve signs ends in defeat at the hands of his own son Mordred. And whereas the challenging and defeat of the father by the son should indicate the normal succession of one generation, one era by another, in this instance the defeat was ignominious and the son a product of dark magic and incest whose life came to nothing.

The Round Table also fails to function at the levels we would perhaps expect from such a cosmic symbol. There are no clear planetary associations and, as we have seen, there is no one clear solar hero. Some, such as Gawain, or even Lancelot, are pretenders to the role, but there can only be by definition one solar hero. There is no representative of the Moon sitting at the Round Table, whether priest or priestess, nor are there any stellar attributes. Some versions of the story describe the table as part of Gwenevere's dowry, given to her by her father Leodogrance of Cameliard, who had it from Uther Pendragon. It was constructed by Merlin as a model of the table of the Last Supper, but here the comparison fails in that it lacks the chief celebrant of this holy feast. The gods and goddesses of our lands should also be seated about the table, but they are absent. The children of Dana—Lugh, Mananaan, Arianrhod—have long since disappeared, all except Bran the Blessed, whose head was dug up from under the Tower of London by Arthur in a revealingly misguided attempt by him to prove his equal status with this giant.

In fact, there are few stories of inspired leadership or true and lasting love within the Arthurian mythos. The disjointedness that Hamlet found in the state of Denmark has also fallen upon the court of Camelot, and one wonders what sustains the existence of its inhabitants other than our own questioning.

Fundamental to the problems of confusion in levels and the deadness and sterility that sets in when there is lack of proper polarity is the lack of higher levels in the mythology. On the one hand the characters seem to be so very nearly human that we are inclined to speak about them as if they *were* human, and to interpret them in that light. On the other hand, because the higher levels of existence are not properly represented in the stories, they can be falsely elevated to roles they are not able to fulfill, and the failure that results is a thread that runs depressingly throughout the mythology, culminating in the sad list of those who, for reasons of "human error," are prevented from reaching the Grail. The message of the Arthurian stories is that the Grail is not the culmination of the heart's desire, but is a spiritual trophy reserved for those who have already achieved perfection. And even then, as with Dindrane, the sacrifice that can be demanded by it is neither noble nor necessary.

We should therefore not be surprised to find that there are an equal number of "problems" with Gwenevere. One of the basic premises and functions of polarity is that the man is typically "positive" in the outer worlds and the woman is typically "positive" in the inner worlds. We do not suggest for a moment that these roles can't be reversed; the ability to work equally well in either mode should be the aim, but either way things don't work well if both are negative at the same time on the same level! As we have seen, when his outer battles are over, Arthur gives up the challenge of functioning in the outer world. However, there is little evidence that his queen functions positively in any world.

We know even less of Gwenevere's origins than we know of Arthur's. Her name means "white shadow" or "white phantom," and because of the telltale "wen" or "wyn" element in her name we know that she is not human but comes from the inner world of faery. It is very important that we are clear about this. *Gwenevere is not human, she is faery.* The odd thing is that just as we seem to have a collective mental blockage with Arthur that keeps him trapped in his outworn image, we also seem to be unwilling to accept that Gwen-evere is not human. And yet once this fact is taken on board it means that we can begin to look at the whole of the Arthurian mythos, particularly those parts that refer to the relationship between Arthur and his queen, in a different light. Apart from anything else it reveals another problem of level and polarity at the heart of the legends. Marriages between human and faery are very rarely attempted at a physical level, yet we have Arthur and Gwenevere apparently existing and married in the outer world of physicality.

Our reluctance to see Gwenevere as she really is has resulted in some unhelpful interpretations of her over the years. In general, writers have taken her name "white phantom" as indicative of a sort of paleness, an overall impression that she was not quite all there. There may be some basis of truth in this, as she might well have ap-peared "pale" and lacking in earthly physical substance, but this has been interpreted as an ineffectual wishy-washiness or lack of char-acter rather than an accurate description of a faery woman in a human, physical world.

What lay behind this marriage between the two races? Following the tradition of many ages, Arthur's kingship would have been rati-fied by his union with a representative of the inner land—that is to say with a faery being. But as we have seen, it was normally the case that this union took the form of an inner mating in which the human king was initiated into the deep wisdom of the land by the faery representative of the great earth goddess, who withdrew once her task was done. This act of empowerment enabled the king to properly carry out the requirements of his goddess the sovereignty of the land; without this inner validation he would not be able to fulfill his true role as king and serve the inner queen. He was her champion or regent in the outer world. It was neither intended nor generally considered possible that the relationship between them should be as of the normal human partnership of man and wife, and the marriage of Arthur and Gwenevere was one of those few.

There are other stories of such marriage between the two races, but most of those ended in sorrow because the rules that governed faery behavior were not understood by mortal partners and were broken through ignorance or curiosity. It is worth making a short digression to look at one of these because it can shed some light on the marriage and general situation of Arthur and Gwenevere.

Legend tells of the half-faery Melusine, born of the faery Pressine and a mortal king of Scotland, Elinus. Pressine agreed to marry Elinus only on the condition that he never saw her giving birth. When she gave birth to three daughters—Melusine, Melior, and Plantina, he broke his vow—and so she returned instantly to Avalon. Melusine later became the wife of Raymond, Earl of the House of Lusignan, but only on condition that he left her in seclusion every Saturday. This, unknown to him, was because of a curse put on her by her mother that every Saturday for twenty-four hours she would become a serpent from the waist down. Raymond kept his promise for many years; they were happily married and, unlike Arthur and Gwenevere, produced many children. However, all of the children were deformed. The first had one red eye and one blue, the second a face red as fire, the third had one eye lower than the other, the next had a face scarred by a mark like a lion's claw, the next had only one eye, another had three eyes, and so on. But Raymond eventually discovered her secret and blurted out to her that he knew she was a faery. At this she climbed onto a windowsill and jumped into the air, where she turned into a great winged snake and flew away. Although she was never seen again, it was rumored that she returned regularly to care for her last two sons who, after all the previous problems, suffered no deformity and who presumably continued the Lusignan line—which from then onward contained faery blood.

This story, so similar in principle to that of Arthur and Gwenevere, shows some of the problems that exist in human/faery marriages that also apply to Arthur and Gwenevere. But once Gwenevere is seen properly as a faery or inner world being rather than a nondescript and failing human, then much that is otherwise unsatisfactory or inexplicable begins to make more sense. In fact, if we "take her seriously" as a faery being, we can ask some very relevant questions, such as: Why was she married to Arthur? Whose decision was it, and what was the intended outcome? Indeed, these questions should more pertinently be asked of Gwenevere herself, rather than presuming her to be silent on these matters. Somehow over the centuries she has lost her voice and her power.

The conditions laid down by the faery partner in the stories of Pressine and Melusine are not made in idleness but speak of the great physical problems they have in taking on physical form and, even more so, in giving birth. Allowing for the interpretation of events added by the storytellers, it would seem from such accounts that the faery's continuing existence in the mortal world relied upon a certain suspension of disbelief on the part of the humans with whom she lived. It would once have been said that a form of magic, of shapeshifting, of alteration in appearance was needed on the part of the faery in order to present a consistently human form to those who saw her. In more modern terms, beings from the faery worlds exist at a higher "vibration" than those in the mortal world, and for faeries to appear consistently to human sight, they either have to lower their rate of vibration and/or the humans to whom they appear must raise theirs so they can meet halfway. This is not always possible, and gives rise to the human perception that faeries have a habit of suddenly disappearing. When the faery "glamour" of assuming a form that is not theirs is broken, or when the human partner breaks the spell and confronts the faery with the bald truth, then the conditions in which human and faery can meet are also broken. "I'll believe in you if you believe in me," is not an invitation to fantasy but a necessary prerequisite for both human and faery to maintain that halfway state in which each can meet the other. When this is no longer possible, then the result is the faery's disappearance to human sight.

Other tales of faery/human encounters suggest where further problems lie. When Thomas the Rhymer is taken into the faery kingdom by the queen of Elfland, his passage from the physical to the faery world is marked by a river of blood.

> For forty days and forty nights
> He wade through red blood to the knee
> And he saw neither sun nor moon
> But heard the roaring of the sea.[2]

The river of blood is none but his own human blood, like a river between the worlds, and it indicates a fundamental difference between human and faery physiology. Faery "blood," in the sense of their equivalent of this life-supporting fluid, is a very different substance. It may be that the persistent descriptions of faery as "white" are descriptions of the appearance of their life force, their "blood," which is white, or light, or shining, or without color. Without getting too deeply into the issue of faery physiology, it would seem that the red blood that is fundamental to human life forms presents something of a barrier between the worlds. It is interesting to speculate that perhaps the Washer at the Ford between the worlds is not washing the blood from the dead warriors' clothes in order to wash them of their earthly sins (the association of blood with sin is a later "Christian" interpretation), but in order for them to pass freely into the inner world of faery unhampered by their human blood.

If this is indeed the problem, then it would certainly explain why Pressine was not willing for her human husband to witness her in childbirth, as the circumstances of a faery giving birth to a child in the mortal world would be likely to be somewhat different from a normal human birth. It may also explain why Arthur and Gwenevere did not conceive any children, but that Arthur's child with the faery Morgan was the spiritually deformed Mordred.

Gwenevere, like Pressine and Melusine, also disappears at regular intervals, although her disappearances from the mortal kingdom are generally described as "abductions," a word that implies that she was unwillingly snatched from her mortal surroundings. We can interpret these abductions in several ways. If we look at them from a purely human point of view, then it would seem that at intervals a jealous and ill-minded man in Arthur's kingdom took a fancy to the queen and thought he would carry her off to his country. If we look at them in the light of the mythology of Pluto and Persephone, then we can perceive Gwenevere as queen of both outer and inner worlds who stays with the dark king during the winter months and the bright son of light during summer. But we are left with the problem that she does not appear to function either as a queen should (that is to say, as the embodiment of motherhood) or as the fecund representative of sovereignty. A third and usually overlooked point of view is that of the Otherworld, that of the faery kingdom, but the legends do not, of course, record their point of view.

There remains another point of view: that represented by Merlin. He had already achieved one deliberate engineering of bloodlines by using his magic to bring about the conception of Arthur. This was through the mating of Ygraine, an Atlantean Sun priestess, and Uther Pendrgon of native British stock. He may have continued to have designs on the seed of Arthur by attempting to bring about an interbreeding between human and faery kingdoms of Arthur and Gwenevere. It is at this point that we have arrived at the end of the long thread that has unravelled from our first chapter.

Whatever the reasons behind their union and the physical problems that it presented (which subsequently have been so misinterpreted), ultimately it must appear that they did not successfully bridge the gap between them on any level. It may be that Arthur, knowing of Gwenevere's origins, deliberately sent Lancelot to fetch her from her father. Lancelot, who was brought up by the Lady of the Lake, was nearer to faery than Arthur, and it appears that Arthur did not discover the ability to walk between the worlds. But it seems that Gwenevere, for her part, was similarly unable to relate to the human world in any way that would bring knowledge of the faery kingdom, its wisdom, or its joy, to those of the human kingdom she ruled equally with Arthur. We get no sense when reading the stories that their union was one that encompassed the many polarities that lie between the worlds and their inhabitants. Their task was to reforge the links between faery and human kingdoms; to be, together, a symbol and gateway to the way back, and their combined role was intended to stretch far beyond the problems of individual achievement. In terms of the Atlantean temple structure with which we opened this study, neither the Sun Temple nor the Temple of the Sea and the Stars is properly established at the Court of Arthur, and there is definitely no communication between them!

But there is another additional and apparently extraneous element to the Arthurian mythology, and one that brings the potential for redemption: the realignment of the kaleidoscope's fragments.

In the early years of the first century A.D., Joseph of Arimathea came to Britain from Judea—perhaps only once, perhaps several times. The biblical record affords him an acknowledged historical role by describing his connection with the events of Christ's death: the rites of passage in the cave in the Garden of Gethsamene and the subsequent resurrection. The cave belonged to Joseph, who had prepared it for this purpose and who by virtue of this fact alone played a pivotal role in the subsequent unfolding of heaven and earth that took place in the tomb in the cave. But although the biblical account quietly records the manner in which Joseph provided the physical setting for such cosmic events, as far as the Gospel writers were concerned, the story ended there. However, this one man's actions on earth provided the physical, earthing end of the pole of a universal event that stretched far beyond the time of Christ's life on earth. The significance of Joseph's actions reaches back like a shuttle traveling on a loom from those first years of the Christian era into the early history of the tribes of Israel. It picks up the thread of that time: the thread that was the essence of their religion and of the form in which they would make their worship, as revealed to them by God in the deserts of Sinai, and where we started at the beginning of this book. This thread is looped forward in time by the actions of Joseph of Arimathea to be woven through the life and death of Christ. Then these several strands are knotted securely into the fabric of another time, another land: the Celtic tradition within the British Isles. And in the same manner that he facilitated the physical arrangements within the Garden of Gethsemane while that glorious transformation took place, he was also the prime instigator in the physical arrangements necessary for bringing the essence of the faith of the Children of Israel, as revealed through Christ, the priest-king, to Britain.

This is commented on in Frederick Bligh Bond's book *The Company of Avalon,* in a passage that may sound somewhat politically incorrect to modern ears, but that makes the point very clearly.

> According to the story as received through J. A. From the "Watchers" *[a group of inner plane communicators]* we are to regard the coming of Joseph and his companions as but one episode in a long sequence carrying us back to most ancient times. It is claimed that Ynyswitrin or, as we now know it, Glaston, had been from distant ages a powerful focus of spiritual teaching and nurture. Light had come to Britain from the East, by mercantile channels, for centuries previously, and the traders who brought it, themselves of Semitic blood and sharing the pure monotheism of the Hebrew, carried to these islands a religious ideal which took root among the British and made them peculiarly ready for the reception, in fulness of time, of the Christian aspect of their cult. It is clearly stated in these scripts . . . that the British Isles have been, under the great evolutionary plan, the seed-bed of a select branch of the true Israelitish race (of which the modern Jew is a section largely diluted with alien blood intermixed during the Captivity and otherwise). Consequently we bear in our racial faith a large and necessary ingredient of sympathy with the pure monotheism of the Hebrew race,

and this was expressed in the flower of Druidical culture . . .
it was coloured by the traditions of the temple worship of
the Hebrew, and so we find the script speaking of the same
tradition in connection with a temple at Glastonbury.[3]

This passage is startling in its recognition that the "New Philosophy" of the Christian revelation was brought to Britain as an acknowledged part and parcel of the earlier Hebrew faith. The best
laid plans, even of the highest powers, may often go awry, and if you
want to make sure of something, it is best to have a "Plan B" ready.
If Joseph brought Christ as a child to Glastonbury, then he must
even then have had a pretty clear idea as to what the next few years
would be likely to achieve—or fail to achieve—in Christ's own
land of birth. If the sacred city of Judea was unable to encompass
the earth-shaking changes that Christ brought, then "plan B" was
Glastonbury.

The words "magician" or "priest" come as something of a surprise
when applied to Joseph, yet there can be few who so quietly, so
thoroughly, have performed the right actions at the right time with
full knowledge and awareness of their meaning and significance. This
is the task of the magician: to form the earthly end of the link of polarity between heaven and earth through talismanic action and intent, and in a perfect example of practical magic, the gifts he brought
to Britain were fivefold and reached through all the worlds.

First, he brought the physical presence of Christ to these islands
as a young child. This was to enable his feet to physically mark out
the pattern of what was to be upon the earth of England and the
green grass of Glastonbury. The magical and talismanic significance
of this cannot be surpassed: of physically treading the ground, mark-
ing the boundaries, using the body as a living axis between heaven
and earth.

Second, he brought knowledge: the canon of sacred measurement
that is the divinely inspired geometry of proportion. This law of sacred proportion was first brought into reality through its use in the

construction of the Tabernacle, the Tent of Meeting that was built by the Children of Israel during their sojourn in the wilderness of the Sinai desert. These measurements were contained in the mystery of the rectangle formed by a double cube, and were enshrined in the oldest Church at Glastonbury, the Vetusta Ecclesia. This was eighteen paces wide and thirty-six paces long, according to one of the messages received from the monks and as recorded by Frederick Bligh Bond in *The Company of Avalon*. This "old church" was later enclosed in stone and rebuilt as the Mary Chapel. It stands at the western end of Glastonbury Abbey, in the same way the Holy of Holies stood at the western end of the Tabernacle, which in turn stood stood at the western end of the outer court.

Third, he brought two cruets that contained red and white fluids from the body of Christ, twin streams of life force: the essence of earth and stars, spirit and matter, man and woman, made holy through His flesh. He blended these two streams with the living red and white waters that spurt from the foot of the hollow hill that is Glastonbury Tor. But in these cruets were contained not only the mysteries of the body of Christ, the *Corpus Christi,* but also the essence of the two races of faery and human, for Christ, in his descent into Annwn during the three days between his death and resurrection, undertook that which no savior, before or since, has accomplished: the union of the human and faery races, the red blood and the white blood.

And finally, he planted his blossoming staff in the earth as living witness and symbol of his fitness to perform these tasks of such holy mystery, just as Aaron's rod so many years before had been touched into blossom by the mother of God.

However, these events are only half the story, and while Joseph took to a boat and brought the seeds of Christ's physical incarnation to plant in the cold damp earth of Britain, another boat carried the bearers of a very different shoot to take root in the hot soils of southern France. A tradition equally firm and persistent as the one that associates Joseph of Arimathea with Glastonbury tells that Mary Magdalene, Martha, and Lazarus also sailed west and landed in Marseilles. This second tiny group, reminiscent of the earlier waves of survivors from the foundering Atlantis, grafted another strain of the mysteries onto the root stock of the Languedoc, one that was to flower in this hot-blooded Mediterranean climate in the Courts of Love and the Troubadour and Trouvere traditions, the Black Madonna and the "Holy Blood," the *Sang Real* as embodied by Mary Magdalene.

In the greater scheme of things this divergence is not hard to understand. The chilly, fog-bound island of Britain breeds a race renowned for the stiffness of its upper lip but not for the ardency of its passion. If the full relationship between Mary Magdalene and Christ had caused problems among the disciples when Christ was alive, then certainly Britain would not have been accepting of her. The ecstatic mysteries of Mary Magdalene, of heart, of sensuality, and love would never have caught on in Britain! On the other hand, the south of France has remained much more at ease with her mysteries. Similarly, the slow persistence of the early builders of the Christian faith in England so clearly made manifest in the patient, stone by stone, chapel by chapel manner in which the Abbey of Glastonbury was painstakingly erected over the centuries by a long succession of priests and builders was not the way of the south. (There was a chapel dedicated to Mary Magdalene at Glastonbury Abbey at one time, but it was burned in the Great Fire and not rebuilt.)

While the legacy of Joseph of Arimathea at Glastonbury grew into a far from orthodox stream of Christianity, at the same time there was the development of the British version of the story of the Children of Israel: the story of Arthur, Gwenevere, and the Knights of the Round Table. This may well be referred to as the Matter of Britain, for the stories of these characters provide the basic building blocks, the matrix, the many-faceted jewel through which shine the changing lights of the incoming mysteries of creation. The kingdom of Israel that was founded upon the twelve male (and one female) children of Jacob may be seen as the template of the unfallen human race's true kingdom. It began with the vision Jacob had of the twin serpents, the ladder of DNA, the blueprint of life for every single living creature upon the earth. And just as the recorded stories of the Children of Israel form that place between the worlds where myth and history are interwoven to produce their own multifaceted truth, so the stories of the knights and ladies of the Court of Camelot provide for us in these Western islands the archetypal web through which the truths of evermore become the parlance of everyday. Instead of the triangle of Moses, Aaron, and Miriam, we have Arthur, Lancelot, and Gwenevere. Our Melchizadek is Merlin. The circle of the encampment of the Hebrews about the Tabernacle became the circle of Joseph's twelve companions about the wattle hut, and later, the circle of the Knights of the Round Table. And we too have the indigenous faith of the land—the Celtic faith and the faery faith—which join with the New Philosophy in a sometimes uneasy alliance, just as the Hebrews' recognition of the indigenous people's adherence to the Venusian goddess Asherah did.

So what is the connection between Joseph of Arimathea and the Arthurian legends? At an immediate level, there is none at all. There is no rational, historical, or even obvious reason why this connection should have been made. When the Christ child came with Joseph to Glastonbury there was no Arthur, no Gwenevere, and certainly no Court of the Round Table. During the early centuries of the slow development of Christianity within these islands there was nothing to connect Glastonbury with the story of Arthur. During the last two thousand years they have formed an underpinning to these legends; they have provided a depth, a breadth of world-vision, and more importantly, a spirituality that the Arthuriad otherwise lacks. There is no rational reason why the Arthurian mythology, slowly emerging from the mists of Avalon and the Dark Ages, should have focused in on Glastonbury to such an extent that it has become synonymous in the popular imagination with Camelot, and in esoteric belief with the New Jerusalem. But when the monks of Glastonbury announced that they had discovered the bodies of Arthur and Gwenevere within the Abbey, irrespective of whether this was an early promotion for tourism, it marked the point at which the two threads of Arthurian mythology and the Christian revelation, previously running parallel, became inseparably entwined. The cauldron of renewal of Celtic mythology became the living cup of Christ's blood.

At a deeper level lies Avalon, the Glastonbury of the inner worlds, the mythic island that floats in the sea of the inner consciousness of the folk soul. At this level these divergent streams of the spiritual destiny of nations come together and, moving from probability to physicality, push above the waters of the etheric and into the green hill of Glastonbury Tor and the red and white streams at its foot. It is in response to a far greater, far deeper source that Avalon, that place of unfallen bliss and healing grace, is where King Arthur, the faery faith, and Christianity come together. But it is also the place where not only has Arthur the king been received back into Avalon's healing protection until such time as he should be called back from his sleep into the world of men, but the place where the true nature and message of Christ the king has been safeguarded, sleeping, throughout the last two thousand years.

It is probably true to say that of all the religions the world has known, none has been so thoroughly, so systematically, so ruthlessly misinterpreted and distorted beyond recognition from its original source. It is easy enough to chart the progress of this downfall up to the present time, as we ourselves have done. It is probably also true to say that of all the current religions offered to the seeker, Christianity appears to be one of the least attractive. It is easy to see *how* this situation has come about, but in the greater scheme of things it is very puzzling to know *why* it should be so. The answer to that lies in the movement and evolution of humankind in ways that are far beyond our worm's eye view. Suffice it to say that at the very beginning of the Christian era, seeds were planted for the future. These seeds were not even to reach germination until the full cycle of the age had been completed and the world moved on into Aquarius. And this has always been the case through the Great Ages of the world.

In Glastonbury, at the turn of the nineteenth into the twentieth century, a man named (significantly) Goodchild was prompted by inner voices to take a cup he had bought in Italy to Glastonbury. It was believed that this cup had been held by Christ. He was prompted to hide it within a well in Glastonbury that lay in land sacred to Bride, Christ's foster mother.[4] In this action we find many resonances with the actions of Joseph of Arimathea two thousand years before. However, by the early 1900s the merging of the streams of influence was by now reaching the proportions of a river in flood, as if the closeness of the millennium was acting like a vortex that pulled at and speeded up the flow. Early Celtic mythology was receiving renewed interest through the writings of Fiona Macleod and the Celtic revivalists, stimulating its reemergence in the British folk soul. The symbol above all others of this was the cup, the Grail, the cauldron of plenty, the urn of Aquarius, the vessel held by the mysterious water-bearer seen in Jerusalem at the time of Christ's entry into the City, the vessel of rebirth and becoming.

The divergence of two streams of Christianity had until this time concealed the fundamental message of Christ. But the last one hundred years have witnessed a dramatic resurgence of scholarship, the discovery of texts that have literally remained hidden underground (the Nag Hammadi Scrolls, for example) and the publication of some brave new voices who have dared to question the very roots of the Christian message as interpreted by the Church. But this layering of the streams of esoteric Christian tradition has brought its own problems. One problem is the geographical division of the mysteries of Christ in Britain and of Mary Magdalene in France, endorsing, by default, the very divide approved by the institutional church. Similarly, there is at the heart of the Arthurian tradition the same separation, the same division at a fundamental level: at the apex of the structure of the Court of Camelot the king and the queen are not partners in any real or practical sense of the word, and the division that lies between them forms a schism at the heart of these mysteries. The different worlds they represent still lie far apart.

The magic of all this lies in the fact that we who are part of this living tradition are also the storytellers. In the Arthurian legends we have a unique opportunity to retell the story—just as Malory, Geoffrey of Monmouth, the compilers of the New Testament, or the post-exilic revisionists did. By the actions of Joseph of Arimathea, who brought the Grail of the mysteries of Christ into Britain's native traditions, we are able to work with the tradition's archetypes in a manner that causes ripples of effect to reach very far, and the many "faults" at the heart of the Arthurian legends and the characters and archetypes therin are opportunities for change. In these lie the continuing mysteries of the Aquarian Age. And in the many and everchanging perspectives of polarity that play between Christ and Magdalene, Britain and France, human and faery, Christendom and Camelot, we may, by right thought and action, continue to work toward the birth of the new Child of their union.

CHAPTER THIRTEEN

RAISING ATLANTIS

ISIS AND OSIRIS

Isis and Osiris were twins who knew and loved each other, even before they were born. For they were a unity, a singularity, in their mother's cosmic womb. So these siblings from the source of being emerged like angelic hoarfrost from one gasp in the void. Even so, they were born to individuality, as mortals are, yet in that individuality was perfect unity. But with individuality comes free will, the ability to experience in space and time, to press one's face against the frosted glass of fate and wonder "what if?" So with Isis and Osiris, those dangerous, individual games to test the certainty of being began.

With Isis it was the desire for knowledge and power, pushing back against the dynamic of being, the great god Ra, her father, the eternal animus, and blackmailing him into revealing his powerful secret names. For Osiris it was that opposite pull toward the anima of being in a phenomenal world. So Osiris mated with dark Nephthys, his other sister. For a while Isis represented the brightness of being and the making of life, and Nephthys represented the limitations that life must impose. Isis and Nephthys are equivalents of what physics knows as two of the great four forces that emerged from the source of being, the Big Bang. These two are the strong nuclear force and the weak nuclear force. The first governs the binding and proliferation of matter, the second its decay. These are the making and breaking aspects of the one great goddess, and in mating with both of them Osiris came to know both breaking and remaking as the axis of experience, the experience of the god-man. For from the adultery between Osiris and the dark Nephthys were conceived the dark twins Anpu and Apuat, beginning and ending, the jackals who lie patiently at the birth house and the charnel house, at the beginning and ending of the phenomena that Egyptian mythology collectively labels "Anubis" and that we call "time."

Thus did Isis and Osiris take their individual paths of free will and desire, but in the eternal drama of the expansion and contraction of a universe, in its dispersion and eventual reconstitution, four forces are involved. That forth force was another brother, Set, the husband of Nephthys. Thus while Isis and Nephthys represent the evolution and the limitation of spirit and matter, so Osiris and Set represent order and chaos, each evolving from the contrasting positive and negative applications of free will and desire. The scenario is cosmic and mundane, abstract and human, and it applies equally to the evolution of a galaxy and the evolution of the human soul. Human beings are more than human, having in both their material and spiritual genetics the seed of stars and the inherited traits of angels. The dichotomy they know, of the equal cravings for independence and experience on the one hand and unity and fulfillment on the other, are those same polarized forces that physics calls the Strong Nuclear Force, the Weak Nuclear force, Electromagnetism, and Gravity. These have as much application in the mind and being of humankind as they do in the life of a universe, albeit in other terms.

Set, like most human beings, had a checkered career. In the long hard process toward Maat (or Tsdeq), toward the cosmic harmony represented by the god-man Osiris, which humankind aspire to, Set is the selfishness in every man. Sometimes early Egyptian religion praised him, but with the evolution of Osiris, he became the personification of evil. But the judgment was harsh, for in the god-man, Osirian aspiration Set is to all purposes the "man" part of the equation, grumbling and kicking the cat. All of that is of course emblematic of kicking for all he's worth against Maat, which he (wrongly) sees as some sort of cosmic dictatorship! Ironically, his wife and sister Nephthys was one of the two Maat goddesses, but this only goes to show that even Set has his place in the scheme of things. Even so, in the later mythological annals, it is said that many of the gods took on their animal totem forms to disguise themselves and avoid Set's spleen!

Set's scheme in the story of the Isis/Osiris was born of the usual catalog of motives. Firstly, he was insanely jealous that his revered brother, the head of state of an idealized Egypt, had bedded his beloved, and that his beloved had in her turn sold out to this cosmic adversary. His wife Nephthys, goddess of material limitation, had mated with the god of resurrection and transcendence, and Osiris had thus imposed his values upon Set's world. Worse still, the product of Osiris' divine interference with Set's world and wife was the birth of time and death, the divine gift most resented by unenlightened, Set-like humankind.

Set's revenge, as the opponent of the divine qualities in everyman, was symbolically appropriate. He fashioned an ornate sarcophagus to Osiris' exact godly dimensions and offered it as a gift to whomever it happened to fit. Knowing that Osiris would try the sarcophagus and claim this doubtful gift, Set would be returning the god-king's gift of time and death, but with no resurrection. Accordingly, he played his macabre Cinderella game of "Whomsoever This Coffin Fits" at the court of Osiris. Inevitably, with the usual naivete of the pious, Osiris got into the sarcophagus and Set slammed down the lid and sealed it. There was no *coupe de grace,* no mummification or magic to ensure resurrection, only slow anonymous death and decay. Set took the sarcophagus to his realm in the Delta marshes and then, like the bag that contained the Celtic Taliesin, it floated away across the anonymous, trackless sea. Set knew that such an ignominious death really meant death, for without either provision for the afterlife or the memorial offices of the living, Osiris had no hope of any mode of post-mortem survival or resurrection.

When Isis heard what had happened she went looking for the coffin of her love. But the sarcophagus was far away, the tides had taken it to the coasts of Lebanon, where it washed up and lodged in a Tamarisk tree. Time passed and the tree grew around the coffin until the trunk was cut and taken away and used as a pillar in the local king's hall. But eventually Isis found it and brought the body of Osiris home. Set, however, learned of this and found where the body was concealed; he cut it into pieces and distributed the pieces across Egypt so that Osiris would never be whole again. With great patience and no little magic, Isis set out again and bit by bit found the corpse of her love. At last the body was complete, except for the phallus, which had been eaten by a fish. Yet with her magic, Isis conceived a son from Osiris and raised him in secret with the aid of her sisters, Hathor and Nepthys. Thus Horus the Savior God was born and raised in secret to become the Sun hero and to overthrow Set and become the god-king of mighty Egypt. Horus was of course the reincarnation, or more properly, "resurrection," of his father Osiris.

It is a story of the evolution of the universe and the story of both the magical and mystical journey of the human soul. Its personae are the powers within both the universe and within ourselves. Some say that Horus, immaculately conceived and born of Isis, was the mythical anticipation of Christ, and that Isis and Nephthys fulfill much the same roles taken by the Blessed Virgin Mary and Mary of Magdala. But the important thing about the Isis/Osiris myth is that it shows the *complete* cycle of being. In this complete cycle what is destroyed is remade, what was dispersed is reconstituted. All except for the phallus of Osiris, which, after being consumed by a fish, returns to the deeps from which it arose.

But then, in the latter stages of the myth, Osiris' phallus is no longer necessary. The god-man has become more god than man, and desire is no longer needed. For Anibus, who is time, no longer needs to be fathered, for the round of experience (signified by the zodiacal thirteen pieces of the reconstituted corpse) has been made. Conditions in creation become raised with the birth of Horus to the level of Maat, of "as above so below," and it is no longer necessary for the "what if?" question to be asked again. Free will has had its run and done its job. Desire has become redundant.

The agency most responsible, however, for the positive outcome of this quest is undoubtedly Isis. For despite the failures of the other three characters, Isis is the one who toils to redeem things and bring them to a satisfactory conclusion. In the detail of the many Egyptian versions of the myth, she appears as both bountiful and motherly, austere and magically powerful, bright and dark, but all her toils and all her aspects and the exercise of her powers are essentially focused by love. For the essence of the state of Maat that she enables *is* love.

It is this enabling by the Isis of many names, resplendent in the stars, the inner earth, and in the body and spirit of every human woman, that this book has attempted to evoke. Yet her most important lesson must be her own myth, and we must dwell finally upon its implications.

BACK TO ATLANTIS

For the definitive mythology of Isis and Osiris we are indebted to the Greek scholar Plutarch. From him and other Greeks who spent time in Egypt during its Ptolemic sunset years we also inherit the Greek renderings of Egyptian mythological names like the Greek "Isis" for Ast, "Osiris" for Asar, and so on. But beside the considerable mythology of the Ennead that the Greeks learned from the Egyptian priests of Heliopolis came that seemingly separate myth of what the Greeks called "Atlantis." In the general run of Egyptian mythology, Atlantis seems something of an oddity, but it actually provides a very substantial connecting thread.

Somewhere in the inner deeps of creation, in what Solon told Plato was "Atlantis," we find the bare bones of the Isis/Osiris myth, or rather we find the beginning and middle but not yet the end of the myth. The myth of Atlantis is the myth about a very real inner state, a "place between," where archetypal unity steps down into potential and elaboration, and in that elaboration knows fragmentation. But it is said that "Atlantis will rise again on a higher arc" and in this "rising on a higher arc" that fragmentation and alienation will be reconstituted in a more spiritually developed "unity from diversity." It is not difficult to see this process mirroring the Isis/Osiris myth.

One of the most recent visitors to this "place between" called Atlantis was Dion Fortune, whose novels *The Sea Priestess*[1] and its sequel, *Moon Magic,*[2] were essentially based upon the transpositions of a long series of Atlantean "memories," into fiction. These Atlantean memories significantly rubbed shoulders with Egyptian memories in that the first story, *The Sea Priestess,* pivots around the Atlantean myth, while its continuation in *Moon Magic* connects the same character to an ancient Egyptian background. Dion Fortune's successor in seership, Margaret Lumley Brown, also provided a good deal of material concerning Atlantis, and with these and other accounts a composite inner picture of this "place between" begins to emerge.

As we saw in chapter 1, Atlantis was an island, or series of islands, centered about a central island called Ruta, considered to be the solar center of the Sun-worshipping Atlantean empire. The Sun Temple stood at the summit of its seven tiered mountain just as the seven tiered Glastonbury Tor now stands at the center of Avalon, representing the sevenfold Celtic "place between" of Annwn. Significantly, Dion Fortune's home at the time of her Antlantean seership stood in the shadow of Glastonbury Tor. The Tor is surmounted by the tower of the archangel Michael, who is the archangel "like unto God." Similarly, on that inner island of Ruta, the Sun, the star that spawned the seven planets including this earth, was considered to be the tangible face of God.

Yet behind the Sun the Egyptian mythographers saw the greater glory of the sea of space, in which countless other Suns form the patterns of a greater reality in their wheeling constellations. So it was that behind the Atlantean temple of the Sun stood the empowering Temple of the Sea and the Stars, the Temple of Naradek. This was the temple of the power that would come be called the universal Isis, for the constellation of Sirius, the Isis star, is known as the "Sun behind the Sun."

The mythographers called the Naradek Temple "the withdrawn temple," because while the mysteries of the Sun Temple abutted the material world, the mysteries of the Naradek Temple abutted the archetypal world. This world of Tsdeq (or, in Egyptian terms, Maat) comprised, as Isis came to know, the secret names of Ra, that hidden ingredient of the divine plan by which heaven and earth may be as one.

It is said that in Atlantis the Naradek Temple provided the priestesses for the Sun Temple, for without this mediatory link to the greater inner reality the Sun Temple was unable to function. Its job was, after all, the externalization of that greater reality, as a focus around which material reality may germinate. Without a valid link to that higher reality, without the priestesses of the Naradek Temple, the Sun Temple would loose its way, and inevitably, it did!

Initially all went well, the priestesses of the Naradek Temple were connected to the archetypal "Lemurian" world, which other terminology would call the angelic realm. Tradition says that this contact was never broken and that the Naradek Temple never fell. Its priestesses went to the Sun Temple with one proviso. If a priestess believed that the Sun Temple was not following the archetypal guidelines that her seership provided, then she could depart from the Sun Temple, severing its contacts with the higher "Lemurian" (that is, angelic) worlds. In essence, as the Sun Temple assumed greater political and material power, this is what happened.

It is in this negation and later abuse of the feminine wisdom power we begin to see that Edenic "blaming of Eve." Without the mediation and moderation of the Naradek Temple the solar mysteries of Atlantis became readily abused and the ethereal, elemental, wave/particle "structure" of Atlantis began to fragment. As these inner islands began to submerge, like the coffin of Osiris, back into the Sea of Space, what are known as "the three great migrations" began. The enlightened of Atlantis, priests and priestesses alike, were charged by the higher Lemurian powers to migrate to the material world "across the sea." Mystery lore cites these three migrations in the founding of the great mystery traditions of the mortal world. All these traditions will, it is said, be reunited when Atlantis "rises again on a higher arc."

In the specifics of the Isis/Osiris myth, this Atlantean fragmentation is very readily described: first in the mythical dislocation of the relationship between Isis and Osiris; second in the "pull" of selfish Set's lower world bringing about Osiris' demise; and third in the complete fragmentation of the body of Osiris, or more pragmatically, of the Osirian priest-king ideal of humanity reclaiming its divinity in reunion with Godhead. Those parts of the body of Osiris, scattered to the corners of our world, describe in a sense the mythical emigrations from doomed Atlantis. In other words, the fracture between the Naradek Temple and the Sun Temple, rather than sowing the seeds of individuality and free will as the crowning glory of the divine plan, actually precipitated cosmic anarchy on the border between the inner and material worlds. But as Isis showed and as the "root" mystery traditions showed, the anarchical fragmentation is recoverable; indeed, it is the feminine "Isis" principle that makes it recoverable.

The fall of Atlantis was that inevitable collision of worlds giving rise to the eternal abrasion between the Tsdeq of spiritual principle and the expediencies of material existence. The Naradek Temple sought to convey archetypal principle and polarize with the Sun Temple to externalize that principle into the daylight of the world.

But the "gravity" of the free-willed proto-human world dragged the Sun Temple out of alignment, so what should have been balanced and fruitful polarity between two modes of existence became spiritual anarchy. What should have provided one correct pattern for material existence provided as many conflicting patterns as budding free will and self-interest could imagine.

Much the same mythology is described in the fall of Lucifer, the light bearing angel who later became so demonized by the medieval church as the perpetrator of cosmic anarchy. In fact, it is the "gravity" of proto-human independence that causes fall and fragmentation. It is the freedom of "what if," which is the final piece in the jigsaw. This is consequential upon the gift of Divine love, being allowed to find its own expression until it levels off and returns to the polarized unity of the Divine lover and his or her beloved thoughts. The emerald scrystone once cited as the emblem of office of the high priestess of the Naradek Temple became the light bearing gem that fell from Lucifer's crown. Thus it became the emerald that gave substance to the hermetic doctrine of "as above so below." Later it became cited as the stone from which the Holy Grail was fashioned when "above" and "below" were seen to become fused in the Melchizadekian cup of Christ.

J. R. R. Tolkien, either through mythological guile or unconscious collision with the roots of the Northern European folk soul, called the green gem the *Elessar,* or "Elfstone." He set it as the token of betrothal between the archetypal realm of the faery/elven, Arwen Evenstar, and the proto-material realm of her Atlantean lover, Aragorn. Having done this, he set them as man and wife, king and queen, over the first material human age of the world.[3] Whether Tolkien realized it or not, this very well describes the Atlantean "ideal" in the initiation of the marriage of heaven and earth. His final word on this in *The Lord of the Rings* tells us that Arwen Evenstar (Venus, if one prefers!) lies forgotten beneath her burial mound in the paradisal forest "until the world is changed." In other words, until this universal Isis figure, representing the divine feminine, again comes to the fore. Or, to put it yet another way, until the priestess of the Naradek Temple is invited to return to the Sun Temple.

MATING WITH THE COSMOS

The principles of the polarity magic instituted by the priests of the Sun Temple and the priestesses of the Naradek Temple are reflected in the various mystery systems of the ancient world that this book has described. The priestesses held the keys to the archetypal worlds signified by the sea of space and the stars. For as bright Isis had known the secret names of mighty Ra, so the priestesses of the Naradek Temple were entrusted to convey the archetypal keys, the Maat, the Tsdeq that comprise the secret ingredients of the Divine plan.

A priest of the Sun Temple would be initiated by the priestess to be elevated to those archetypal realms beyond the Sun to represent its source in the seeding of the stars across the sea of space. In this the priestess would represent the dark Isis of all potential, the dark sea of prime space into and across which the galactic Milky Way of the God's seed may be ejaculated. As in the Welsh Arianrhod and Gwydion myth (in its original form), the priestess as goddess would spiritually stimulate the ejaculation of the star seed from the priest--as-god and proceed to magically gestate that seed. This would not be done in any passive way, but in the building of a definite archetypal matrix. Thus in that gestation the priestess represented the change from dark Isis to bright Isis, or in other terms, from Hathor to Nephthys to Isis. These functions are paralleled by the Welsh Celtic goddesses Bloudewedd, Arianrhod, and Ceridwen, and we are reminded by that last gestative phase of Ceridwen's pregnancy, transforming and patterning the seed that would become Taliesin, the archetypal bard. These various archetypal roles and situations were shown in the situation, behavior, and influence of specific constellations and stars, and in the assumption of those archetypes, the "Atlantean" priest and priestess embodied them. In this it was what we might now call a "faery marriage," a mating between two levels of being in two proto-human beings. In other terms, it was the mating of a priestess who represented Isis as queen of heaven, and a priest who represented Osiris the god-man in earth. They in turn represented their primordial parents Nuit, lady of the stars, and Geb, the father of earth. Their rare meeting in this Atlantean realm was the kingdom of Shu, who stood in the ethers separating Nuit and Geb, the ethers of desire.

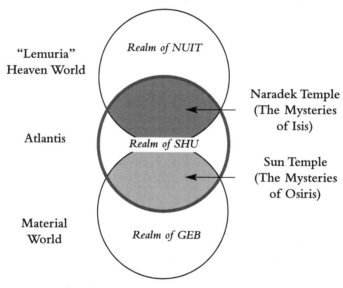

"Lemuria"
Heaven World

Realm of NUIT

Naradek Temple
(The Mysteries
of Isis)

Atlantis

Realm of SHU

Sun Temple
(The Mysteries
of Osiris)

Material
World

Realm of GEB

Earth (The Mysteries of Nephthys and Set)

Atlantis

The union of the priest and priestess was assumed to be magical rather than "physical," although as we have seen from our studies of "the inner fire," in true union *all* the levels of being are experienced. From this union, entities were "conceived" in astral/etheric sense to embody archetypal forces. This conception was, not least, through the consciousness of the souls, or "higher selves" of the priest and priestess, and brought to birth in their integrated personalities. In this latter respect the priests and priestesses acted as "foster parents" to these "solar externalized" entities. Gwydion had done so with Llew, Merlin (and later Ector) with Arthur, Isis and her sisters with Horus, Elphin with Taliesin, and Brigid with Christ. In this fostering such entities were honed by their originating priests and/or priestesses "in secret," or more accurately "in themselves," to fashion them for externalization into and empowerment of the proto-human world. The myths of the Beni Elohim of Genesis reflect this mystery practice of inducing angelic, archetypal powers into the human genetic chain. In as much as the mating was the talismanic mating of the powers represented by the priest and priestess, it was anonymous. The entities conceived, whether or not they eventually became incarnate in the material world, were therefore to all purposes "immaculately conceived" and/or "virgin born." Such "immaculate conceptions" may be seen in that of Merlin (himself an exponent of these sacred genetic tactics), who was said to have been conceived by the intercourse between "a demon and a nun." For "nun" we might read "priestess," and for "demon" we might more constructively suggest an inner entity or a priest representing such an entity.

The Atlantean temple in which this magical mating took place was a small chamber just below the great image in the Sun Temple. Thus, behind the tangible solar face of the divine, the mechanisms that would "angelically" seed the corporate body of God among humankind were set in motion. For in the chamber below the image of the Sun the archetypal essence of each Star/Sun of the greater galaxy was distilled in the conceptual rites of the priest and priestess. In this the forces of a particular constellation would be focused upon the two participants. The womblike construction of the Great Pyramid of Giza, with its star shafts and exact stellar alignments, may be seen to provide for this practice. This does not of course deny a funereal connotation to the pyramids. The dead pharaoh was "an Osiris," and the magical mating of Isis and Osiris takes place after Osiris' death. Moreover, the pyramid depicts the ben ben, the primordial island that rose up from the inner sea, a veritable Atlantis. Exactly the same criteria may be applied to the mounds, circles, and burial cists of Bronze Age Britain, not least in the Osiris-like dismemberment of the sacred kings whose rites were conducted there.

ATLANTIS ON A HIGHER ARC

But if these were the practices of either ancient Atlantis or ancient Egypt, how may they "return on a higher arc?" Let us assume for a moment that Atlantis represents an "inner Egypt," with the projection of ancient temple practice onto an inner landscape and through that inner landscape to the stars, with, as we have seen, that "place between" acting as a catalyst. Such formats are still in fact used in advanced magical work. Let us say, for argument's sake, that the Great Pyramid at Giza, being the most impressive of sacred structures, represented the island of Ruta, the Egyptian ben ben, that "place between." Below that place is the physical rock of the Giza plateau, the material anticipation of Egypt. Yet these are not "separate modes of being." As our illustration indicates, they "overlap." For while Atlantis existed, and exists, upon another wavelength of creation, that wavelength is available to human perception. Indeed it is myth, like a pair of special spectacles fashioned for the folk soul, that makes it so. The fact that Atlantis is thus humanly, if dimly, perceptible is in fact its whole *raison d'etre,* for how may its patterns be otherwise conveyed to mortal consciousness?

Even so, those wavelengths shift constantly in the cosmic ebb and flow, even as the stars do. What is certain however is that Atlantis is a quantum realm, a realm of potential, and we are therefore unable to fix its position in space and time. Just as it is behind appearances, so it is beyond time and not, as many have suggested, set in some very distant prehistoric epoch. Atlantis is about possibilities, not about facts. But this is not to say that with the turning of the stars and the shift of wavelengths, the catalytic mode called Atlantis may not in some time have more closely abutted material creation (or at least human perception in material creation). Indeed, saying that "Atlantis will rise again on a higher arc" is another way of saying that it will become as available to human consciousness as it once was, so that the opportunities that were available in the "Atlantean" situation will again become available. If that availability is matched to a "higher arc" of human spiritual experience and maturity, we may enter upon those final Osirian re-integration and birth of Horus phases that the Egyptians anticipated.

That anticipation is the heritage of ancient Egypt, and indeed of all the many mystery systems cited in this book. It is the heritage bequeathed to us in the Isis/Osiris myth and in the Atlantean myth itself. It is also bequeathed to us in the sacred structures that gave substance to those myths, not least the pyramids of Giza. But while ancient Egypt codified these truths with rare precision, it by no means held a monopoly on them. Egypt, as we have seen, did not stand in isolation from the rest of the ancient world. Her sacred structures and her myths knew kinship with the Ziggurats and myths of Sumer, the barrows and circles of prehistoric Europe (and the myths that the Celts later attached to them). And not least was that kinship extended to Canaan, which, as "Israel," gave focus to the secrets of being in the great structure of Solomon's temple. To this temple, Solomon's daughter brought the Asherah, symbol of the divine feminine, for even as the tabernacle had been clad with dolphin hides, so Solomon charged Hiram of Tyre, the father of the "sea people," to set the mysteries of the sea and stars in his Edenic temple on the rock above the waters. And what is the "cedar from Lebanon" used in the temple's construction? It was the Tamarisk that contained the sarcophagus of Osiris, which the Egyptian priests foresaw would form the pillar in a priest king's hall.

Eventually, these ancient glories, which had anticipated the marriage of heaven and earth, were scuffed out by the expedient sandal of Rome. The legions tramped across those older worlds of Egypt, of Jerusalem, and of Celtic Britain. Yet even in the dispersal of those ancient dreams and the coming of new, forgetful faiths, a cloud of ancient dust still hung in the air. Upon it were carried the seeds for that "Atlantis on a higher arc" and the completion of the Isis/Osiris myth. So even as the marching legions faded into history's distance and the new faiths took root, the secret tendrils of what Atlantis was yet to be reached out and wove themselves together in the twilight. They wove themselves to what remained of Akhenaten's grafting of his solar mysteries to the royal line of Bronze Age Ireland. To this the Celtic mysteries of Britain and Ireland were doubly woven when Joseph of Arimathea brought the revived seeds of ancient Judaism to Avalon. Atlantis, Annwn, the inner Avalon, and the New Jerusalem are all names for that one device that shall rise on a higher, integrated arc to enable the marriage of heaven and earth.

Dion Fortune later realized this Aquarian anticipation in Avalon. Like others, she sensed, behind the myths and the pyramidal hills and islands, a time when the priestess would return from the Naradek Temple to the Temple of the Sun. In that priestess she saw (if not always accurately) the personification of the universal Isis, who reintegrates what has been fragmented. She saw the Brigid who weaves all the sundered threads together and nurtures the Horus, the Christ, the Child of Light, the angelic spark of Divine essence, which is within each human soul. She knew the time was close, but had not yet come, because that rainbow arch of heaven, that "higher arc," was still in the making. Yet she herself had contributed in no small way to that making, and in those long ago Egyptian lives she had once lived, the priesthood knew exactly when the true reintegration would begin.

That they did so appears to be confirmed in Mark Vidler's fascinating book *The Star Mirror.*[4] In this book the pinpoint alignments of the Great Pyramid angles to the bright stars of 2450 B.C. "tell" the Isis/Osiris myth. But more remarkably, they appear to concede that the myth had yet to complete its cycle, and anticipated when the archetypal patterns of the stars would align to indicate that completion. As the reader may know, or may have guessed, that "completion," that repetition and restatement of the pattern "on a higher arc" commenced in A.D. 2000. This is not vague soothsaying but the sophisticated mapping of star myth to precise astronomical occurrences. The priest astronomers of Egypt both mythically and scientifically "remembered" a past long before their own time and a future far ahead of it.

One of the many examples that Mark Vidler gives indicates that the Pyramid builders of 2450 B.C. were well aware that in A.D. 2000 their structure would show Orion carrying the solstice Sun through the Milky Way below the galactic equator for the first time in 25,830 years. In terms of the Isis/Osiris myth, this means that Osiris "carries" (or rather, *is*) Horus for the first time in 25,830 years, and is upon the Milky Way that the Egyptians equated with the Nile, the ("milky") succor of Isis. This image of Isis rising up to, in a sense, provide succor to the fledgling Horus that Egypt will one day become, was seen in the inundation of the Nile. This annual flooding was and is announced by the rising of her own star, Sirius, which is itself precisely spotlighted in the Great Pyramid's stellar alignments. In Atlantean terms, the Nile is the river Naradek that, again as the Milky Way, provides the stellar/archetypal/angelic succor that the Sun Temple needed to function properly to ultimately bring Horus the Savior Sun Hero into the world. The fact that the Pyramid priests anticipated this time of the proper conjunction of the priests of the Sun Temple and the priestesses of the Naradek Temple may also be seen in their anticipation of A.D. 2000 as the time in which the stellar alignment of the "sword" of Orion becomes vertical to the meridian. They appear to have anticipated this rising of the Osirian Dagger, or in more apposite Egyptian terms, phallus, by sighting the Auriga stars that would in our time "pro-vide" the erection directly over the Great Pyramid. As Mark Vidler puts it, Osiris will have an erection for the first time in some ten thousand years! To confirm this alignment of myth to anticipated astronomical fact, Mark Vidler further reminds us that the Orion Nebula (the source of our galaxy) at the center of Osiris' erect phal-lus is often called "the mouth of the fish." So in a sense the renewed phallus of Osiris has (jests of "on a higher arc" notwithstanding!) resurrected to mate with the Isis impulse in this new millennium.

Not content with predicting such things in their own mythol-ogy, the Egyptians may also have realized that the "star triangles" they mapped in the Great Pyramid had application to other regions and cultures, not least in Britain and Ireland, where their three stars representing the head of Draco, the Pendragon stars, now fall ex-actly upon Ben Nevis (the highest mountain in the British isles), Mount Brandon, the most westerly mountain in the Eurasian land mass, and Silbury Hill, the greatest manmade mound in Europe. In this latter case, it appears that the Egyptians anticipated the move-ment of the eye of Draco from their pyramid in 2450 B.C. to the Silbury Hill "pyramid" in A.D. 2000. But we shall speak of the Pen-dragon, the head of the dragon, again shortly.

THE KINGDOM OF SHU

The marriage of heaven and earth was in Egyptian mythological terms the marriage of Nuit and Geb, the parents of Isis and Osiris. The priestly Egyptian mythographers had probed the inner worlds and found that "place between" the two. An inner island beyond the stream of time where, in Celtic terms, potential seethed in the cauldron of being upon the fires of "what if?" That secret fire burned perpetually in the deeps beneath the Temple of the Sun, the secret home of the Sun. In mythological terms, it was the misuse of the fire of desire, the fire of "what if?" that caused the Atlantean fall.

The Egyptians had told Solon the Greek that Atlantis was in the west, and the west was where the Sun disappeared into the inner regions of sevenfold Duat, even as the home of the Sun was in the Atlantean temple upon the seven-tiered mountain. That island mountain, the ben ben mound of primordial creation, reared up from the sea of being as the Egyptian "place between." Like the Jerusalem temple that rose up over the waters of chaos, it held sway over the etheric, watery world behind matter, the world that Osiris traversed in his boat of a million years. It was in this realm, encompassed on the one hand by the starry body of Nuit and on the other by her earth mate Geb, that the god Shu insinuated himself, for Shu was sky and light and air. His body provided the four pillars between earth and the starry heavens, which in their upper aspect were the foundations of heaven and in their lower aspects the four cardinal points of earth. In this we may see where Plato's assertion that Atlantis was "beyond the pillars of Hercules" came from; he had, after all, received the account through a string of intermediaries. Similarly, his assertion that the sacred beast of Atlantis was a bull may be accounted for by the fact that the heavens, the goddess Nuit, whom Shu supported, was represented as a cow in one version of the myth. Text and illustration of this appear in the tomb of Seti I in the Valley of Kings.

The kingdom of Shu was thus that Atlantean "place between," and once Shu was in place, heaven and earth were separated, yet able to know that "desire," that "what if?" that separated their children Isis and Osiris, and gave free will the opportunity to do its painful but necessary work. Every pharaoh went through the "pillars of Shu" into the Duat to mate with the archetypal patterns of the stars, for most male pharaohs were mummified with an erect penis and lay like the aroused Geb, father of Osiris, facing the representation of Nuit on the ceiling of the tomb above them. Unlike most other Egyptian deities, Shu and his mate Tefnut had no particular cities dedicated to them. Many temples, however, like Dendera, dedicated to Isis, and Edfu, dedicated to Horus, had a portion of their halls dedicated to Shu and Tefnut. This would seem to imply that they fulfilled some all-pervading function in the dialogue between heaven and earth. Indeed, the air itself, the ether, was often referred to as "the house of Shu." The "pillars of Shu," seen as the entrance to the Duat (the underworld, the kingdom conquered of Osiris) implies the change in the ethers, that "other wavelength" that Atlantis is, that enchanted lake that is the entrance to the Celtic Annwn.

That the Egyptian myths "prove" Atlantis as a mythological realm in no way obviates its "reality." It was and is very real, and its "loss" through the abuse of human free will, resulting in the fracture of the link between heaven and earth, between Nuit and Geb, and later Isis and Osiris, is a demonstrable reality in the world that we know. What was made by myth must be remade by myth through myth being lived by humankind.

Behind human life stand the "what if?" worlds of quantum mechanics, an Atlantis that science might recognize. For as the Egyptian priests charted its progression, decline, and reemergence through precise astronomy, we may make similar statements through astrophysics. Nature, as she is, is no random backdrop to the story of Nuit and Geb and Shu, of Isis and Osiris. The stuff of super nature is seeded in the being of angels and of men, for how else may the genetics of the eternal be grafted to the human strain? Consciousness and matter are as intimately entwined as the waves and particles that lie behind them, for in this is the rationale of magic. Human physiology and psychology employ the same four forces that govern the life of a universe. Our psychology reflects and effects the wave functions of matter and our physiology the particle function.

Perhaps that melee of waves and particles, having expanded itself to universal proportions, has at last reached some Aquarian zenith, and from that zenith the universe begins to compress again.

The astronomical signs are presently otherwise; the universe is still expanding and if it continues to do so it will give itself enough rope to hang itself. For as the distance between planetary and stellar bodies increases, worlds like our own will become isolated from their Suns and die. But as Heisenberg showed, our consciousness may intrude upon the quantum realms that govern a universe, and in doing so effect changes. We may, to put it another way, find that it is our responsibility to draw the universe back toward its primal intimacy, but on a higher, more experienced arc. We may thus revive a perception of the lost "wavelength" (rather than "continent") of Atlantis, and through it readdress the opportunities that were thought to have been apparent in an earlier epoch.

The capability that Heisenberg indicated on a quantum level, the human ability to intrude consciousness and change things, is that original "what if" of free will, and free will is the inevitable gift of divine love. Like so many aspects of human love, it is both a blessing and a curse, the source of untold joy when things go well and untold misery when they don't! Now perhaps the time has come to apply free will as "love under will" and do something constructive with the universe as if it really were the conscious projection of God.

REWRITING THE MYTHS

To do this we must adjust the myths, for myth is the mindset that humanity uses to project its consciousness into these quantum realms. Myth is not canonical, it is evolutionary, just as human perception evolves through time and experience, so myth must evolve, for what was appropriate in another epoch may not be appropriate now. In addition to this, a good deal of myth is badly warped and tainted. Egyptian myth was lucky to submerge itself for centuries out of the reach of dogmatic Islam and largely beyond the tampering of Christianity. Other mythologies have been less fortunate, for the canonical approach of the "peoples of the book" shunned the very premise of mythology. We have already seen the sorry results of entrusting myth to the Jewish Deuteronomists and the early Christian Fathers, a situation akin to encouraging people who hate children to become foster parents! Yet myth is the very framework set in the folk soul of a race, from which both spiritual and material consequences will inevitably follow. It is our realm of "Atlantis," and with its ability to convert possibilities into actualities, we cannot afford to make the same mistakes again.

Myth must be properly equipped to ask the questions, because magic, or whatever we choose to call the activation of myth, can only provide answers to the questions that myth poses. The theological remedy of divine grace works in and through this cosmic process, but it cannot overrule it. To do so would break its own rules. Free will is the essential gift of Divine love, and love by its very nature cannot compel. Divine love allows the beloved, that other part of itself, to roll its own dice. God seeks unity not uniformity, a marriage, not a dictatorship!

Meanwhile, ass-eared Set stalks the halls of myth, for much mythology (not least British mythology) tainted rather than informed by faith, highlights the pious sacrifice of disintegration without the affirmation of reintegration. These unhappy endings overflow not only into our psyche but in the methods that we use to heal it. Like a boy with an electrical appliance, psychoanalysis tends to tear the thing apart and see how it works, with little idea of how to put it back together. Even C. G. Jung, the father of archetypal psychology culled from an understanding of myth, confessed that the only cure was ultimately a "religious" one. But it was the "religious cure" of myth that framed this unhappy situation in the first place. True mythology is not a medieval morality play that marks the feminine within us as the heritage of original sin. Nor does it take us down from the cross and ignominiously bury us in platitudes. True myth gives us all the opportunity to walk from the tomb, with an Isis to pick up the broken pieces and a Mary of Magdala to greet us in the garden of a new morning.

Despite the fact that the Arthurian legend is as alive now as it ever was, it remains a fragmentation that shows no sign of reintegration. Our national mythology is dragged down behind that cynical veil of tears with which medieval Christianity constantly flagellated itself. The marriage of heaven and earth is just a hopeless dream, as far as our extant mythology goes, and Arthur, Gwenevere, and the rest of us—but especially fickle Gwenevere— should have known better!

THE FABLE OF THE WRONGED WIFE

There is an old Welsh folktale called *Morwyn Llyn Fan y Fach* (The Faery Woman of Lake Fan y Fach).[5] The story goes that a young farmer from Myddai met a beautiful woman who came out of the lake (that is, Annwn, "the deep"). The faery promised to marry him with the proviso that if he gave her three blows without cause she would leave him. They were married, and her dowry from the lake was a selection of the finest cattle in Wales, a veritable "gift from paradise" in Celtic terms! For many years they lived happily together and raised three sons, but on three occasions the man lightly struck his faery wife: once when she refused to attend a Christian baptism, once when she cried at a wedding, and once when she laughed at a funeral. Following this last episode the faery wife returned to the lake and took her cattle with her, only to reappear from time to time to teach her sons bits of esoteric lore, notably magical herbalism.

This wronged wife is not any wife. She is the faery mate of many a Celtic myth who readily "marries" mortals, very much on her own terms. Her appearance from the lake (a favorite Welsh gateway between the worlds), and her paradisal cattle and qualities of paradisal original innocence show her to be the emissary of an unfallen state where the archetypal patterns still hold good. This original innocence that makes her unacceptable in a fallen material world are shown in her denial of baptism (and thus denial of original sin), her dismay at a Christian wedding (which to all intents makes her the man's property), and her laughter at a funeral (for she is an immortal). Her story is one of many folk branches that extend from the main corpus of Welsh Celtic myth, which, before the advent of revised Arthurian myth, had their own version of the mysteries of Atlantis. In these mysteries as goddess and wronged faery spouse she is of course the priestess of Naradek.

Her story and the story of what we may call "autumn in Atlantis" is most vividly evoked in the Mabinogi tale of Bran's sister, "Branwen Daughter of Llyr,"[6] which we considered briefly in chapter 7. This is not only the quintessential tale of the wronged wife and queen, it is also, as are all the Mabinogi stories, a tale about the sovereignty of Britain. This "sovereignty" theme that was in fact just as relevant to the stories of Christ and of Osiris, was emphasized by the Celts. It stresses that the stewardship of the earth, embodied in the king, can only be rightly achieved if that sovereignty is informed by the patterns of what we have been calling Maat and Tsdeq, and that such are conveyed to the king by a representative of the Goddess. That representative is, again, in Atlantean terms, the priestess of the inner or "withdrawn" Naradek temple.

Branwen, the sister of Bran, was such a "priestess." Her name, with its "wen" suffix, immediately tells us that she is from the underworld of Annwn. To the extent that Atlantis/Annwn is hidden or "lost," the priestess must cross the wavelengths. She does so as ethereal queen or faery mate to touch the figurative Sun Temple that has dispersed into the material world that it was meant to serve. The Branwen tale is therefore told from the inner side of things. In this myth Britain, or specifically Wales, is a magical island not unlike Atlantis, and "Ireland" is the material world across the ethers of the Irish Sea. It is *from* Britain that Branwen sails to become the wronged faery wife in the world of men.

As we saw earlier, the myth opens when the Irish king, Matholwch, comes to Wales to court Bran's sister Branwen. After initial misunderstandings, for which Bran makes up by giving Matholwch a magical cauldron, Branwen and Matholwch set off for married life as king and queen of Ireland. All appears to go well until Branwen becomes pregnant. She gives birth to a son, Gwern, against a background of mounting hostility against her from the Irish people. Having got what he wanted (a faery wife, the magical cauldron, and an heir to secure the royal Irish bloodline to the paradisal faery world), Matholwch caves in to public pressure. He makes Branwen a prisoner rather than a wife, putting her to menial tasks in the kitchen, where the head cook has orders to regularly beat her (an interesting comparison with the Morwyn Llyn Fan y Fach myth). At this point all communication with mainland Britain is cut off in case Bran hears of his sister's plight.

Branwen does however manage to establish magical communication with her brother by teaching a bird to speak and then sending it across the sea to Bran (this evokes the practice of the faery and mortal worlds using the animal "wavelength" as a bridge between the two modes of being). Bran responds by invading Ireland to rescue his sister. This results in the murder of Gwern, the half human, half faery heir to both the material kingdom of Ireland and the inner kingdom of Britain, cutting off the possibility of bridging these two wavelengths of being. The cauldron, the essential device of commerce between the two worlds, is destroyed. In this alienation of the material and inner/faery worlds, Bran becomes mortally wounded. He instructs his seven companions to cut off his head and take it back to Britain with his rescued sister, but when they reach that inner Britain, Branwen, like so many faery women before and since, dies of grief. Bran's head is still alive, however, and its animation gives comfort and council to the seven companions.

As the head of Bran instructs them, these seven withdraw to an island, so that the faery impulse is in some senses isolated but preserved. So it must be, for Branwen, the emissary and faery hieros gamos, is no more. The feminine link with the world of men has, as in Atlantis, been abused and lost. On a magical island (said to be Lundy) the seven companions remain, waiting perhaps for a time when the wavelengths may again be fused. There is however one thing that Bran, their king, has told them *not* to do, and that is to open a window that faces toward Cornwall. Inevitably, one of the seven does this and so the head of Bran dies and begins to putrefy. The modern assumption is that the opening of that gate to Cornwall is an invitation for Arthur to be born at Tintagel, but it may also have been a reference to the early Judeo-Christian temple said to have been established there. Either way, this ends the epoch of Bran and commerce with the inner worlds that facilitates the mediating linkage between heaven and earth.

As was Bronze Age custom, the head of Bran, the sacred king, was buried in the "White Mount," doubtless a burial of the Newgrange type covered with white quartz. This mound supposedly became the site of the Tower of London, and from here Bran's head guarded Britain. When Arthur came he is said to have dug up the sacred head, with Set-like arrogance, to obliterate the memory of Bran. But more than this he abducted Bran's daughter and stole her dowry. For Arthur is Matholwch of Ireland, and it's that dismemberment of the link to heaven and the fall of Atlantis all over again. The "Math" prefix of Matholwch's name suggests that he is similar to Arthur, for Arthur was modeled upon an earlier mythological king, Math ap Mathonwy[7] (Bear son of bearlike). The later Welsh word for bear was (and is) *arth*: hence "Arthur."

ARTHUR OF MOURNFUL MEMORY

So for all of Merlin's hopes, Arthur was born on the wrong side of faery, for his myth indicates that same old "Atlantean" abrasion between spiritual principle, the customs of the archetypal world, and mundane expediency; the mores of our fallen world. Indeed, the very confusions that saw the departure of the faery woman of Morwyn Llyn Fan y Fach see the departure of Gwenevere (or Gwenhyfwr, as she was originally known).

This gave the Taliesin bards, who understood these things, their "Arthur of mournful memory."[8] Their hope is shown in Merlin's first vision of the coupling of the red and white dragons beneath the toppling tower of Vortigern's sovereignty. Vortigern's Britain, misruled by treacherous expediency, needed that balance with Annwn, that polarity between the inner and outer kingdom, for its restoration. This polarity of the white dragon of Annwn with the red dragon of mortality was that same Atlantean mating that could seed right rule. It was the same vision seen in the Joseph of Arimathea legend. In this the red and white springs that ebb out from the sacred sevenfold hill, that Atlantean island, that sevenfold Annwn of Glastonbury Tor, were joined as blood and seed in Joseph's Christ. A Christ "fostered by Brigid in Avalon" to be the fulfillment of a mythical Osiris, who had risen up as an historical Horus.

We see the hope of this mating and seeding of the archetypal heritage to humankind through the names of the mythological characters involved. In these we may trace those tangled bloodlines that crisscross the wavelengths of being. The later Norman French traditions tell us that the father of Gwenevere was, for example, Leo de Grace ("the great lion"). It has been shown that this name is an adaptation of the Welsh Ogyr Fran, which means "Bran the baleful." The fact that Bran was at one time considered to be Gwenevere's father is confirmed in another piece of Arthurian myth, which says that at one time Gwenevere fled to the Tower of London for refuge, which was the site where Bran's head was interred. Her "dowry," the much-prized Round Table that Merlin is said to have brought "from the stars of the Great Bear," is of course the archetypal plan. The Round Table therefore represents what we have been calling Maat and Tsdeq, and in its provision Merlin becomes a Melchizadek figure. But the Round Table, the archetypal plan, was the dowry of Gwenevere, for she was to be the new Branwen, the restored Narakek priestess who would empower Arthur's sovereignty.

Then we find that Arthur is not appointed by the powers of Annwn, or if he was, the appointment was summarily revoked. In Atlantean terms, the Naradek priestess who is Gwenevere forsakes the temple; she cannot mate with Arthur. Something has gone disastrously wrong! Arthur will have none of this, so, as we see in the Taliesin poem, *Y Prieddu Annwn,* he raids Annwn. Indeed, all the later tales of Gwenevere being abducted by underworld powers turn out to be tales of Gwenevere's abduction *from* Annwn by Arthur. The vaunted quest for the Holy Grail fashioned from the fabled green gem that was once the emblem of the high priestess of Atlantis is not so much a spiritual odyssey as a pillaging of the inner worlds. The poem itself tells us why there is this change from the original Arthur, the second coming of Bran, to this gung ho king of Christian legend. It castigates the court bards, the expedient Roman clerics who twist myth without knowing what they are doing. "Beyond Caer Wydyr (Glastonbury) they know not Arthur."[9]

For Arthur was the successor of Uther Pendragon, and in being so placed by the Welsh mythographers, he found himself in that epoch of a fragmented Atlantis. This division of epochs is as clearly defined in Celtic astronomy as it was in the Egyptian astronomy of the Great Pyramid. For the astronomical names of "Uther Pendraig" and "Arthur" mark two distinct phases. The axial tilt of the earth toward the Pole Star at the center of the heavens, the precession of the equinoxes, was the distinguishing feature of those epochs. The situation of the Pole Star in the constellation of Draco, the dragon, marked the Bronze Age times that Uther's reign brought to a close. This was the time when the powers of faery held sway in direct reflection of the archetypal patterns of the stars, the patterns of Arianrhod. Then came the movement of the Pole Star into the Little Bear, and what we might call the "post-Atlantean phase." This time marked the fading of faery and, in Atlantean terms, the departure of the Naradek priestesses. This departure of the empowering feminine, the starry Arianrhod of the Celts, was noted in *The Prophecies of Merlin:* "None thereafter shall return to his wonted duty, but Ariadne (Arianrhod) shall lie hidden within the closed gateways of her seagirt headlands."[10] It was the demise of Atlantis and the end of the story of Bran.

This was not the way that Merlin, or the Taliesin bards that Geoffrey of Monmouth had "Merlin" represent, had wanted things to remain. The Arthur they had intended was the one who would build that "Atlantis on a higher arc," and translate Arianrhod's starry patterns of heaven into the kingdom of earth. He would revive the Atlantean ideal that had been seen to fade with the mythical Uther Pendraig. Geoffrey of Monmouth's *Uther Ben,* "Uther of the Head," was the archetypal sacred king whom their ancestors had known as "Bran the Blessed," the Osiris-like god-king of Bronze Age Britain who had possessed Ceridwen's cauldron, that essentially feminine, Atlantean device that was the catalyst through which the patterns of heaven may be apparent in earth. Their hope had been that the age closed by Uther/Bran would be reopened and taken to greater heights by Arthur. They had wanted their Arthur to be another Osiris, but Christendom turned him into Set, a Set who would take those female faery powers by the scruff of the neck in the name of Christ, and through their intransigence fail heroically.

So it was, from this tangle of mythical aspiration, that the pragmatic court bards and orthodox Christian clerics in the world beyond Wales concocted the greater tangle that we now call the "Arthuriad." With their monopoly on communication and their dogmatic allegiance to the Church of Rome, the clerics knocked the Arthuriad into what they considered to be the right theological shape, despite the best efforts of esoteric detractors and the infusion of Templar heresy imported during the Crusades.

Uther Pendragon had been a Bronze Age king, Arthur had been an Iron Age one, and that trite tradition that tells us that faeries are alienated by iron indicates the problem that the bards were facing. The Taliesin bards fashioned their Arthur to overcome this alienation; the politically motivated Christian mythographers had other ideas. In Atlantean terms, Arthur starts off as the new solar hero of the Sun Temple, but, after the expedient interference of the uninitiated clerics, ends up shunning his priestess queen and thus losing touch with the higher archetypal contacts to enable right rule. As far as the Taliesin bards are concerned, he becomes an example of all of us as stewards of the kingdom of earth, who depend upon the illusion of the patriarchal strong arm of self-will and pay mere lip service to the priestess of wisdom. The result then, as now, was a wasteland where neurosis thrived like weeds. It is a battlefield landscape on which Arthur, the macho hammer of the Saxons, lays mortally wounded. Such a representation suited the new Norman masters of Britain very well.

They started off by making Arthur Christendom's favorite warrior and hacking him away from his Celtic mythological roots. They placed the image of the Blessed Virgin on the inside of his shield, the only female character to command their biblical respect, as a substitute for the Goddess or her representative. This was to all purposes a Christian "spell" to ensure his celibacy. They made him just a little Christ-like, but so flawed as to deter any direct comparison. Their pseudo-Christ was Galahad, an impossibly ethereal, truly celibate figure whose useless piety soon had him quit the quagmire of earth to be taken up by God to the marbled halls of heaven. Meanwhile, Gwalchmai, the old Mabinogi hero, became the vengeful Gawain, and Lancelot, the old pagan Sun hero who had been Llew, became a superb warrior, but as the monks assumed of all successful soldiers, an adulterer. Not content with mere adultery, they also blamed his sexual charisma for the death of Elaine of Astalot, who apparently died from unrequited love.

Even Merlin was not spared. As Geoffrey's thumbnail sketch of a Taliesin bard, Merlin became a caricature of those bards who had courted the Goddess. The wonder of the polarity magic he had conducted with Gwenddydd was replaced by an old man's infatuation with the magical femme fatale Vivienne, the loss of his powers, and his failure to provide support when he was most needed.

The women of Arthurian romance fared worse still. Morgan le Fey, a Ceridwen-like figure from the pagan Celtic past, became a demonization of the priestesses of the Naradek Temple. Not only was Morgan made responsible for thwarting (rather than illuminating) the sovereignty of Britain, but in a gross parody of the Atlantean sacred mating rites, she was made to conceive Arthur's bastard Mordred as the incarnation of all evil. Ladies of ethereal substance and dubious virtue were set in magical castles to lure every knight from his quest for the cup of Christ. Gwenddydd became the devious Vivienne, seducer of wise old men, and Gwenevere, Arthur's queen, became jointly responsible with Morgan for the collapse of Britain and the loss of the Holy Grail. Augustine of Hippo and the editors of Genesis would have been proud of what their priestly successors did with Arthurian myth.

The Arthurian raising of Atlantis on a higher arc, which the Taliesin bards had initially anticipated, was successfully destroyed. The Church was waiting for the Second Coming to solve the problems of being (on its terms!), and it was going to make sure that nobody came up with any counterfeit versions in the meantime. The marriage of heaven and earth would be as it was prescribed by the Church of Rome. After all, Christ had awarded St. Peter the franchise.

Meanwhile, we have followed biblical precedent by making Britain's native mythology all but canonical. We have stopped asking the "what if?" question, discontinued myth's open-ended accessibility, and stunted its growth. Only Christ is allowed to rise gloriously from the dead; Gwenevere, like Branwen, dies of grief; Arthur, mortally wounded, sails off to some Avalonian purgatory; and the Holy Grail is withdrawn to cosmic abstraction. But it cannot be allowed to stop there!

THE HOMECOMING

As Jesus observed, we have little hope of new wine if it is put into old wineskins. Both British mythology and biblical mythology must evolve if we are to push past Osirian fragmentation and move toward recollection and unity "on a higher arc." It is time to write the myths that will get us home.

Myth is the source and the index of human creativity, and its parameters are infinite, because the wellspring of mythical inspiration never runs dry. The creative imagination through which human beings polarize with that source is initiated by desire, for like Eve in Eden, desire constantly wonders "what if?" When human beings cease to ask the question and desire dies, human priesthood becomes extinct. Myth teaches us to frame questions, and magic enables us to obtain answers, even if they are not always the answers that we want to hear. Each answer prompts further questions as well as refinements of questions, and so little by little we build that inner dialogue that forms the inner world span between "the world" of how things are, and Tsdeq, the archetypal, heavenly way that things should be. It is a courtship, a long and exacting process of two states of seemingly independent being getting to know, trust, and love each other, and to conceive something greater than themselves. There is therefore no more precise metaphor for the building of the relationship between heaven and earth than there is for the building of the relationship between a man and a woman.

Great Isis knew this, and swallowing her grief she drew the fragments of her love together so that something greater then she or Osiris could be conceived. She understood from the secrets of Ra that in some alchemical moment of metaphysics and memory the zenith of individual experience is passed and urgency for reunion begins. Eventually, the universe draws its fragmented galaxies, its disparate moving groups back together, back to the union from which a greater singularity will form. So it is with stars and souls, galaxies and gypsies, planets and popes. The keys to the self are held by another self, and that electric something that animates us also magnetizes and polarizes us. We must, as a bleak Wystan Auden observed in the fragmenting world of 1939, "love one another or die."[11]

We have, like Isis, suffered the pangs of fragmentation; now the time comes to pick up the pieces and head for home. In that eventual homecoming, man and woman, heaven and earth may look into each other's eyes and no longer ask "What if?" but say "I know." For every priest and priestess should work toward the day when they may relinquish their priesthood. On that infinite day, when time ceases, the "cure of souls" will have become an obsolete function. In the New Jerusalem there is no temple; it is absolutely unnecessary. But in the meantime, men and women of good will must become the equitable and loving partners in the magic of "Atlantis on a higher arc."

Isis, above all others, knew this, and these pages have touched upon her sermons to the forgetful congregation of humankind.

NOTES

Introduction
1. Quoted in *A History of White Magic,* by Gareth Knight (London: Mowbray, 1978).

Chapter One: Autumn in Atlantis
1. C. S. Lewis in conversation with J. R. R Tolkien, September 19, 1931, taken from Tolkien's poem *Mythopoeia.*
2. Jerusalem Bible, Job 38.4.
3. *Corpus Hermeticum.* Extracts in English translated and compiled by Willis Barnstone in *The Other Bible* (San Francisco: Harper, 1984).
4. Jerusalem Bible. Luke 10.27–28. Actually said to Jesus by a lawyer, then confirmed by Jesus, who replies: "Thou has answered right. This do and thou shalt live."
5. Allan Bloom, *The Closing of the American Mind* (London: Simon and Schuster, 1987).
6. Jerusalem Bible, Gen. 1.2.
7. J. R. R. Tolkien, *The Silmarillion* (London: Allen and Unwin, 1977).
8. *Preiddeu Annwn* (The Spoils of Annwn), trans. D. W. Nash in *Taliesin or the Bards and Druids of Britain* (London: J. Russell Smith, 1858).
9. Mike Harris, *Awen: The Quest of the Celtic Mysteries* (Oceanside, California: Sun Chalice Books, 1999).

Chapter Two: Akhenaten, Nefertiti, and Sun Magic

1. Lorraine Evans, *Kingdom of the Ark* (London: Simon and Schuster, 2000).

2. David Rohl, *A Test of Time* (London: Century, 1995).

3. Joann Fletcher, *Egypt's Sun King* (London: Duncan Baird, 2000), 20.

4. Ibid., 12.

5. Bower, *Scotichronicon,* trans. D. E. R. Watt (Aberdeen University Press, 1993).

6. *Book of Leinster,* Irish Texts Society, Dublin.

7. Evans, *Kingdom of the Ark.*

8 Christine Hartley, *A Case for Reincarnation* (London: Hale, 1972), 123–126.

Chapter Three: The Life and Death of the Goddess

1. New English Bible, Gen. 11.30.

2. Ibid., Gen. 4.7.

3. Ibid., Exod. 19.18.

4. *Preiddeu Annwn* (The Spoils of Annwn), trans. D. W. Nash in *Taliesin or the Bards and Druids of Britain* (London: J. Russell Smith, 1858).

5. New English Bible, Song of Songs 3.1–4.

Chapter Four: The Priest King and Temple Weaver

1. Leigh Baigent and Lincoln, *The Holy Blood and the Holy Grail* (London: Jonathan Cape, 1982).

2. New English Bible, Second Epistle to the Heb. 5.11.

3. Ibid.

4. Ibid., 5.5.

5. Cameron, *The Other Gospels* (Philadelphia, Westminster Press, 1982).

6. New English Bible, Song of Songs 4.5.

7. Ibid., 5.3–6.

8. Aleister Crowley, *Moonchild* (Mandrake Press, 1929).

9. Dion Fortune, *Esoteric Philosophy of Love and Marriage,* 4th ed. (London: Aquarian Press, 1967).

10. Cameron, *The Other Gospels.*

11. M. R. James, *The Apocryphal New Testament* (Oxford: Oxford University Press, 1924).

12. Ibid.

13. Ibid.

14. Josephus, *Works: Antiquities,* trans. R. Marcus (London: Loeb Classics, 1961).

15. Ibid.

16. J. A. Stevenson, *New Eusebius* (London: SPCK, 1990).

17. Elaine Pagels, trans., *The Gnostic Gospels* (London: Widenfield and Nicolson, 1980).

18. D. W. Nash, *Taliesin or the Bards and Druids of Britain* (London: J. Russell Smith, 1858).

19. New English Bible, 2 Sam. 15.8.

Chapter Five: The Priestess from Magdala

1. New English Bible, John 2.5.

2. Ibid., 2.11.

3. Ibid., 4.46.

4. Meirion Evans, *Credaf,* trans. C. Davies, in *Cydymaith y Pererin,* comp. B. O'Malley (Gomer, 1989).

5. New English Bible, Matt. 28.8.

6. Ibid., Mark 16.9.

7. Jerusalem Bible, Mark 7.9.

8. J. M. Robinson, *The Nag Hammadi Library, Gospel of Philip,* trans. W. W. Isenberg (San Francisco: Harper, 1987).

9. Epiphanius, *Heresy XXVI,* quoted in The Gospel of Philip in M. R. James *The Apocryphal New Testament* (Oxford, 1924), 12.

10. J. M. Robinson, *The Nag Hammadi Library, Gospel of Mary* (San Francisco: Harper, 1987).

11. Ibid.

12. New English Bible, Song of Songs.

13. New English Bible, John 20.13.

14. Jerusalem Bible, Song of Songs 1.5.

Chapter Six: Taliesin, Ceridwen, and the Mysteries of Britain

1. Robert Graves, *The White Goddess* (London: Faber, 1961).

2. See Huws, ed., *Llyfr Aneirin* (Aberystwyth: National Library of Wales, 1989).

3. Geoffrey of Monmouth, *The History of the Kings of Britain,* trans. Lewis Thorpe (Middlesex: Penguin, 1966).

4. Geoffrey of Monmouth, *Vita Merlini,* trans. (Chicago: Parry, 1925).

5. G. Jones and T. Jones, trans., *The Mabinogion* (London: Dent, 1974).

6. *The Song of Amergin,* restored and trans. Robert Graves in his introduction to *The White Goddess* (London: Faber, 1961).

7. *Preiddeu Annwn (*The Spoils of Annwn), trans. D .W. Nash in *Taliesin or the Bards and Druids of Britain* (London: J. Russell Smith, 1958).

8. G. de Santillana and H. von Dechend, *Hamlet's Mill* (Boston: Godine, 1977).

9. Mike Harris, *Awen: The Quest of the Celtic Mysteries* (Oceanside, Calif.: Sun Chalice Books, 1999).

10. *Thomas the Rhymer,* Scottish Traditional Ballad.

Chapter Seven: Owain and the Lady of the Fountain

1. G. Jones and T. Jones, trans., *The Mabinogion* (London: Dent, 1974).

2. Chretien de Troyes, "Yvain, the Knight with the Lion," from *Arthurian Romances,* trans. D. D. R. Owen (London: Everyman, 1986).

3. Fiona Macleod, "The Washer at the Ford," from *The Collected Works of Fiona Macleod,* 7 vols. Selected and arranged by Mrs. William Sharp (William Heinemann, 1910–12).

4. G. Jones and T. Jones, trans., *The Mabinogion.*

Chapter Eight: The Inner Fire

1. Dylan Thomas, *The Force that through the Green Fuse Drives the Flower,* from The *Oxford Library of English Poetry* (Oxford: Oxford University Press, 1993).

2. See Alder, *NLP, the New Art and Science of Getting What You Want* (London: Piatkus, 1994).

3. R. J. Stewart, *The Underworld Initiation* (Wellingborough: Aquarian, 1985).

4. *Preiddeu Annwn* (The Spoils of Annwn), trans. D. W. Nash in *Taliesin or the Bards and Druids of Britain* (London: J. Russell Smith, 1858).

5. Israel Regardie, *The Middle Pillar* (St. Paul: Llewellyn Publications, 1970).

6. Gareth Knight, *Experience of the Inner Worlds* (Cheltenham: Helios, 1975).

7. Anthony Duncan, *The Lord of the Dance* (Cheltenham: Helios, 1972).

8. *Preiddeu Annwn* (The Spoils of Annwn).

9. Duncan, Anthony, quoted in Gareth Knight's *Experience of the Inner Worlds* (Cheltenham: Helios, 1972).

10. Gareth Knight, *The Rose Cross and the Goddess* (Wellingborough: Aquarian, 1985).

11. Jerusalem Bible, Luke 22.19–20.

12. Allen Bloom, *The Closing of the American Mind* (Simon and Schuster, 1987).

Chapter Nine: Merlin and Gwenddydd

1. Geoffrey of Monmouth, *The Life of Merlin (Vita Merlini),* ed. and trans. John Jay Parry, University of Illinois, 1925, as reprinted and amended by R. J. Stewart in *Merlin: The Prophetic Vision and The Mystic Life* (London: Arkana, 1994).

2. Alan Richardson, ed. *Dancers to the Gods* (Wellingborough: Aquarian Press, 1985), entry for February 3, 1938.

3. D. Wace and Layamon, *Arthurian Chronicles* (London, 1937).

4. *Affalannau,* trans. John Matthews in *Merlin Through the Ages*, ed. R. J. Stewart and John Matthews (London: Blandford, 1995).

5. *A Dialogue between Myrddyn and his Sister Gwenddydd* (London: Blandford, 1995).

6. "The Story of Myrddin Wyllt," from *Chronicle of Elis Gruffudd,* National Library of Wales, MS 5276D, reprinted in *Merlin Through the Ages,* ed. R. J. Stewart and John Matthews (London: Blandford, 1995).

7. Geoffrey of Monmouth, *The Life of Merlin (Vita Merlini).*

8. D. Wace and Layamon, *Arthurian Chronicles* (London, 1937).

9. Geoffrey of Monmouth, *The Life of Merlin (Vita Merlini).*

Chapter Ten: Practical Polarity Magic

1. Janet Farrar and Stewart Farrar, *The Witches' Way* (London: Hale, 1984), 171.

2. Dion Fortune, *Moon Magic* (London: Aquarian Press, 1956).

3. Dolores Ashcroft-Nowicki, *First Steps in Ritual* (Wellingborough: Aquarian Press, 1982), 27–31.

Chapter Eleven: Dionysos and the Bacchae

1. All indented text from Euripides, *The Bacchae and Other Plays,* trans. Philip Vellacott (Penguin, 1973).

2. Gen. 3.14.

3. Jane Ellen Harrison, *Prolegomena* (Princeton: Princeton University Press, 1991), 448.

4. Marvin W. Meyer, *The Ancient Mysteries* (Philadelphia: University of Pennsylvania Press, 1999, by arrangement with Harper Collins), 63–64.

5. Janet Farrar and Stewart Farrar, *The Witches Way* (London: Hale, 1983), 58–59.

Chapter Twelve: Arthur and Gwenevere

1. Thomas Malory, *Le Morte d'Arthur,* ed. Janet Cowen (London: Penguin, 1986), 40.

2. Traditional Scottish Ballad.

3. Frederick Bligh Bond, *The Company of Avalon* (Oxford: Blackwell, 1924), 105.

4. The story of this is told by Patrick Benham in *The Avalonians* (Glastonbury: Gothic Image, 1993).

Chapter Thirteen: Raising Atlantis

1. Dion Fortune, *The Sea Priestess* (London: Aquarian Press, 1957).

2. Dion Fortune, *Moon Magic* (London: Aquarian Press, 1956).

3. J. R. R. Tolkien, *The Lord of the Rings* (Unwin Paperbacks, 1968).

4. Mark Vidler, *The Star Mirror* (London: Harper Collins, 1998).

5. See *Chwedlau Gwerin Cymru* (Welsh Folk Tales) comp. Robin Gwyndaf, National Museum of Wales (Cardiff, 1989).

6. G. Jones and T. Jones, trans. *The Mabinogion* (London: Dent, 1974).

7. Ibid.

8. *Preiddeu Annwn* (The Spoils of Annwn), trans. D. W. Nash in *Taliesin or the Bards and Druids of Britain* (London: J. Russell Smith, 1858).

9. Ibid.

10. Geoffrey of Monmouth, *The Prophecies of Merlin,* from *Geoffrey of Monmouth, The History of the Kings of Britain,* trans. Lewis Thorpe (Harmonsworth, Middlesex: Penguin, 1966).

11. W. H. Auden, from his poem *September 1939* in *The Oxford Library of English Poetry* (Oxford: Oxford University Press, 1993).

BIBLIOGRAPHY

Ashcroft-Nowicki, Dolores. *First Steps in Ritual*. Wellingborough: Aquarian Press, 1982.

Ashe, Geoffrey. *King Arthur's Avalon*. London: Collins, 1957.

Baigent, Michael, Richard Leigh, and Henry Lincoln. *The Holy Blood and the Holy Grail*. London: Jonathan Cape, 1982.

Barker, Margaret. *The Gate of Heaven*. London: SPCK, 1991.

Barnstone, Willis, ed. *The Other Bible: Ancient Esoteric Texts*. San Francisco: Harper San Francisco, 1984.

Benham, Patrick. *The Avalonians*. Glastonbury: Gothic Image, 1993.

Bligh Bond, Frederick. *The Company of Avalon*. Oxford: Basil Blackwell, 1924.

Bright, John A. *History of Israel*. London: SCM Press, 1991.

De Santillana, Giorgio, and Hertha Von Dechend. *Hamlet's Mill*. Boston: Godine, 1977.

de Troyes, Chretien. *Arthurian Romances*. Translated by D. D. R. Owen. Everyman Classics.

Duncan, Anthony. *Jesus: Essential Readings*. London: Crucible, 1986.

Euripides. *The Bacchae*. Translated by Philip Vellacott. London: Penguin Books, 1973.

Evans, Lorraine. *Kingdom of the Ark*. London: Simon and Schuster, 2000.

Farrar, Janet, and Stewart Farrar. *The Witches Way*. London: Hale, 1984.

Fletcher, Joann. *Egypt's Sun King*. London: Duncan Baird Publishers, 2000.

Fortune, Dion. *The Sea Priestess.* London: Aquarian Press, 1957.

———. *Moon Magic.* London: Aquarian Press, 1956.

Gardiner, Laurence. *Genesis of the Grail Kings.* London: Bantam Press, 1999.

Graves, Robert. *The White Goddess.* London: Faber, 1961.

Harris, Mike. *Awen: The Quest of the Celtic Mysteries.* Oceanside, Calif.: Sun Chalice Books, 1999.

Harrison, Jane. *Themis: A Study of the Social Origins of Greek Religion.* London: Merlin Press, 1963.

Hartley, Christine. *A Case for Reincarnation.* London: Robert Hale and Company, 1972.

Hazlett, Ian, ed. *Early Christianity.* London: SPCK, 1991.

James, Montague Rhodes. *The Apocryphal New Testament.* Oxford: Oxford University Press, 1924.

Jones, Gwynn, and Thomas Jones. *The Mabinogion.* London: Dent, 1974.

Knight, Gareth. *The Secret Tradition in Arthurian Legend.* York Beach: Weiser, 1996.

———. *The Rose Cross and the Goddess.* Wellingborough: Aquarian Press, 1985.

———. *Experience of the Inner Worlds.* Cheltenham: Helios, 1975.

———. *The Magical World of the Inklings.* Shaftesbury: Element Books, 1990.

Lesko, Barbara S. *The Great Goddesses of Egypt.* Norman: University of Oklahoma Press, 1999.

Macleod, Fiona. *The Works of Fiona Macleod.* 7 vols. Selected and arranged by Mrs. William Sharp. William Heinemann, 1910–12.

Malory, Thomas. *Le Morte d'Arthur.* Edited by Janet Cowen. Penguin Books, 1969.

Matthews, John. *Taliesin.* London: Aquarian, 1991.

Metzger, B., and M. Coogan, eds. *The Oxford Companion to the Bible.* Oxford: Oxford University Press, 1993.

Meyer, Marvin W., ed. *The Ancient Mysteries: A Sourcebook of Sacred Texts.* Philadelphia: University of Pennsylvania Press, by arrangement with Harper Collins, 1999.

Osman, Ahmed. *Moses, Pharoah of Egypt*. London: Grafton, 1990.

Pennar, Meirion. *The Black Book of Carmarthen*. Lampeter: Llanerch, 1989.

Picknett, L., and C. Prince. *The Templar Revelation*. London: Bantam Press, 1997.

Rabinowitz, Jacob. *The Faces of God*. Woodstock, Conn.: Spring Publications, 1998.

Richardson, Alan, ed. *Dancers to the Gods*. Wellingborough: Aquarian Press, 1985.

Robinson, James M., ed. *Nag Hammadi Library*. Leiden: Brill, 1988.

Rohl, David. *Legend*. London: Random House, 1998.

———. *A Test of Time*. London: Century Ltd., 1995.

Stewart, R. J. *The Underworld Initiation*. Wellingborough: Aquarian Press, 1985.

———. *Merlin: The Prophetic Vision and The Mystic Life*. London: Arkana, 1986.

———. *The Power Within the Land*. Shaftesbury: Element, 1992.

———. *The Underworld Initiation*. Wellingborough: Aquarian Press, 1985.

Stewart, R. J., and John Matthews, eds., trans., and comps. *Merlin Through the Ages*. London: Blandford, 1995.

Tolkien, J. R. R. *The Lord of the Rings*. London: George Allen and Unwin, Ltd., 1954.

———. *The Silmarillion*. London: George Allen and Unwin, Ltd., 1977.

Tyldesley, Joyce. *Nefertiti*. London: Penguin, 1998.

———. *Hatshepsut*. Viking, 1996.

Vidler, Mark. *The Star Mirror*. London: Thorsons, 1998.

Wallis Budge, E. A. *The Gods of the Egyptians*. 2 vols. London: Methuen, 1904.

INDEX